ALWAYS
EAT THE
WEIRD
STUFF

WHAT OTHERS ARE SAYING

Bo Kitty's work should come with a warning: inhaling this material will make you feel reckless, invigorated, and free. It can move you to touch base with a deeper self. Bo Kitty's voice is authentic and confronting. She goes to dark places where others fear to tread then brings the reader back to a higher ground, more steady than before. Her vitality is contagious as she walks you through adventures across the globe. Take the dare and read this book. I couldn't put it down.

Clémence Overall, author

This book is an arrow straight to the heart. It aims for the core of what makes us human and hits the mark. *Always Eat the Weird Stuff* will have you laughing out loud one minute and heartbroken the next.

Aubrey Rhodes, artist

As a life-long lover of words, Bo's evocative style will transport you to another place and time. Grounded in reality with an overlay of glitter, emotion and poignant imagery, her writing will take you on a ride that will linger in your mind long after you have read the last page.

Mel Lancuba, communications professional

Always Eat The Weird Stuff is an exquisite dance through an extraordinary woman's life. Detailed with such intimacy and unique humour, you journey through both unbearable and joyous moments with grace and painful candour. This book is a love letter to all who have overcome the shit that life has flung at them. As Bo so aptly puts it, "I've found a million ways to say I love you in my lifetime." In this book you will read those million ways.

Jeanne Reynolds, multidisciplinary creative

WHAT OTHERS ARE SAYING

Bo has gifted us with an invitation to her extraordinary life. Each vivid scene evokes a deep response, promising to linger in our minds long after the chapter has ended. An evocative and poignant story, filled with unforgettable life events punctuated by not-so-sugar-coated lessons. It triumphs in its humanity, showing us the beauty in struggle and the grace in authenticity. Bo's narrative is more than just a recounting of her life; it is a powerful testament to living fully and fearlessly. Her ability to capture the essence of life's highs and lows, with a touch of whimsy and a great deal of courage, makes this book a compelling read. It is a reminder that within each of us lies the potential to be extraordinary, to embrace our vulnerabilities, and to find strength in our true selves.

Rose Inserra, author

Always Eat The Weird Stuff is expressive and expansive, filled with gritty magic, deployed in the service of truth. Equating stasis with death, this book rattles with life.

Stu Taylor, screenwriter

These stories are a magic-carpet ride through echoes of places, people and phases of life—at times frighteningly familiar, this book will take you by the hand down some seedy, graffiti-ladened and much-loved laneways and to psychedelic nature-filled fields. You'll laugh, and cry, and maybe find a little slice of yourself along the way.

Pheelix Mclelland, artist

Published in Australia
by True Grit Publishing
PO box 7111 Reservoir Victoria 3073
Email: me@bokitty.com
Website: www.bokitty.com

First published in Australia 2024
Copyright © Bo Kitty 2024

All rights reserved. No part of this publication may be reproduced, stored in a retrieval system, or transmitted, in any form or by any means without the prior written permission of the publisher, nor be otherwise circulated in any form of binding or cover other than that in which it is published and without a similar condition being imposed on the subsequent purchaser.

National Library of Australia Cataloguing Publication entry

 A catalogue record for this book is available from the National Library of Australia

ISBN 978-1-7635864-0-6 (paperback)
ISBN 978-1-7635864-1-3 (hardcover)
ISBN 978-1-7635864-2-0 (ebook)

Cover design and typesetting by Sophie White Design
Printed by Ingram Spark

This book is a creative memoir based on non-fictional experiences. The stories recounted herein are rooted in truth, but their presentation is subjective and reflective of my personal perspective. To protect the privacy of individuals involved, names have been altered and specific details have been withheld. The only people who will recognise the characters in these stories are the characters themselves. This work is intended as a literary exploration of life experiences and should be interpreted as such. In addition—if you find the portrayal of any character unflattering, please remember that actions speak louder than words. All contact details given in this book were current at the time of publication, but are subject to change.

ALWAYS EAT THE WEIRD STUFF

A REBEL WOMAN'S QUEST FOR LOVE,
IDENTITY AND BELONGING

Bo Kitty

This book is dedicated to the seekers.

You are not alone.

I WOULD LIKE TO HONOUR THE TRADITIONAL CUSTODIANS OF THE LAND ON WHICH MUCH OF THIS BOOK TAKES PLACE—THE WURUNDJERI PEOPLE OF NAARM, ALSO KNOWN AS MELBOURNE, VICTORIA.

I PAY MY DEEPEST RESPECTS TO THEIR ELDERS AND ANCESTORS, THE FIRST AND MOST ENDURING STORYTELLERS ON THIS LAND FOR OVER 60,000 YEARS. I ACKNOWLEDGE THEIR ONGOING RELATIONSHIP WITH COUNTRY, AND THAT SOVEREIGNTY WAS NEVER CEDED.

CONTENTS

Note from the author — 11
Prologue — 12

Chapter 1	Fuck Authority	15
Chapter 2	Vagabond Saints	18
Chapter 3	Ode to McKean	26
Chapter 4	Ode to McKean Revisited	29
Chapter 5	One day in Melbourne	31
Chapter 6	Lest We Forget, Hanoi, Vietnam	34
Chapter 7	Home	38
Chapter 8	My Place	39
Chapter 9	National Australia Bank at Midnight	41
Chapter 10	Dog Walk	42
Chapter 11	Internet Love	47
Chapter 12	I Still Love You	50
Chapter 13	Seeking a Sign, Ubud, Bali	52
Chapter 14	Birth of a Mermaid, Gili Trawangan, Indonesia	55
Chapter 15	I Am in the Right Place, Lombok	60
Chapter 16	Because You Can	62
Chapter 17	The Art of Eating Alone, Koh Tao, Thailand	63
Chapter 18	No Limits, Koh Tao, Thailand	65
Chapter 19	Question Everything, Vang Vieng, Laos	68
Chapter 20	Thanks for the Stories	70
Chapter 21	For Women Everywhere	73
Chapter 22	Rape is not a dirty word	75
Chapter 23	I Used to Be a Real Tomboy	81
Chapter 24	Sexy Trouble, Far North Queensland	85
Chapter 25	Moving North	87
Chapter 26	Solar Eclipse of the Heart, Far North Queensland	89
Chapter 27	Horrible Movie Scenes, Far North Queensland	92
Chapter 28	Broken, Whole, East Coast of Australia	93
Chapter 29	Twelve Hours to Make Mistakes	96
Chapter 30	Reality Check	97

Chapter 31	On Being Tattooed	104
Chapter 32	Single Motherhood	107
Chapter 33	Eternal Moment, Koh Tao, Thailand	108
Chapter 34	Eat Me	110
Chapter 35	Gone Again	112
Chapter 36	Dance It Out	113
Chapter 37	Compost	114
Chapter 38	On Junigudira Land, Exmouth, Western Australia	116
Chapter 39	A Bungalow Somewhere, Amed, Bali	118
Chapter 40	In a Dimly Lit Room	120
Chapter 41	Never an Easy Choice	122
Chapter 42	All Silent	124
Chapter 43	Exhausted, Dirty and Happy as Fuck	125
Chapter 44	Landing, New York, USA	129
Chapter 45	Occupy Yourself, New York, USA	131
Chapter 46	Love Story in Two Chapters, New York, USA	133
Chapter 47	Struggles, Tikal, Guatemala	136
Chapter 48	Island Politics, Caye Caulker, Belize	139
Chapter 49	Glow Sticks, San Diego, USA	147
Chapter 50	Burning Man, Nevada, USA	151
Chapter 51	In Transit, Fiji	159
Chapter 52	KFC Island Style, Tasmania	161
Chapter 53	Microdosing Diary	164
Chapter 54	It's Real	174
Chapter 55	Love Is	176
Chapter 56	Alcoholism	177
Chapter 57	Missing You When You Are Right Here	178
Chapter 58	Ode To Yoshi	180
Chapter 59	Thirty Ways to Mend a Broken Heart	187
Chapter 60	Mom Arrives	189
Chapter 61	The Biggest Secret Ever	190
Chapter 62	Identity	192
Chapter 63	What Happens and What You Do With It	196
Chapter 64	Parasites, Canggu, Bali	200
Chapter 65	Homecoming	202

Chapter 66	Invocation About Not Settling	204
Chapter 67	When a House Becomes a Home	207
Chapter 68	Alessandro	211
Chapter 69	Happily Ever After	212
Chapter 70	Uluru, Northern Territory, Australia	213
Chapter 71	The Letter	216
Chapter 72	Things Mother Said	219
Chapter 73	When It Hurts	221
Chapter 74	A New Family	223
Chapter 75	At The Airport	226
Chapter 76	The Most Arrogant Man on Earth, Rome, Italy	227
Chapter 77	When in Rome, Date a Roman, Italy	232
Chapter 78	Not Quite Yet, Firenze, Italy	236
Chapter 79	Pandemic Blues	240
Chapter 80	Small Wins	242
Chapter 81	Fraying	245
Chapter 82	Lockdown Ends	246
Chapter 83	The Longest Love Affair	250
Chapter 84	Fuel for the Fire	254
Chapter 85	Ten Years Coaching	256
Chapter 86	So Many Beautiful Men	259
Chapter 87	My Legacy List	263
Chapter 88	You've Got This, Babe	267
Chapter 89	Goals for Joy	270
Chapter 90	Earn the Right	274
Chapter 91	Safari, Tanzania	278
Chapter 92	Coming Home to Yourself, Zanzibar	292

About The Author	298
Reality Check—Holistic business coaching for rebels	299
Power Up Cards and App	300
The Real Army — B2B solutions by creatives for creatives	301
Acknowledgments	302
Author Contact Page	303

NOTE FROM THE AUTHOR

Hello dear reader,

This book encapsulates more than two decades spanning multiple continents. My wish is that these stories act as a beacon, wayfinding through darkness towards light. I've dedicated my life to exploring the edges of things but there is no courage without vulnerability.

Spoiler alert: This is not a traditional novel.

In this space of post-modern auto-fiction, narrative conventions fade and the essence of human existence emerges, unfiltered and unadorned. There's no linear plot to follow, no neatly-tied narrative threads; instead, expect a mosaic of short stories, vignettes, and musings that invite you to ponder, question, and interpret. The men in the love dynamic stories are nameless for a reason. They represent the 'him' that is the polarity to 'me' or 'her'. Apologies for the hetero-centric language, hopefully these stories have value for all genders and combinations of people.

In addition, a content warning: this book explores themes around generational trauma and contains references to sexual abuse, drug use, drug addiction, alcoholism, emotional abuse, abandonment, abortion, grief, and pet loss.

I fully believe we heal from trauma as a community, not in isolation, and that we create belonging rather than 'finding' it. May these words resonate, provoke, and inspire as you consider your own journey of self-discovery, and remember there is magic in storytelling.

So yell it louder for those in the back. Enjoy.

PROLOGUE

It was 1985 and we had wild parties at our house in San Mateo, California when I was five years old. Mom wore a purple studded belt and would spin me around on the lawn by my hands, and everyone was high.

I ran away from home when I was six, hiding under the loquat tree at the dead-end road of South Eldorado Street with a suitcase full of tea towels and my imaginary friend 'Pond', plotting our escape.

Soon after, we moved to Australia to look after my grandparents, who were both dying of cancer.

I remember smoking pipes of weed in the front yard in Aldgate, Adelaide Hills when I was fourteen, and thinking that the blue spruce was the setting for a mediaeval fairyland. I never really fit in either place.

When it came to my education, I finished high school two years early, and started a Bachelor of Arts at Adelaide University but dropped out at sixteen. My parents said I couldn't live at home and work a job, *but* I could live at home if I was attending university—to "use my actual brain", apparently.

Shortly after, I was kicked out of home for a weed plant that was dying on the roof outside my bedroom, but I'd been stealing Dad's weed for months.

So, I packed my shit and I left. It was the very first time I was deserted on a hot road with my worldly belongings.

It wouldn't be the last.

I lived in share houses, and worked three hospitality jobs because mother wouldn't sign the dole forms to say I couldn't live at home. So, I hopped a bus in 1997 from Adelaide to Melbourne the moment I turned eighteen, with three hundred dollars in my pocket, still just a girl. From a teenage life hovering on the edge of circles, to creating circles of my own.

There was a big world out there I wanted to see, so I left. Melbourne called me. A place I'd never been. There were more challenges, violence, opinions, competition, and art on every corner. Not the biggest pond in the world, but big enough for me to become a part of the ecosystem, to love and fear and forgive and try and then start another cycle. To do it again. Wiser.

Thus was the true beginning of Bo Kitty and the unfolding of this story...

Thank you, younger me, for being brave enough to leave, a catalyst to find so many incredible people all over the world who think like you do.

This book is for my extended community and my chosen family of freaks.

I am only a reflection of all of you.

CHAPTER 1

Fuck Authority

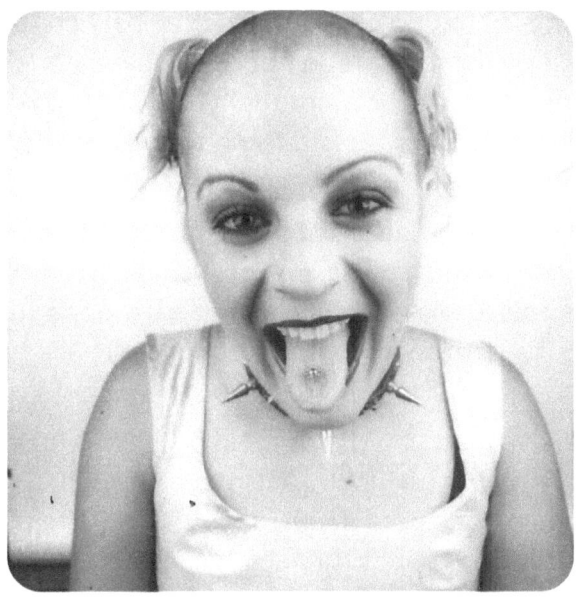

STUDIO SHOOT, CIRCA 2000

Let me state for the record: I have a healthy distrust for both authority and bureaucracy pretty much everywhere. Basically, most red tape and rules are set up to fuck us, especially the little people—cent by cent, signature by signature.

Okay, so, I'll be honest. I break laws. All the time. I smoke weed, drive illegally at times, I lie to the government, to the tax office, to employers... there are probably hundreds more laws I've broken once (or more) as well. I believe in following the 'spirit' of the law, not the letter.

I do not live the way most people do. I haven't got a degree, I'm not married, don't have a regular job, don't drink every night, eat spam. Don't go to church, don't eat three regular meals a day, nor sleep every night. I've spent much of the last couple of decades living with artists, dole bludgers, computer dudes, ego trippers, and fringe dwellers of all ages and from all walks of life. Lived in houses ranging from the utterly middle class to the grungiest of warehouses. Spent many years living the life of one immersed in electronic music. Talking about punters, clubs, fliers, acts, music, money, hype, reputation, decor, budgets, overheads, door lists, mixers, amps, decks, live acts, copyright, licensing, commercialism, competition, promoters, posters, rivalry, backstabbing, sabotage, support, and networking. Just to name a few things!

Living a life of fast food, rising at noon, eating at five, going out at eleven, coming home at six, sleeping fitfully for a few hours, then rinse and repeat. Dodging the system at every opportunity, giving each other tips and showing each other where the holes in the fence are.

Having those around you act psychotic, unstable, suicidal, from bad families, with no rulebooks, trying to make sense of it all, pay bills, go shopping, and care about the Earth while also trying to find some answer to the imposing question of why we are here. You can bet these people ask that question of themselves more than the average Joe Blow living in a sweet haze of constructed denial. The fringe dwellers always do.

So, if my life is like this, has been like this, and (as I am loving it) will be like this till the day I die, then I must realise that NONE OF THE OTHER RULES APPLY.

None.

Just as I made this reality of sparkles and spontaneous occurrences because I expect my life to be a constant state of chaos and wonder, it is also unchartered territory. There is no rulebook for the life I've chosen.

So, none of the old pathways, none of the trails down which logic walks, will lead me to happiness. I am going to have to unlearn and relearn a new way of being.

I will have to learn the rules, and then break them.

WOOMERA DETENTION CENTRE BREAKOUT PROTEST, 2002

CHAPTER 2

Vagabond Saints

Living at McKean Street warehouse in Clifton Hill around the turn of the millennium, the drug dealer, Zed, says to me, "My friend is coming to stay, he's American... and he's a DJ."

"Well," I remark with a smirk. "You'll have to introduce us."

We both laugh and I don't think much of it.

Little do I know...

A few days later, I was standing at the first-floor window in the living room where only one pane has unfrosted glass. Through the tiny portal, I see a yellow van parked in the driveway. Zed's and another voice drift up the front stairs. The American is gorgeous; baby face and blue eyes, short hair with the typical t-shirt and shorts uniform of a billion travellers worldwide. He dons a cheeky smile and his left arm is entirely tattooed with colourful, cartoonish designs.

"Hey, how ya doin," he drawls.

"Well, hi there," I purr.

The next night, around midnight, James, Sascha and Mike are in the lounge; I'm in the kitchen talking to them while I make toast. The American appears, plonks himself on the couch near the kitchen and says to me, "Fuck, I really need a beer. Is there anywhere to get beer this time of night?"

"Yeah," I tell him. "There's a bottle shop up the road. I'll come for a walk with you."

We take orders from the others and find that the drive-in at the end of the street is shut.

"Let's go to the twenty-four-hour place. Jump in my car."

I'm excited at the thought of a fun night; anything spontaneous is okay with me. He starts the conversation with, "If there's one thing I hate, it's Canadians who sew their flag on their backpack. What the fuck is that? I even met an American who had a Canadian flag on his pack because he said it was 'safer'. What an idiot."

I like him already.

"Yeah, well, I've spent ten years in Australia being an ambassador for the fact that not all Americans are gun-toting, obese, suing-your-arse-off patriots. It might be safer, but who wants to be safe?"

"Risks are where the real fun is at," he replies with a wink.

Finally, someone who is just as forthright and assertive about what they feel. That's the moment I decide I'm going to seduce him. We buy beer and drive home, talking passionately and joking after knowing each other for around twenty minutes. We spent the night talking with the others. Sascha and her boyfriend Mike bring out their whips and a raucous whipping session happens in the living room. The American loves it; I don't think he's had any light-BDSM lately. He brings out a tape recorder and asks us for some stories.

"Well," I tentatively begin. "I've got a travelling story for you…"

"Please do," he says, hitting the record button.

And so, I began my story…

…When I was fourteen, I left for a three-month cultural exchange program to Nepal. When I arrived, my host-brother picked me up on his motorbike and hooned off. Kathmandu is surrounded by a ring road, and beyond, there's not much civilisation, but we ride on a dodgy motorbike way beyond this road to his house.

There are no white people out here and I feel very out of place. He takes me to his home, where my host-sister seems to be his maid and hides in the kitchen. He shows me to a small, sparse room and begins to talk in halting English, "For two weeks, you eat only oranges to purify you, I ask your father for your hand in marriage, we stay three months here, then we go to Australia and I start business with you."

The whole time he speaks, he is staring at my long, curly hair, not at my face. Perhaps because most Nepalese people have straight hair and I had bouncy ringlets.

I freak out and explain he's got it wrong, that I was not, in fact, his bride. He suddenly loses his English and denies there is a telephone anywhere and leaves me there. Makes it clear that I can't leave the house without him. A couple of days later, I escape when he isn't around and make my way to a temple I'd seen on one of our walks. I had been practising Hinduism with my mother before I left Australia and thought a Hindu temple would be the best and safest place to work out my next move.

I sat in the courtyard of this temple, breathing with relief, writing poetry and feeling good, watching the tattered flags blow in the breeze. An elderly man, stooped with age and wrapped in orange robes, walks into the courtyard and smiles at me. I return it. He comes over, gesturing to me. He seems like a very old monk, and wants to show me something. So, I follow him into the temple, and he ushers me up a collapsing concrete staircase to a room missing one wall. It's filled with rubble and dirt, rebar sticks out of the walls, but the view through the rubble is beautiful. He waves his arm towards the view, and says, "You like this?"

"Oh, yes, it's so beautiful. I love it," I reply enthusiastically. We repeat this same exchange a few more times until I realise he is in fact saying: "You like sex?"

I'm saying, "oh, yes, it's beautiful" like an idiot. Fuck.

With a quick excuse of a fabricated Swedish boyfriend, I beat the hell out of there, find a phone box and call the organisation. I tell them what happened with the host-brother and ask them to come get me. They put me up in a hotel in Thamel while they found me a more suitable host-family. At fourteen, I lived like a solo traveller in the city for two weeks. Nearly got killed a few times.

Got molested on a packed public bus when a man rubs his cock against my butt for a two-hour trip and I'm powerless to move or say anything. Those damn cotton hippie skirts with the bells, thin as toilet paper; I could feel his breath on my neck and his pubic hair pushing against me.

There were a bunch of rebels from Australia that I made as friends, and we got into some adventures and some trouble. I trek the Annapurna range, smoke hash with Sadhus and get trapped on an island full of head-hunters without knowing, but that first week of imprisonment was hell. After three months, I got off the plane with Jimi Hendrix in my Walkman, and a headband on, feeling about 30 years wise...

RETURNING FROM NEPAL, 1993

"See," says the American. "I love that. Real travellers come home with stories like that, tourists just return with their Lonely Planet tattered and a few snapshots, they don't really experience the countries they visit."

He is doing a book he calls the 'Vagabond Saints', reminiscent of Jack Kerouac's *On the Road*, the lonesome traveller who finds wisdom and glory in all the people he meets on his travels. His trip to Australia is the first leg of this journey. Now he has my story to add to it.

I ask him, "Do you take amphetamines?"

"Sometimes."

"Wanna have some with me?"

"Why?" he says, looking at me sideways with a cheeky grin.

"Well, so I can seduce you." I wait for the answer to this very forthright statement. He seems like the kind of guy who can handle it and, well, I take risks.

As we have ascertained already.

"If they are good amphetamines," he finally says, "I just might have to seduce *you*."

"Well then, it's settled. Tomorrow night, you're coming on a date with me."

We say goodnight and he heads downstairs to sleep in his van parked in our driveway. The next day I venture into the city early and get tickets to see *Blade Runner* in the botanical gardens, trying to act like it is no big deal, but I am actually really excited.

We drove to the botanic gardens in the late afternoon, and while walking from the car park, we take a seat on a bench and eat some ecstasy, wash it down, and hold hands as we head to the movie, which is screening on a big hill overlooking the city. It feels cute and comfortable.

After spreading out a blanket and cracking a beer, we watch people cover the hillside with blankets and wine, chicken and salads, talking and laughing. Soon, bats start to fly around the trees and as the sun descends, the number increases till the sky is thick with swirling masses of wings and screeching.

The American is so excited. "I've never seen that many bats before! They're fucking amazing!"

A black swan comes up to say hello and he takes photos of it very enthusiastically while everyone else throws bits of bread at it. I tell him how the bats have gone rampant and are reaching pest proportions. The city has started to talk about culling them. We agree that no matter how pest-like they become, they are the most beautiful thing to watch; stars appear, city lights flicker on in the warm, blue dusk, and critters whirl through the sky.

Next to us, a wealthy middle-aged couple sit down. They have blankets and matching chairs, sushi on little lacquered plates and matching chopsticks, champagne in a cooler and frosted glasses. Both wear expensive, tailored, 'casual' clothes—muted tones of brown and green, wool and fine gold jewellery. They unpack everything silently, settle down, and immerse themselves in newspapers—him reading the financial section, her, the lifestyle. The bats and the brightening stars go on around them unnoticed. They are right next to us, not speaking. They have everything one could possibly want for the ultimate romantic, decadent evening at the movies in the park, yet it appeared they didn't even know it. Or didn't appreciate it.

Meanwhile, we are laughing on a tatty purple rug from the car with bottles of beer, cigarettes and nothing else. Should have brought some crackers at least. As soon as the lights go out and the movie begins, he sits between my legs and hugs me, rushes rippling through me, spreading warmth and goose bumps simultaneously. My eyes are on the movie, but my mind is on his hands squeezing my legs. We kiss briefly; a smooth, soft exchange and then back to the screen. The film is dark, slow and intense, but very beautiful. As

I watch, rain threatens to pour.

When the movie ends, he says, "Let's get outta here."

He pulls me to my feet, taking off at a run through the still sitting people, weaving and dipping through the crowds where a pathway opens up magically before us. We talk easily, holding hands, walking back to the car. There's no mistaking the sexual energy between us, surging and pulsing. Once home, we find there are loads of people in the kitchen. It's only midnight but feels like early morning. After a bit of small talk, I know I'm better off shutting myself away with him.

"Have a shower with me?" he says, looking me straight in the eye.

"Sure."

We light candles in the bathroom; flames play with the shadows—flickers and distorts. I'm nervous about being naked in front of him when we've only known each other for two days, but he's so comfortable that it puts me at ease, and I undress with a cheeky smile. We hold each other under the cascading, warm water, a cool summer breeze blowing through the window.

"Your face is so beautiful in this light," he says with awe, and I believe him.

We kiss slowly, languidly in the warm orange rain, the water cascading endlessly. Hours, we spend lying on my red satin sheets, naked, reading our writing to each other, both of us amateur anthropologists looking for answers. I love the way he puts his thoughts to paper. We play with each other but the drugs mean we are content to just lie, stroking bodies and speaking, feeling skin. Near dawn, we meet with sleep, comfortable in our small world of a sea of bed.

The next day, I head to a warehouse party a few suburbs over. It's a 'gangsters and molls' theme and I cannot persuade him to come with me. Dressed in a pinstripe mini skirt, giant platform boots with toy guns tucked into each, multiple silver chains around my neck, thick black eyeshadow and a white, collared shirt. I walk into the party and hug a few friends but immediately something doesn't feel right. Still, I crack a beer anyway, and start playing ball with four dogs as I stand in the middle of the empty dance floor.

I lean down to grab the ball and suddenly I am on the floor, surrounded by concerned dog-faces and one guy looking at me with fear in his eyes. In that instant, I am fixated on a white-hot tunnel of pain. The guy had done a dive roll, attempting to break-dance, and snapped my foot in its six-inch platform boot, right out from under me. Both tibia and fibula bones of my leg are broken and no longer joined to my ankle. I spend days in hospital, unable to walk or use crutches. My cast is huge, heavy, and cumbersome. Can't even get to the toilet at the warehouse; it's two flights of concrete stairs from my bedroom. I am given a bucket to pee in and the housemates procure a TV, the first we have ever had.

I ask Mom if I can come to Adelaide to stay with them to be looked after, and the answer is a resounding "No".

The American is lovely at first, pushes me around in a wheelchair stolen from a chemist down the road. However, he is on holiday, a traveller, and in a short time finds a girl who can run with him, explore with him.

Meanwhile, I am left in my bedroom on the third floor, waiting in the dark for someone to come home to turn the light on for me.

CHAPTER 3

Ode to McKean

The warehouse is falling apart, bean-bag balls blow listlessly around the living room, kicked aside by numerous feet. Walls come down each day, opening studios up to become the giant shell it was in the beginning. One minute there's twenty people around you, then you blink, and it's only the wind whistling, cats sleeping, nobody in all these thousands of square feet.

There have been moments here of pure belonging, pure bliss. Mornings when you rise with a thousand goals and, before you know it, it's 3 or 4pm, you've had ten coffees and just talked the day away with your housemates. Of having the weirdest family on Earth, populated by artists, cooks, adventurists, comedians, performers, filmmakers, strippers, power trippers, couch surfers, sword swallowers and drug dealers. Hailing from all over the world with a million experiences and aspirations. All living and learning, eating and drinking, striving and playing under the same huge, asbestos roof. Relationships born under this roof—both destructive and those I hope last as long as forever can mean. Friendships formed every day because there are so many people passing by. Jumping the abyss from window to roof to lie outside and stare at the city skyline. Buildings; tall, glistening monoliths, blue lights contrasting with the few stars that penetrate the orange glow.

People arrive home and join us, and before you know it there are ten of us jumping around, singing and playing instruments as the sun drops behind our city sanctuary. Dinner parties begin with four people and by the time the tacos, roasts, salads, wine and desserts all arrive on the table, there's thirty hungry mouths and sixty sparkling eyes feasting like it's so good to be home. The ping pong table is dusted off and set up. Fierce tournaments go till all hours of the morning, screams and groans echoing throughout as another arse is whipped. Boredom is pretty much non-existent here. If there's ever a lull, it's time to do washing, pay bills, read—all that life admin that gets put aside when fun stuff is happening.

The sound of coffee brewing, endless dishes, weird music and movies that get showcased, and the ones we make ourselves too. We shoot a film of Stan's nipples being pierced by two piercers at the same time, and everyone emerges from their rooms dressed in crazy costumes for the scene. Footsteps echo through wooden floorboards as we stagger upstairs at dawn. Belly dancing, kickboxing, painting, sculpting giant heads and *Dr Who* Daleks made from bikes and cardboard, graffiti pieces appearing on the walls in the dark of night. Jams in the living room, drums, double bass, guitars, flutes, mouths, and tapping toes all round. A fleet of vehicles constantly coming and going, docking at the driveway, bringing stories from afar.

A blue bus in the driveway as big as a ship with bed, spa, and cranking sound system inside. Plus a caravan, three vans, ten cars, and twenty bikes moving through, blocking doors and cruising around inside the warehouse.

Just as half your stuff goes missing here, amazing things you don't expect turn up as well, rotating in some kind of twisted yet beautiful way. So inspiring to see all these people have successes, so intriguing to glimpse into their lives, even if only for a day or a week. So reassuring to help, comfort and have impact when it all seems lost to them. A place for when the world out there is all too much, and you can retreat to a universe of your own. When there's always someone laughing or crying or eating or playing or challenging or suggesting or fucking or leaving for somewhere exotic.

The backyard decking is removed by the landlord; a jungle of weeds sprout, reaching to the sky, flies and little bugs swirling in the sunlight. The drums sound great out there, concrete walls and open roof rebounding the beats till there's a whole orchestra echoing, filtering up to the kitchen where fruit smoothies are going down. The debris scattered around me has many stories to tell, roller skates left abandoned till someone gets that disco urge again, remnants of a billion art projects, some past their moment of glory, left to gather dust and decompose; some in the middle of years of process, others hoarded with visions of their future glory in mind. Wisteria has found a gap in the high windows that curls and grows down, feeding on the heat and stretching into the rehearsal space, cascading green and purple flowers.

I could spend a week wandering, touching the walls, breathing in the dust, pain and memories. Eyes drinking in the dents, patches, and art from this little industry we have. I spent only eight months here, and fear overcomes me at the thought of forgetting any of it.

Now, we go our separate ways, gentrification forcing us out with a giant yellow planning permit stuck out the front for months of trepidation. I made a yellow cardboard 'PLAN TO STAY' permit about community and art and connection and stuck it next to the other one.

Some of us move back into small suburban homes while others hit the road, unwilling to commit to anything, unsure where they fit in.

We will remember, for a while, the politics, the edges fraying, people yelling and being totally selfish. Then, as we grow older, walk different paths and gain perspective, we will forget all that stuff. What will remain are the reasons we gathered here in the beginning, the reasons for excitement at the thought of waking up or coming home from work. We'll cherish the visions that occurred here and pine for the moment we shared.

McKean Street warehouse will be frozen in time, in the memories of a thousand people, an oasis of beautiful chaos that can never be recreated. We'll all take a little bit with us, a small piece of this place, and carry it somewhere deep inside, smouldering, quietly glowing, reminding us gently of this time we had.

This twisted, beautiful family we've left behind.

RAVER STYLE, 2002

CHAPTER 4

Ode to McKean Revisited

Six months after the last wheels rolled out and the big party, six months after I sat in the warehouse and wrote about this place with a broken leg. Still, I can't say goodbye. I'm working as an Associate Producer for the Fringe festival on Queens Parade in Clifton Hill and each day I think of the lost warehouse. It whispers to me under the sound of the traffic. With an hour to kill today, an urge has me pull up to the familiar driveway. Breathe a deep sigh.

I get out of my car on the deserted street, do the obligatory side-to-side check to see if anyone is watching, and sneak in broad daylight to the gate on the right side. The latch is still unlocked; I lift up the window and hoist myself in. The front hallway is littered with glass and junk mail. Tags are sprayed up the stairs and on every window. Smashed bottles crunch underfoot and I hear the echoes of drunken kids. I search the debris for signs of life, of art, of what used to occupy this space. The bean-bag balls still blow around in the whirlwinds that come from the backyard.

I walk the long expanse, my footsteps echoing in the shell that remains. At the back, a bar stool lays embedded in the glass of an interior window, shards gripping it and breaking as I pull it away. There is a little note on the floor, tiny in this huge expanse.

To read it, I have to shake the broken bottle from it. 'THIS IS SOMEBODY'S STUFF DON'T TRASH IT'. I have to lean hard against the door to the backyard to shove it open. There, the giant, burnt pile of stuff we just couldn't get rid of in time. Couches, cardboard, stray stuffed animals that have wandered too close to the flames. Plants have grown into thick bushes, wind whistles through the open roof. Vibrations from long-past drumming sessions are imprinted in the cracks between the bricks. The bottom of a forty-four-gallon drum with frayed metal edges was a favourite of many drummers; now, it sits disintegrating with rust and filling with rain.

I walk slowly through the remains of pictures and postcards from around the globe sent by absent friends and lovers. A chest of drawers holds old movie postcards and book covers. One, *Danse Macabre* shows a big-haired, dewy-eyed woman wearing a nightgown, asking, 'What drove her from lover to lover, and to death?'

I think about the nature of warehouse life and how it trembles in the grip of the sweaty mitts of redevelopers, liquidation, and property values. It's the early 2000's and all the warehouses are almost gone. So goes the fate of McKean Street… was this sanctuary ever real?

As I walk, I pick up pieces: a wooden kit-butterfly, a plastic baby with wings. Her foot has been cut off and two plastic guns, one green and one red, are shoved in her leg. I decide she is the fairy angel of the cyborg death patrol, and she comes with me. Inside, the floor is sodden and muddy. A blanket of mushrooms grows in the morning sunlight, a little village thriving. Five plants stand in the middle, sprouting under a hole in the roof. The gnome that always watched them is still there, but he fears for his safety and comes with me too.

Upstairs, the protection symbol—apparently from a UFO found at Roswell, New Mexico—is still painted on my door. Silver swirls on the sky blue. In my old room, there are no tags, no rubbish, just paint peeling in giant flakes and dropping from the high ceiling, exposing a pink of long before, a feather and a flyer from a gig I ran. In the living room, leaking insulation and chipboard, holes have been kicked through the graffiti that has appeared since we left. In the kitchen and bathroom, signs of a sledgehammer, piles of rubble and gaping pipe-ends. In some rooms, a Stanley knife has been run around the edge of the floor, the carpet removed. All the doors are missing.

Everyone has come and taken the bits they can use, the bits they want, the things they want to remember. All that remains are the rejects.

I close the only door left on hinges at the front.

Who knows how many times I will have to come back to say one last goodbye.

CHAPTER 5

One day in Melbourne

I walk to the train station in the rain. 11am pours a steady, slanting drizzle. I drop inspirational cards changed to cynical and comical things into letterboxes along my way, for the purpose of humorous culture jamming, not hitting houses that appear to be inhabited by the elderly. They've got enough to worry about, I think to myself.

The city passes; concrete grey and graffitied. People on the train are silent; rustle of newspaper, tinny sound of techno from a Walkman, breathing, bodies swaying. My reflection is pale and freckled, black hair shiny and spiky against my head. I seem to split in two as the train doors open and I step into the rush of people. Don Don is an institution, a hole in the wall by the library and RMIT university with cute Japanese staff who always play the blues loudly. Meals are five to seven bucks, only ten things on the menu. Teriyaki Don is delivered to me as I sit on a stool at a tiny table sticking out from the wall. A black wooden bowl filled with rice, chicken, seaweed, ginger and broccoli, pungent with simple flavours and break-your-own chopsticks. The crowd is varied: mod punks with asymmetrical hair, English professors and students, some standing with steaming bowls in their hands as they wait for a table.

After lunch, I go to Degraves Street and check out the new art, place a couple of bondage babies, glue them to the building with liquid nails and take photos of them. Most people do graffiti or street art to 'get up big' but I prefer to be noticed in micro, so I make hundreds of tiny plastic babies and animals with Mohawks and googly eyes and bondage outfits made from string, and stick them in public places.

A guy drops his lollipop wrapper on the ground, looks me in the eye, and lights a cigarette. He spits in the same spot twice.

I think about how you meet someone in another country, and anything is possible. You meet them and they happen to live on the south side of the river, and it's goodbye forever.

A guy gets on the train and starts playing guitar. The Beatles song, 'Something In The Way'.

The sun comes out, and I give him three dollars and a smile.

BONDAGE BUNNY & BONDAGE BABY, 2000'S

CHAPTER 6

Lest We Forget

Hanoi, Vietnam

It is dusk in Hanoi, and a fine mist is falling, turning the myriad coloured lights into a haze and causing the riders to don raincoats that cover their bikes. The streets are full of caped BMX-bandits rushing to get to a pho shop or bi ha noi bar as soon as they can. I amble along the wide gutters, crumpled map in hand, beside Rachelle, a triathlete from California who I just met while lost on the street. She is travelling solo as well.

We are hunting for the 'Kangaroo Bar' where the *Lonely Planet* tells us we can get cheap and tasty vegetarian fare. After a few spins on street corners with confusion and laughter, we find the bar and enter to see smiling Vietnamese girls welcoming us. Rachelle spies some men she met at the airport and they greet each other like old friends. We sit at their table to have the most amazing conversation I will witness during my time in Vietnam. There are four of them, in their fifties and sixties, grizzled, tattooed, smiling, and one of them wearing the tell-tale 420 t-shirt of American cannabis culture. There's Chuck and Gary from Oregon, Charlie from New Hampshire, and Wolf from Colorado. They joke with us right away, with the sharp wit I identify with the real yanks of my childhood when I grew up in San Francisco. On the outside, these guys look like hippies on the road to Saigon but they are on an altogether different mission in this part of the world.

All are Vietnam Vets.

They came here in the late '60s as teenagers, some as young as seventeen, to put their lives on the line for their country, for a war they knew little about. They went with heads held high and hearts full of hope, only to return home plagued by nightmares, the effects of Agent Orange and memories that would shape the rest of their lives.

During the war, which is known on this side of the world as the 'American War', they fought as helicopter crew, medics, tank commanders, as supply men in South Vietnam, where the foot soldiers were deployed while the B52 bomber planes took care of destroying the north. Years later, while the nightmares continued, they met again at a Vets gathering in the States and decided to do something to help. They wanted to help rebuild the lives they destroyed, and they needed to do something to help themselves heal. A team of men and women began to rebuild and retrace their steps of destruction forty years ago and replace their painful memories with hope. The first group of returning Vets landed in Vietnam in 1989 with a team of thirteen and spent two months helping to build a clinic. Then, they began to build schools, hospitals and orphanages, and this group of men I met are part of the 'Team XXIII' of the VVRP or Veterans Vietnam Restoration Project.

This first team drew plans, carried baskets, broke rocks, and talked with the local villagers about what everyone's lives had been like since the war. Tears flowed from both sides. Chuck was part of the team in 2001, which was a crew of three Vets, the wife of one and the daughter of another. The daughter chose to come so she could see what had so affected her Vietnam Veteran father, so she might make tangible some of the endless nightmares and fears that haunted him still.

One of the members of the team 'XXI' battalion, was Joel, known as 'Buddha' to his friends for his Buddha-like frame, loving personality, and smiling eyes. During the war, Joel always connected with the kids in the villages they passed through and was a loyal friend to all of them. He left for the war with love and his friends. He was seventeen.

Upon his return to the United States, Joel worked hard to integrate and be 'normal', studying at night to become an attorney, connecting at home as best he could despite the damage done to him in his formative years and the constant uphill struggle to offset it. With his wife Jane and son Gabe close by him, he died in America from the after-effects of Agent Orange—cancer of the oesophagus. Joel wanted his remains scattered across his homeland of New York and other parts of the US. However, to the delight of his family, his final request was that a portion of his ashes be taken back to the school they helped build in 2001, and to the battlegrounds of Vietnam to rest.

Chuck and Gary then had the daunting mission of getting permission to honour their friend's—a veteran's—last wishes in the country they had fought against. After a few incredulous phone calls trying to explain to the government officials that Joel was, in fact, an American soldier who wished to lay at peace in Vietnam, they received an official letter from the Socialist Republic of Vietnam stating that they would be honoured to have his ashes brought back here, and attached was a tourist visa for him.

They met at the airport and Chuck carried a Ziploc baggie of their friend's ashes (he shrugs and points out that it was the best way to transport him). They boarded the plane, made the trip to Hanoi, and presented the letter to officials at Customs.

The man behind the desk asks, "Where are [sic] he?" when the letter and visa is presented.

Chuck holds up the baggy, points and explains that Joel was, in fact, right here.

The official's eyes grew wider and wider, then he quickly stamps Joel's visa.

Nobody has ever been rushed through Customs so fast in the history of the world. Chuck and Gary make their way to the northern village where Joel had helped build the school in 2001. On the way there, and over several weeks, Gary and Chuck scatter Joel all over Vietnam. They throw him from the deck of a junk into the churning waters of Ha Long Bay, east of Hanoi, down to Ho Chi Minh City (previously Saigon) from the coast to the HCM (Ho Chin Minh) trail, often from the backs of their bikes while hooting, laughing, and crying.

While doing this, they say goodbye prayers for their lost buddy, Buddha.

When they arrive at the school Joel and Chuck helped to build, the entire village and students are formally dressed to receive them and are prepared for a formal Buddhist funeral. One of the headmasters of the school brings forward a refined lacquered tray, one of the local craft specialties. Gary and Chuck give each other a meaningful look, shrug, and reverently place the plastic Ziploc baggie of grey dust on it. After the formal gathering and the placing of Buddha's ashes in a temporary shrine, they gather in the headmaster's office to talk.

The headmaster built a large shrine on the school grounds, and when he knew that Joel was coming there to rest, added a second storey onto the shrine just to hold Joel's ashes. The shrine would only be accessible from the second storey of the buildings. When Chuck and Gary asked why the tall shrine, the response was: "So he can view the whole valley."

The men take turns telling this story, peppered with swearing and raucous laughter. Their mission was to fulfil their brother's final wishes in a land to which they were terrified to return. So terrified, that the first time they landed, they had to pull each other off the stationary plane, unable to cross the runway and confront what had happened, what they had done all those years ago.

Chuck shows me a tattoo on his left forearm—a beautiful black and grey rendition of Buddha. He points to the bottom and says, "There are the children, Buddha's children." Sitting below are three tiny, plump faces smiling happily.

As night falls, we wander out into the street. I am arm in arm with Gary who practises spiritual paths of the Sioux and Navajo Indigenous peoples, and the boys light up a smoke as we walk the misty evening around the lake, where the sacred turtle of Hanoi is rumoured to live.

Parting ways with email addresses and hugs, feeling as if I just met a group of long-lost fathers who love me, I am left humbled and in awe. I'm left hurting inside for the choices those men in power make in boardrooms, in every country, and the people it affects forever.

Those who will bravely fight for their countries, even now, in wars we should not be fighting.

For everyone who is brave enough to admit when they are wrong, for everyone ripped from the Earth for an agenda not their own.

For Buddha and the others I met that night, lest we forget indeed.

CHAPTER 7

Home

We fly over the Northern Territory, and I look down from 11,889 metres in the air.

My blood rushes to see the expanse of red land below me, to know it is home.

The desert is etched with giant ripples, like waves from the pulsating winds. Clouds are the same. Patterns repeated in nature everywhere.

So much space here.

The tributaries and rivers are so visible, they look just like the roots of a tree that winds and grows in the sand. No signs of industry save for the odd power line keeping everyone connected.

Dusk falls and the sky turns rainbow, fading from cool blue to green, yellow, and orange to meet with the red earth that turns purple in the night.

This is Australia. I'm glad I'm home.

CHAPTER 8

My Place

Just finished reading Sally Morgan's *My Place*, and I can't stop crying. It's the Australian story of a woman who was told she was of Italian ancestry along her mother's side when in fact she was of Indigenous lineage, tracing her family roots to find belonging.

I've been saying I'm American, but I'm not really that American at all. My ancestry runs, I've been told, German and French, Scottish and Irish; a descendant from Nazi lines on one side and convicts on the other. Hectic line up. That's all I know. I'm in my mid-twenties and I have no real idea of who I am.

Who were my ancestors?

Were they happy? Educated? Artistic or musical? Am I one?

And where are the women in my family? The nannas long gone, were they strong?

Did anyone laugh like me? Whose hips do I have? Whose lips?

I don't want my history to start with me.

It's the forces and faces that came together to shape me that I want to know. I would love to sit around a table and shell peanuts or trim peas with all the women of my past. Nanna and Grandma and Jade and Cherie and Danielle and Mom and all the ones I don't know.

We'd talk about being women. Our links and history. About each other and finding our likenesses.

So I can laugh.

So I can know.

So I can see that these freckles and eyes and the shape of my thighs have reason, are meant to be, were not some accident I'm supposed to be fixing, but were given to me with love, with purpose, handed down from my grandmothers to me with glory and belonging.

I want to know the goddesses that came before me.

So now, I will create a special place in my mind.

A room that is timeless.

Where I can go and talk with the women who made me.

Who love me, help me, and teach me about myself.

Sitting there, too, will be the little girl I left behind.

They are waiting.

They are watching.

I am coming home.

TEEN HIPPY YEARS

CHAPTER 9

National Australia Bank at Midnight

I meet him in a dark club across town known for its risqué crowd, where upstairs is members-only and at the top of the stairs there's a clock with various vulvas instead of numbers.

He's wearing a shirt that says 'I like girls'. So far so good.

After dancing and flirting, we catch a cab into the city together, the night is nowhere near over. He swipes his card over red LEDs at the revolving glass doors. I'm giggling like a schoolgirl as we enter the hangar-like foyer. We're met with slick marble surfaces and hushed air conditioning, like being inside the Vatican or a mausoleum. We're humming with the thrill that we are inside, with no business to be there at all. Well, not that kind of business anyhow.

We pass through the open security gates and catch a smooth, silent elevator to the 21st floor. Opens to a cavernous open-plan office space with wood-grain desks and hundreds of silent, grey computers. The windows look over the Melbourne skyline; orange, blue and white lights as far as the eye can see, black sky reaching beyond the edges of the city. There is a thoroughfare between offices linking one wing of the floor to another, curtains at each end. No cameras in here. He pulls the curtains closed and we plunge into darkness, hidden from the fluorescent lights and glass doors that are etched with inspirational finance words.

We fall upon each other, more fuelled by the strange location than anything we've consumed.

The sound of our breathing breaks the silence, he grabs at me like he grabs at money during the day, trading on the stock market. Smooth chest and tensed muscles, a half-dressed tumble of skin, underwear tangled. Lips that find each other in the dark, his cock fits perfectly.

I'm on all fours pulling at the curtains groaning as we cum together, spent, my knees raw from carpet rash.

I don't care if the security cameras spot us because I've just been fucked in National Australia Bank after midnight.

CHAPTER 10

Dog Walk

Yoshi and I live in a cream brick house in Thornbury, one of Melbourne's inner suburbs.

Our explorations of the roads and alleys around us have exposed a myriad of stories, or even favourite places to eat if you are a hound. When we wake an hour after dawn, we drink some water and head off, turn left at the steel gate at the bottom of our front walkway, and head up the hill shaking the sleep from our eyes under a pink sky. We pause at the roundabout and sniff the wind, check for cars and cross the road. Yoshi waits for the ok and bounds ahead, the leash crammed into my pocket. Go right down the sidewalk and past the decrepit house that seems to put up a hand-lettered 'For Lease' sign every few weeks. Today, the sign is gone and there is an empty beer bottle and pile of vomit on the nature strip, which Yoshi finds too easily. Past some modern apartments, some not so modern, the inhabitants ranging from friendly to freaking out and running onto the balcony when I call his name, causing me to call out "It's only me!" and then feeling idiotic because who is 'me' to them? I giggle to myself as we hit the third roundabout, the one where the park is visible, and pause for discipline rather than necessity, and then flee into the park upon my "Ok".

Our park—Penders Park—is the best park ever. We aren't loyal like a kind of football team locality thing, it's just the people and the dogs that frequent it are united by how perfect the small park is. A playground, one BBQ, dodgy toilet block that is definitely a gay beat, basketball hoop and benches scattered around. It's perfect for not only the dusk dog walks and dawn breakfast BBQs with little kids, but also the midnight drinking sessions and illicit things that leave the grass flattened.

When you look in the MELWAYS street directory, there are little pictures of a dog silhouette crossed out with a big red NO, specifying which parks are not dog parks. No dogs at all. Not even on leashes. They seem to have omitted the little dog with a halo over it telling you where you can go with pooch in tow, nor are there any signs that read 'Run Free All Liberated Puppies Here.'

However, our park is an off-leash park. It tells you as you arrive and provides you with a padlocked roll of poo bags for your moral obligation. The dog-park thing is pretty new to me, having been a cat owner for most of my adult life so far (RIP Shiba Mowie). It's true that cat people can live a happy, solitary life, occasionally interrupting private reveries to acknowledge each other. Dogs explore, seek, stick their nose in as far as they can and sniff, force you to get out there and grab the rope with all your might and swing it around, yell, scream and laugh.

Then there is dog-park etiquette, of which I am now aware and sometimes makes me feel like a nervous tourist unsure of the local customs. If an older woman comes up and does not look at me, yet says to him, "And how old are you then?" do I answer for Yoshi or is she waiting for a bark and a half to issue forth? If someone says, "What a cute dog!", am I obliged to return the sentiment, even if their dog looks like a Skeksis crossed with an emaciated racehorse? If your dog is playing with another dog, should you always speak to the other parent? Or can one remain autonomous around the perimeter, perhaps with only a nod on arrival? If you do speak to the other owners, it's usually about breed, age, sex, names, balls, training, perhaps a mention of the weather—if it's going really well. Say you meet the same dogs in the park and you begin to chat to the owners, on more than one occasion, what subjects are okay in the dog-park dynamic? Exchange names perhaps, but jobs? Addresses? Marital status? How about your recurring nightmares involving a tunnel and giant octopus tentacles?

Then there is the extraction, when the dogs are just having too much fun and the parents are yelling in a restrained way so as not to appear abusive, and the moment when the more conscientious dog breaks away and we are free to go on our way again, silent, unheeded, mobile. We proceed out the opposite end of the park from which we enter, cross the street past squat, red-brick units and quiet alleyways, most of which always seem to have some kind of food waiting just a short distance down for Yoshi to find and remember each day.

YOSHISCAPE, PHOTO BY MARK BURBAN

We pass the giant house on the corner—wooden and peaked—the entire thing painted a soothing shade of lilac that makes me dream of living there and dressing in all hues of purple, hanging out on the porch drinking Frangelico in the golden afternoon light. Cross a few small streets and blocks with fences and flats on them, choose which left to turn depending on our energy, our time, the weather and a variety of other factors. Three streets then left if we are the laziest, four then left if we are lazy, five standard, and six if we are extra determined and sprightly. It's these parallel side streets that have way more tales to tell. Each house we pass, I imagine in a split second the scenario of living there. I transport myself into the house by a quick glance over the fence, but if it's one of my favourites, I am unable to break my gaze as I travel past.

Each house is more appealing than my own because I imagine that each could actually be mine; not rented. Some of these houses are like a breath of sweet relief, like if I owned that house, it wouldn't matter what else was going on in my life. If that small plot was mine, if that porch, those windows, trees and gravel driveway was actually mine forever. I have dreamt of a place to call my own my entire life, both in my waking life and in recurring dreams. One of my favourite houses is the little old one whose front door is flanked by two windows. The house has been renovated and had this double-storey, glorious hacienda added onto the back of it. Beautifully done. Old-world colonial with huge art deco windows, soft green grass curving around to the hidden backyard. If I lived here, I would carry a parasol each time I went out to water the garden. I'd wear pearls and stockings inside on the dark, wooden floorboards, and hold parties in the giant bathtub with ecstasy and champagne.

Another of my favourite houses is modern. Wooden with ochre walls and green trim. Gum trees and natives spill their dappled light onto the driveway; asymmetrical windows and bizarre angles suggesting interesting levels inside. In this house, I would wear organic cotton underpants, bake wholemeal cupcakes and sit in my home office drinking green tea, thinking about moving to the country while writing about sustainable energy. There are not as many stories on the actual street in these side roads, instead they hide behind fences, quietly watching from behind closed screen doors, tinnily blaring out of lace curtains and open windows. The traffic is barely audible, the streets we cross are barely dangerous but we stop anyway for discipline. We pass the elderly lollipop man at the primary school, he wishes me a great day each day, not a good day, but a *great* day, and on Friday he says, "have a *great* weekend" as we walk through the mothers with their handbags, sneakers and kids running around at knee-height.

On the footpath, someone has graffitied in the once-wet concrete, so now and forever it says, 'May the force be with you' in scratchy writing. I walk over it and smile because I think it just might be.

There is a surf shop on Victoria Rd; a surprising place to find on a suburban back street miles from the ocean. The door is almost always closed with a sign in the window that reads: 'Gone Surfin'. Perhaps the surfers merely choose to hang their boards there occasionally. When the sand, the waves and the heat gets too much, they return, clean the dead flies from the windowsills and open-up shop to encourage young, bored teens to take up a hobby—a lifestyle of extremes and adrenaline.

I marvel at the small units who have impressive veggie gardens in their small 3x3 metre patch of land, enough to be out there picking and eating each night, and the old man who says good morning as I walk past while he is watering it lovingly. I pick the head off a lavender flower, and squish it between my fingers as I walk, savouring the smell left behind long after I toss it to Yoshi to sniff, who rejects it.

As I pass jasmine cascading over fences, I pause, taking deep breaths of it as though I am inhaling spring itself. Wisteria has erupted on the purple house, pouring out into the street, and I smile and admire the many different kinds and shades of purple flowers around the purple house, and know that the person who painted and planted them had some different sensibilities to the norm.

We hike up the last hill, which I find harder going but for some reason Yoshi always runs up, as if he knows that we are on the home stretch. We pass with our noses in the air (well not Yoshi's, he is permanently stuck to the ground, even when running towards me) and head up our street to meet with the front walkway again. Now full of the stories of our 'hood, his belly a little fuller from the spoils of the street too, ready to start our day of working, talking and breathing around the other humans.

We quietly wait for tomorrow morning when the sun peeks over the hills and we are sniffing impatiently for our next walk, the next chapter in our suburban epic.

CHAPTER 11

Internet Love

In the days before social media, there were forums. I frequented a street-art forum called Stencil Revolution where I was the female with the most posts out of 16,000 members worldwide.

One night there was a ping.

'What time is it in Australia?'

That is how it began. So brief yet so frozen in time. We began to message each other day and night like nothing else mattered. I hadn't seen his face before, this was pre-Skype, and he was a graffiti writer, so there were no photos of anyone's faces online. We sent thousands upon thousands of MSN messages, many of which I copied and saved, poetry that kept coming. He sent me a hard-copy letter. A perfumed letter, sprayed with aftershave in my mailbox with a picture of him wearing a white t-shirt holding a huge semi-automatic gun in the desert.

I wanted to consume that picture.

He was nineteen, a few years out of high school. I was twenty-five. The words did not stop pouring from us. It was the first time I would cross an ocean for a man. The first time I would cross the globe for love.

From him:

I want to take off your clothes to take me away from here. Where to begin? I seem to be in the same predicament as last night, too little time and so much to share. You are now out meeting a stranger in a cafe and I've missed you since the sun went down. It's so dark outside, still musty and unbearably hot but there are flickers of lightning and no chance of rain.

I can't help but think of you or the smell of your hair when it's wet and fresh from a bath. When I'm talking to you, there is nothing else I'd rather do.

Flowers I will give to you. I want you to be my girlfriend, put your hand in mine please. Don't worry if things get a bit too heavy, in the end it will all be worth it. You and I should get away for a while. My love is so deep as the blood in my veins.

I don't think I'm in love, I know I am.

When you laugh, everything is okay. I'm so melodramatic, I feel empty like dead leaves. If only I could hear your pretty voice. I just want you to know you are not alone. Now where do we go from here?

To him:

Now it's my turn to sit in the still of night, in the quiet freezing with a sky that has no stars. I got my passport and ticket today. The travel agent knows I am coming to see you and wished me luck. I feel like everywhere I go, there are signs pointing to good luck.

Fuck, the need to kiss you is so strong.

I'd stop you in the street, make the world melt away, and kiss you for a whole minute in the rush of people passing like water. I want to know about work, is it good, are you going to like it, was it easy to get up early, did you ask for the day off, was your work day at the hospital okay?

I feel I might miss talking to you real-time with all the early nights you're going to need. I seem to have to-do lists everywhere, the satisfaction comes when you get to crumple one up and throw it away. Baby, this letter feels disjointed. Too much mundane information, writing to you is all I can do to stop watching the clock, waiting for waiting. Maybe I shouldn't tell you some things. Tell you everything. But something in me feels like you'll know the important stuff from the scenes which I've been a part of, random scenes I can't believe myself sometimes. You know the important bits.

I am sitting in the dim light trying to get my fleeting thoughts into order but simply, I am crazy, it is cold. I haven't touched you yet but I love you.

So I flew to Arizona, and you drove across three states for the first time in your life to collect me at LAX.

CHAPTER 12

I Still Love You

I went to Arizona and lived with his family; the tattooed Australian girl six years older.

We did a lot of his 'firsts' together. His first ecstasy pill, which I sent ahead by slashing a teddy bear and hiding it inside. First road trip without his parents to the Grand Canyon and beyond. Many first sexual things he wanted to do, and we did them all.

He always looked at me with wonder. I felt loved. We adored each other.

We road tripped and tagged shit, I stuck bondage babies in churches and we drank beer. We nature hiked and kissed and tagged rocks. DEMO 4 GKITTY

When I had to leave, we both cried for days. I bought a doll from the thrift shop and drew my tattoos on her in marker, added pigtails, and left her on his bed as a little 'me'. I left love notes in his drawers and tucked into the pockets of his scrubs.

I invited him to Australia, but it was too scary, too far and too hard, and he gradually faded away after I left. The messages became fewer. The time between them, longer.

I'd call and he would hardly pull his attention away from video games. My dear man with three names, thick glasses and endless messages, one of my sweetest stories to this day.

We didn't fall out of love, but it never had a lifetime beyond a million typed words and one brief month together. It's still sweet when I reflect on it now.

Geography got in the way. I haven't heard from you for a decade.

Then you found me on Facebook. Two kids later for you, a lifetime later, and the love still remains. However, our different lives got in the way. Back then, you weren't brave enough and that's totally okay.

I still love you.

I probably always will.

ARIZONA DREAMING 2004

CHAPTER 13

Seeking a Sign

Ubud, Bali

Reading back over my writing, I touch these pages of my past to try and understand where I come from, where I am going.

So many love poems. They blend together. Often, I can't remember who they were even about. Some I read back now and I'm ashamed of myself, of the raw emotion, the same patterns repeating.

I realise that both my long-term unions were not committed relationships. Both times those men were always about to leave, never really mine, never saying they wanted to be with me. Two years each, with men both eleven years older than me, who were always one foot in, and one foot out. These were my first relationships, and they were nothing but challenging. Neither was a place to rest.

This means I have never been in a committed, healthy relationship that has any sort of lifespan past six months or so. This thought depresses me. Even ten years ago, I wrote similar things, hoping for impossible loves, transcribing my realisations, looking back afterwards and feeling stupid. Always stupid. For hoping, for wanting, for trying so hard with so many incorrect matches, each time with certainty, that THIS IS THE ONE.

I am starting to think there might be only one, and I'm pretty certain I haven't found him yet. Some of them were the ones-for-right-now, but that is no longer enough. None of it is. I can't wait around hoping for them to grow from a half-baked dude, from a floppy, smudgy, squishy potato, that suddenly blossoms into a dragon, fringed with glitter wings. To metamorphose the moment he meets me to become sensual, loving, happy with himself and spiritual at the same time. It just doesn't work that way; he has to be like that from the beginning, on his own.

I don't know if I've met anyone like that yet, or not at the right time and place for me anyhow. Always so many options. They exist in so many dimensions but then fade away to nothingness, and too often, don't even end up my dear friends. I have dreamed of it since I was ten. Can remember that first pull of longing for some love other than from parents, that outside validation that I am me and am worth loving, regardless of obligation. The movie *Bagdad Cafe* and the haunting soundtrack, listening to it and watching the autumn colours change, the wistful hoping began back then. So many years ago; years before sex was even a factor. I know it is not the sex I crave. Sex can be got anywhere, like cigarettes, like food. Stuff to sustain you for a few hours until another need surfaces. Love can surpass all these needs. Love is and always will be, the only answer.

OCEAN DREAMING

Now, I'm in Ubud, Bali. Another solo mission across oceans to find myself somewhere out in the world, a clearer definition of myself. Complacency is my greatest fear but I'm still glad the urge is there, pulling me away from comfort zones even if only on a self-fulfilling pilgrimage once or twice a year. Perhaps, this is enough. I cannot help but think of the parade of lost boys that knock on my door. They bring hope, they satisfy a regular urge for attention of some kind, but they do not sate my desire. These are younger men from whom I cannot learn enough to keep me and my mercurial ways delighted. I date and remove, date and remove, often putting in all the work on my own, and then a conclusion arrives, and I pull away from the chase which often, I started. They leave, and I am not sad but relieved. Relieved that, in fact, I will never settle.

I want it to be amazing. Know it is possible. It is out there. This is why I stayed with the first two even when they would never commit to me. They took me along on their spiritual journeying, and when we broke up, I thought that perhaps my self-discovery would end with them.

It didn't.

It hasn't.

It won't.

It's inside me, driving me to have these experiences, driving me to write.

Today, I went to see the traditional healer from Elizabeth Gilbert's *Eat Pray Love*. I tracked her down hidden alleyways, and she read my palm among other things. She said I will have three great loves in my life—two deep and one not too deep—and I have already had one.

She said I can choose to marry one of these men who is coming, that I will have a long life. Said right now it's easy for me to find good work, and I work close to my home, but in the future I may have to travel to work. She said there are three children for me, if I want them. I like that marriage and children are there for me *'if'*

I want them, they are options within my realm of possibility but aren't necessarily preordained. That's how I feel about the future; I could decide with the man I'm with if we want these things, and when. We are in control of our own destiny.

The healer also said that four people will love me but I won't love them back. She said maybe because they are too ugly for me. I laugh. I don't know if any of these have come to pass but I will keep this in mind! I am still seeking the connection, the moment. I guess when it's right, I will know. Will I know?

What I do know, is I am ready, and ready for it soon. I have been waiting so long, and I have so much to share. The healer also put leaves in my underpants, told me to leave them there for two days, and hands me a script of 'pretty pills', which I laugh at, and then take religiously.

Come on universe, I'm doing the work, please give me a sign.

CHAPTER 14

Birth of a Mermaid

Gili Trawangan, Indonesia

The ocean. Hugo. Unrelenting. Timeless in its constancy but always telling us the movements of the moon with its tides that suck and pull at the edges of the land we inhabit.

Though we may be able to fuck it up by pouring oil into it from human mistakes, and we overfish it to feed our ever-growing population, though we have worked out how to profit from it, and traverse it with ease; hopefully, it will remain never tamed, never conquered, never portioned off and developed.

It's still the largely unknown and unmapped deep, deep blue.

Hopefully, the ocean will always assert itself somehow and remind us that we are only human. Tsunamis are caused by the plates shifting, by earthquakes below us, but the end result is destruction by a simple and powerful force: water.

Here, on this tiny island off Lombok, they previously used dynamite for fishing, to blow up huge portions of coral and then scrape the stunned fish from the surface. Not the best karma for what you are about to eat. Often, we think we have found effective ways of doing things, and only later are they revealed as damaging to the sustainability of precious life. Now there is an established environmental trust fund—you must pay a tax to come diving here, and there are giant structures on the seabed that send electromagnetic pulses into the sea to regenerate the coral. It is working. Slowly, slowly, we realise our mistakes and create new technologies to rectify them. Hopefully, this will be a constant process of learning and changing behaviour.

Some people grow up around oceans. They frolic on the shore and in the surf from a young age, and they understand this elemental force almost intuitively. Others grow up in cities, where beaches are boardwalks and promenades built into safe bays, full of people parading their manmade, lurid fancies in the sunshine.

I used to be terrified of deep water, and remember as a kid irrationally freaking out in my uncle's swimming pool when I couldn't touch the bottom. Even though I knew this wasn't real, the fear of a shark in the deep end would often propel me to the shallows in a flurry of adrenaline. We did grow up in the era of *JAWS*, right?

Everyone has some irrational yet primal fears. As a teen, watching my Aussie cousins jump off the end of yachts into the open ocean with no fear was hard for me. I respect the ocean and the creatures that live there. Yet, I have feared it for a long time. Being dumped in the sea when you don't know which way is up, coughing and spluttering, full of sand can also help that fear, as happened to me the few times I was lost in real waves. I still think scuba diving is a crazy concept, not far removed from space travel, really—humans entering an environment that is totally foreign and hostile to our sensitive lungs and fleshy bodies.

So much heavy gear, I strap myself in, buddy-check all equipment, and do a rear entry by crossing fins in front, left hand on weight belt, of which mine has five kilos, right hand holding both regulator and mask so it doesn't fall off upon entry.

After only nine dives, I no longer baulk at the idea of deep water. I float calmly, BCD inflated, mask on, and raise the inflator hose in the air as we go down. As soon as your head is below water you are more comfortable, when you can see there is no shark below you, no jaws about to pounce. I focus on my breathing, slowly, regularly, so I don't use too much and limit my bottom time. For the next hour I am aware of every breath, almost like meditation—three seconds in, six seconds out—the regulator humming in my ears, bubbles spiralling towards the surface. We communicate with hand signals. Are you okay? How much air do you have? Come up or down to my level. It's a new sign language that feels good to master.

Sea life has its own symbols too, so you can point out a turtle, an angelfish, some sweet lips or a puffer fish. I love the names of all these fish, as colourful as their amazing neon hues. Too many to identify, they circle and swirl around the coral, hide in crevices, school in tiny pods near the bottom, alternately hide and disperse, hide and disperse, as if of one mind. I love the tiny fish who have attached themselves to a bigger guy, for protection perhaps, or to ride in his wake with ease. Often, I come face to face with a huge fish—a groper or snapper—and see its eyes on me and I cannot help waving. The coral is mind-blowing, breathtaking. Giant, majestic columns and trees that look so beautiful moving in the swell, betraying the hard, poisonous reality they actually are.

Some look like satellite dishes—solid, spreading out in myriad colours. Others move gently in the currents, like the hair of mermaids, stuck to a rock while clown fish hide in the poisonous tentacles—the only creatures immune, safe from the bigger fish who circle looking for a bright, tasty morsel. Some are elegant, mauve tubes hiding secrets, or giant brain-like pods, alien skinned and solid. There are entire cities down here, whole ancient ruins that I imagine Poseidon and his disciples left behind, regenerating themselves quietly underneath the fishing boats. Some of it resembles trees on land, the formula for growth the same, the golden mean, sticking out from the coral wall like divine latticework. I cannot tell if it is soft or hard because not much is as it seems down here. When you descend deeper than 30 metres, all colour is lost. Even a tomato looks blue, and this is where the most bizarre of creatures dwell.

As I circle a huge coral pinnacle teeming with life, I look upwards. Giant sea turtles circle languidly above me, flippers wheeling with prehistoric shells and eyes that survey their surroundings with the wisdom that only comes from being a species alive for so long, against so many odds. The survival rate for green sea turtles is one in 200, yet they are still here. On the ocean floor, spotted stingrays search for food, their plate-like bodies moving like the pool cleaners we have fashioned after studying the effectiveness of their physiology. I hear a flickering, the hum of an unknown life force behind me, turn slowly and am engulfed in a school of thousands of silver fish no longer than my finger, all moving as one, the sunlight from above reflecting off scales, almost blinding me with the intensity.

I love them, all of them, each tiny being a part of a whole, and I can't help but think this is Gaia in action, the connectedness of everything in motion, right here, only a few metres below the choppy, azure sea.

When I look up, the weight of the water presses down on me, but as I watch my breath ascend to meet the sky—a column of shining bubbles erupting like jellyfish—there is no fear anymore, only wonder.

AT ONE WITH THE OCEAN, FINALLY

CHAPTER 15

I Am in the Right Place

Lombok

Dolphins arc in the sea as I sit on a fast boat back to Bali, tears in my eyes because I've left another home-away-from-home.

A quick mission to escape Melbourne has turned into feeding the fire again; I remember who I am. Lombok is different to Bali, the ratio of sunburnt, raucous tourists is lower, the people are poorer and the travellers a bit more open to adventure over resort life. One dress, a swimsuit and a rash shirt became my wardrobe. A dry bag is my handbag. A bike my transport, riding under pink frangipani trees. Spicy, rice-based food and very little political correctness—honestly, it's a fucking relief. Sometimes Melbourne's hipster, moral high-ground perspective exhausts me, especially when there is so much poverty in the world. Let's focus on living instead of just batting around righteous ideologies online. I had other plans: riding a horse, going on a paddleboard, working on my projects even. Instead, the days blended into a routine of eating, sleeping, diving, smiling. Riding bikes in the rain. The diving—that magical, exhilarating underwater land we don't visit enough; that I fear we don't appreciate enough.

A night dive revealed so many extra-special creatures you don't see during the day, dropping in at sunset and following the shore, our torch beams like lightsabers. Cuttlefish like tiny aliens and octopus that squirt us with ink as they shoot away, tiny fluorescent nudibranchs, a lionfish more beautiful than I can even describe, the shape of its fins echoed in our boats, tribal headdresses and kinetic technology worldwide. Out of this world, something I'll never forget.

I stick my iPod in my ears as the boat slams into the waves and play my 'coming and going soundtrack' for chapters of change.

For these missions to faraway places and for the sweet goodbyes, I feel like the luckiest woman alive. But it's not luck. It's my determination to have the most amazing life possible and spread love everywhere, and go as far as I can, as often as I can afford. However, I know I'm not hardwired to be transient forever, I really love home. My things. I collect a lot of things as well as moments. But I'm a traveller over a tourist, and I'm already planning the next chapter of exciting projects at home, as well as the next plane out of there, to find somewhere new to belong again. To chase this feeling around the globe, I take photos and write so I never forget.

Also to inspire anyone making excuses that it's too hard.

It's not.

Sometimes you have to get lost to find yourself, sometimes over and over again.

Just now another dolphin arcs in a shower of spray outside the window.

I am in the right place.

DRINK LOCAL BEER, ENJOY LIFE

CHAPTER 16

Because You Can

Sometimes, it's winter.

It's grey and you want to escape from your life.

So, you fly somewhere on a plane, and see people who smile at you and it's different and amazing. But you miss your walk by the river, and the pillow is wrong and it's raining anyways and then you realise...the most amazing place on earth is YOUR PLACE.

Because you know where everything is, you don't have to ask anyone and you have collected all the pretty things that make life sparkly. You are the boss of your life and you know how to heal yourself.

You don't have to behave any way other than how you want, you choose who you hang out with every day and you breathe a sigh of relief because some people go away to escape their lives, but you go away for perspective and return loving yours even more every single time.

Then you think *phew*, thank crap I'm one of the people who creates their own reality!

I made a damn good choice whenever the fork in the road was 'STATUS QUO' and 'SOMETHING WILD AND UNKNOWN'.

You don't feel trapped, you go home to your colourful house and lots of people smile at you because you love them and they love you and it's a choice. Yoshi dog has a yellow bandana on, the cutest guy ever and he smiles with his entire body at you for about twenty minutes non-stop.

You eat chocolate in your underwear with the heating up, with him on the couch with his paws around your neck loving you relentlessly all night long under twinkling chandeliers—because you can.

CHAPTER 17

The Art of Eating Alone

Koh Tao, Thailand

Food.

I have often said that great food is preferable to mediocre sex. I stand by that.

They may both have associated guilt after the fact but I know which I would choose if I had to pick a lifetime of either. Yet, often when I'm on my own, I lack enthusiasm for food. We say it's hard to cook for one but it's really not, you just halve the ingredients. Most of the time, it's hard to get excited and motivated to fulfil cravings, and to shop and cook and delight in food on your own. It's easy to decide exactly what you and *only you* feel like eating and go on a hunt for exactly that. No compromises. That often isn't the case when eating with other people.

I love cooking for others, and get inherent satisfaction when they eat food I've made, that I am helping them stay alive. When I'm alone, especially when travelling, often I choose healthy, tasty, utilitarian food. Food to keep me alive, with as little guilt as possible associated with it. It's much harder to gorge yourself to be overfull when it's just you eating. There is no encouragement, nobody to lick your fingers in unison or share those groans of satisfaction.

Tonight, I decided that utilitarian just isn't going to suffice.

I did some research, found a place that sounded good. I say out loud to my apartment, "I am taking myself out for dinner", and add earrings and strappy sandals before I head downstairs to my scooter.

The Hippo Bar and Grill is a classy vibe for the island, yet not one person is in here.

Instead, I'm greeted by a phalanx of Thai men in matching t-shirts, trained to wait on customers Western-style. I choose the best table in the house… well, the second best if I'm honest, but still a table for six. I realise now I should have taken the best one. That is what you can do when you eat alone in an empty restaurant. I flick through the menu, tempted by Thai dishes though I'm at a 'rib house'. Order a beer.

"It's two-for-one," they say.

"Can I have one now and one later?"

"Yes."

I ordered the pork rib specialty. Fuck it, I'm in Thailand and they are less than ten bucks. I never usually eat ribs when I'm out at home. So, I sit. I pour my beer into the water glass because if I have a choice, I prefer a glass to drink with. I sip it, and the fizz calms me.

As I listen to the street, I watch the waiters and think. Can't even tell you what about. I enjoy the ambiance of the red lanterns, and ponder the day ahead, the day that has been. I cross my legs and admire my tan… and notice I am tired.

My ribs come. Other people come and take the best table, right next to me, in the empty restaurant. I don't care, and tuck in. I love pork ribs. Sip my beer. Cut my ribs. Pick them up in my fingers and enjoy every bite of that porky, fatty goodness. Lick those fingers unabashedly.

I eat slowly. Think some more. Groan with pleasure, but inwardly. Fifteen minutes later, the plate is clean. No salad, no coleslaw, just a small pile of bones where a caveman's feast was just before. I lean back. Exhale. Lick my fingers one last time.

Sip beer. Relax. Then I just sit. Listen to the soul music playing softly. I don't smoke, nor do I play with my phone. I sit. Alone. Satisfied. Fat and happy, I finish my beer. I wonder about a visit somewhere else for dessert.

I realise, I have mastered the art of eating alone.

CHAPTER 18

No Limits

Koh Tao, Thailand

KOH NANG YUAN ISLAND, OFF KOH TAO

When you stop travelling every few days, and actually live somewhere, you realise how small the planet really is. People you probably passed in the street or on a dance floor in your hometown for the last ten years, but you have to meet them again on a boat on rough sea in the middle of the ocean to connect.

I am simply not content with working a nine-to-five job and partying on the weekends. I never will be. It's not in my genetic make-up or something. I hunt down adventures like a warrior hell bent on getting into trouble, and then delight in laughing about it later when I'm fixing whatever got broken. If I'm scared of something, it's a red flag waving at a bull (me) to do it anyway.

Currently, I'm on an island, which is for many, paradise on Earth. For others, it's a place to live, to make a life, a community of searchers. My hair fades here, bleached with sun and surf, and grows natural, grey hairs no longer hiding. I become an olive-skinned, wild, mermaid-hair woman, kickboxing, diving, reading, writing, being physical instead of dormant, not sitting in front of a computer for hours. Here, the time you do that is an hour or two per day at best. You don't 'hang out' online as I often do in Melbourne, especially in winter. I write more creatively and cathartically in a month here than I have written in six months. Writing which means something, which is relevant later. No memes. Just me.

No shoes, no make-up, no traffic lights, no television, when local news is the only news, the people you see every day. Having a slow internet connection, no car and books instead of TV is really good for the modern, Western soul. Our desires are often at our fingertips but there's too much noise, too much static, too many choices. Faster isn't always better. With simplicity and minimal inputs, contentment is just that bit easier to reach. A billion monks can't be wrong.

Every night you sit by the edge of the sea, watching the sunset, drinking a piña colada and listening to soul music, but you still find yourself in the same thought patterns. Your universe actually inhabits the space just above your shoulders and you take it with you everywhere.

Here, events are immediate. They occur right here, right now. It's like a festival. Lawless. Liberating. At first, you are out of your comfort zone. Then you relax and suddenly, no other way of living is relevant. There is only now. Only free. *Why the fuck would anyone choose to do anything else? I don't want to leave now...*

I will, however. There are whispers every day of the life I have built, which is calling. I am not done with that life yet. There is more to achieve, more to complete and to learn, though I do love piña coladas.

I do the things that I say I want to do. Follow through and make it happen. This feels good to know. It's good to remember. I go on solo missions to crazy places and take on random jobs I have never done before to remind myself of that fact, and am often caught unaware by a sense of beauty so sharp it takes my breath away. I call this feeling 'limitless joy'. From the city skyline to my knowledge of the streets (always a backstreet bandit) to my house packed with love, good smells and artwork, to my beloved doggo to my incredible, inspiring, beautiful, constantly-growing friends, I truly love my life back home.

On this distant beach, I sit with my piña colada and can't help wishing for those friends to share it with me. I think about how good it is to drink amazing coffee and eat decadent, hipster breakfasts. How much I actually like wearing outfits in layers, not just a bikini every day. How I actually really like driving my car, even in traffic. Even how I like doing the dishes (don't tell my housemates!), my hands in the warm water, staring out the window, music playing, in my house, my sanctuary, that I have created. I love Melbourne for its challenges and relationships that change. For my history there, my first ever really, that I created—the home I chose to make in our beautiful lady of the night city, and how goddamn well I made it. I know I will never really leave. Not forever. My family is there, even if my blood relatives live elsewhere. Maybe they will join me soon. Maybe never.

I am American. I am Australian. I live in Melbourne but I want to go everywhere, and I will return to Koh Tao. Subject to change at any whim because I can change my mind at any time and so can you.

On first dates, I often ask men, "If you could eat anything in the world tonight *anywhere*, what would it be?"

It makes me disappointed when they reply, "A Parma at the pub", even if that is what they want. I want to hear crazy stuff, people! I AM GIVING YOU NO LIMITS!

There is not only one reality. There are multiples. Right here, right now is only one grain of sand on the beach of possibilities. Stretch your heart and mind and ask what more you want. What more you can have. I write this for anyone who has never felt home, till you went out and made one. I'm reminding you, there is more than one to make!

There are no ends to the possible 'you's' there are. I promise, there's always more. You can overcome any shitty past, any broken heart, any boring job, any stagnant life. You can make all your places, moments, and people, *amazing*.

You can.

I am.

I want it.

I live it.

I believe it.

I have to.

I have no choice.

CHAPTER 19

Question Everything

Vang Vieng, Laos

You caught a plane to meet me. Spontaneously, I *love* that you decided and actually did it.

A total surprise. We have already had so many goodbyes and now we have another chapter in our adventure before yet another arrives! It's Saturday and you are beside me on our bed in Vang Vieng, post-breakfast, post-sex, sleeping like a baby. I can't believe how awesome it has been travelling with you. For such a fiercely independent woman, I have so enjoyed having you accompany me on this trip.

We are easy together. We don't argue, don't put each other down, I feel safe and respected with you. In fact, it's totally bittersweet that we have got it together now, right before you leave for London, and again, we have not been allowed to settle into each other for any length of time. Perhaps that is how it is meant to be. The universe has some bigger plans for us.

I felt sad when you sent a photo of my name you drew in the sand, for at the time I thought I couldn't teach you or help you grow. So, I ran away. I often run away when I'm not sure. Uncertainty has always made me feel anxious. Now, I see that it was my role—dictated by greater forces—to help you overcome, so that I could enjoy the benefits. I'm proud to hold your hand, I love being out with my arms around you, how we fit together. I'm pretty sad it has to end in only a few short days. I could get used to it. In the past, I have been a very fickle lady, quick to run away. For what it's worth, I'm sorry. I do regret that now. I'm so glad we got to spend this time together too; what a great way to leave things, really. You have been a real trooper with not feeling well, good old South-East Asian gastro. I'm sorry this happened to you but such is travelling. I wish I could wave a magic wand and make it go away these last few days for you. Alas, my witchy powers don't seem to work that way. Yet.

The person I'm with doesn't have to be the same as me; I can be the reader, and you can be the listener. I love reading to you, even and especially when you fall asleep. Love that you love my excitement at things even if they are not the same for you. I love our shared love of feet, our love of food, even when you have to eat bland stuff. Love that you clean up what I can't finish, even if sometimes you try to feed me things I have said no to numerous times—you feeder!

I love that you respect others and other cultures, even if totally foreign. Love that you prayed to Buddha even when it threw you right out of your comfort zone to do so. Many aren't willing to change, to admit moments when they are unsure and forge onwards anyway. I love that you love listening to my voice—we give each other shit about our accents and laugh. Love that we wrestle and tickle on the bed, giddy with silliness. I love that it is easy to do things with you, and just as easy to not do things. Love that I can strip off and lie naked in front of a window for you to take pictures of me. Thank you.

CHAPTER 20
Thanks for the Stories

You are living it up in London on a massive adventure and might never come back. Sigh.

Last night, I spent hours looking through photos of our trip. Not photos of sunsets or elephants or flowers, but of us. Rolling around in bungalows, playing, smiling, sitting on the balcony with each other's feet on laps, smoking and being silly. Some of the most favourite photos from any trip I've been on *ever*. Favourite photos of me with any lover. Ever.

I will look at them repeatedly and wish to be back there. Of course, I'll forget about the semi-bad food and the heat. That's the beauty of being human, we get to forget the crappy stuff and remember the magic moments, like the thunderstorm at 3am, like riding the motorbike in the hot rain framed by mountains with me singing in your ear. Feeling free. Feeling held. Feeling loved.

That's what life is really made of, those are the things we recall when we are old, not running out of toilet paper. I was thinking that you might just be the yin to my yang. Yin and yang are life force, not just the hippy black-and-white symbol. Yin is passive, yang is active. Yin is feminine energy, yang is masculine energy. Yin is cooling, yang is fiery. Yang is me who runs around asking what/who/where/how do I fit in and what do I do next? Yang is devouring books, writing and talking a million miles an hour. Yin is he who quietly decides on the next course of action and works towards it diligently. Yin is he who watches. Who says that he is here to listen to others' fantastic stories. This is important to realise because I've been trying to find someone who can match me—intellectually, energy wise, sexually, spiritually, in every way, and I don't know if that's even possible or even healthy.

That night we smoked a joint and I laughed for an hour at one silly noise you made, and then you laughed at me laughing, on and on till we cried. Then we finally went to bed when we couldn't laugh anymore and had sex by using only our two hands locked together in the dark. What the fuck was that? That was better than so many ecstasy moments for me, so pure, so unplanned, such joy and exploration. Fully clothed, just feeling each other, symbiotic movement in the dark, just hands touching, no other body parts needed. Now that was magic, *real* magic. It went for what felt like forever, and all I could do was feel you, I couldn't even think. You seriously popped my hand-sex cherry. I loved it way more than losing my virginity all those years ago.

The night we dressed up in the only collared shirt and dress either of us had packed, held hands and walked the fifteen metres to dinner, ate next to the pink mountains and walked back to bed. I've imagined that dinner scene my whole life, but never had the chance to do it. Same with flying along a road on a motorbike in a foreign country with my arms around you, singing freely without worry of what anyone thinks. I always imagined it, and never had the chance, so thank you.

Now, I can be a bit of a know-it-all. I said things that turned out to be bullshit. Was wrong sometimes. I will always admit when I'm wrong, even if it's hard to backpedal when I've been so righteous.

Anyhow, I appreciate the gracious way you let me do that, without being mean or arguing with me. I needed that experience; I don't want to argue anymore, with anyone. I've been a scared and sometimes angry lady in the past, but not anymore. I'm well and truly home now, settled back into the craziness that is my life, used to going to bed with Yoshi to cuddle each night and with space to reflect on our trip, on the adventures and trials we endured. Somehow, nothing is different. It just feels wrong that you aren't sitting here, eating my amazing dinners and touching me. I'm doing my thing, as I always have, usually alone. I know how important it is for this space to be here right now, and I freaked out when I thought you were coming straight home because I know how important it is to you and to the man-self you haven't quite found yet.

I don't want you to regret anything. While I did look up flights to London, I am staying here for now. Doing things equally as important to my progress as you are to yours. Things will change, but I know I am loved. You should know you are too. What an awesome thing!

My idea is this: I'm printing this letter and sending it to you in the book you gave me. There is an envelope for you to put a reply letter to me, and send the book back. You can add whatever you want to it, photos, stickers, bus tickets, mud from festivals or whatever. Then I can touch your words, your adventures. We will share the same stories. We might write six letters; it might be thirty. It might be an encyclopaedia of books and you might never come back. I don't know. To claim to know is arrogance and stupidity.

One day, we can read them together, feet touching. Till then, humour me, and keep the beauty of a connection found in Asia, one that was under our noses the whole time.

CHAPTER 21

For Women Everywhere

This is for women everywhere. All of the strong, yet vulnerable women.

The brave and fearless women with realities to bear.

Women with secret plans and the knowing of centuries behind her.

Despite her smile, you do not know the trials she faces.

For the women who will not bend to society, yet do yoga in darkened rooms while the city sleeps.

For the 'wild, opinionated' types who won't accept the demure stereotype, for those of you who propagate against all odds, who survive, and who fight.

For the soccer moms living the great suburban dream, piloting big SUVs in tiny car parks, wanting to break free.

For the women happy climbing trees, being anarchists in their kitchens, who turn heads with self-confidence when they walk down the street.

For the mothers, especially single ones, doing the hardest job with no salary, who are dishevelled, stressed out and with no space to breathe.

For the determined-to-be-fabulous-no-matter-what ladies wearing killer heels, she's fashionable and beautiful and some say intimidating, but her jewellery is armour that hides how she feels.

For the women brave enough to stand up to each other, and those with the humility to hear it.

For the passionate, nurturing, loyal, adventurous, intelligent and imaginative, for the unapologetically wild and crazy and free.

For those travelling mermaids among us who perpetually run to the sea.

For the femmes who climb corporate ladders, manage events and wield power tools, who occasionally feel like Sea World dolphins, jumping through hoops for misogynist fools.

For women with determination fighting uphill for recognition.

For every doubter, let's plant a seed of intent to believe in your own vision.

For any woman in any industry with more honesty, integrity and balls than those above her, for those who strive, and strive and strive, even when it feels like the planets are crashing around her.

For all the women who have made hard choices alone, who've had to be either selfless or selfish to allow themselves space and time to grow.

For the legion of mamas who have given everything, birthed the world, raising amazing, compassionate beings for the Earth.

For those judged for choosing not to be mothers, for the ovaries everywhere that cry out for babies and for the women eternally destined to love the children of others.

For the women who were born in men's bodies and everyone in between who questions and quests.

For outright acceptance among the sisters, all of us included.

For a blanket ban on competitive bitchiness; it's a waste of energy fighting amongst us.

Here's to nurturing each other, because we must.

For those of us with scars from parents or childhood or sex, with nightmares in our waking life we try to suppress.

For any woman who has owned the words abuse... rape... incest.

I want you to know right now, that it wasn't your fault.

I wish I could give you a giant bunch of all the flowers in the world that explode like fireworks, showering you in sparkles and sunshine, faces lit up from inside, and the sweet smell would linger eternally.

I'd tell you all that you are beautiful in a way that would make you believe it.

I'd remind you of your complete uniqueness, your perfect imperfectness, that all the wobbly bits and hairs are meant to be there, that you are actually a divine creation, a goddess of your own making.

I'll tell you the best love story ever; it's the one where you love yourself eternally…

For women everywhere, together.

CHAPTER 22

Rape is not a dirty word

Every woman should know when to use it. The word 'rape' is an intense word to say.

It's a hard word to own, a hard word to feel comfortable using in any context, really. Even the take-no-shit, self-aware, honest, very opinionated of us who are also covered in tattoos and not afraid of pretty much anything, hesitate to use it.

Yet, when I'm honest, and when I am brave enough to say it, I have been raped three times. Always by people I knew, who did not understand that 'NO' actually means no.

You know how you know you have been raped? After consensual sex, you are smirking. You are feeling the imprint of a cock inside you and inwardly giggling at your devilishness, your cheekiness, you feel wanted, you feel sexy.

After being raped, you feel dirty, inside and out. You are ashamed of your body, the things it does to your mind and heart, the way it 'makes men act'. You want to throw up, to scrub yourself raw till your skin hurts. You want to devote yourself to some god you don't even believe in and never have sex again. You can't even remember what tenderness and intimacy feels like.

When you are raped, intimacy does not come into it. Ever.

The first time was many years ago.

A DJ who played at my club in Adelaide. Somehow, we became casual lovers. There was no obligation, and I don't know if I wanted more with him at the time because the subsequent events meant he ended up repulsing me. One night, he calls. Distraught. Crying. Tells me he needs me now, needs a friend now. It is late and he sounds drunk but he says he is suicidal. Being the compassionate person I am, I get in my car and drive to his house. I arrive, ready to confront the worst situation. He opens the door in a robe, wasted, drinking champagne, and tells me to come inside for a drink.

"I don't want a drink," I tell him. "I rushed over here because you sounded really bad and here you are swanning around in a bathrobe, drinking."

I tried to leave. He wouldn't let me. Forces me onto the bed.

I tell him, "NO. I'm your friend, you are not in a good way, I don't want to fuck you."

He pushes me down, drunk, leering, bigger than me, overweight and sweaty. His beard scratches across my face, he is panting. I give up and let go, travel somewhere else in my head. Try to ignore his body on top of mine. Suddenly, his phone rings. He clamps his hand over my mouth and answers it. It's a girl. He gets off of me telling me to shush, and goes into the next room to talk to her.

I can hear, "Oh baby. I miss you, please don't do this."

Suddenly, I realised why he called in tears. I realise why I am there. A stop-gap, good-times girl, the one you call up for a quick, zipless fuck when the girl of your dreams breaks up with you. I leave him pleading on the phone in the other room, and drive off feeling angry, horrible, dirty and used.

That first time it actually took me weeks to realize that he raped me. I said no many times and he did not listen. I felt powerless and dominated and terrible afterwards. At the time, I told a few close friends but never confronted him about it, and never slept with him again. He knew. He knew that the balance had shifted, knew the way he behaved was wrong. I still remained friends with him, civil, he still came to my club every week and part of me felt like it was my fault.

Fast forward a long time, perhaps a decade. I was working at another club in a different city, often hanging out drinking on the balcony with people late into the night. I was with a new male friend, and a friend of his—can't even remember his name now, I have blocked it out so hard—starts telling me how hot I am, that he wants to take me home. All those sweet words that we like to hear yet are often, so hollow. We get drunker and drunker on my endless free-drink tab and I take him to my place. I can't even recall the sex then, but I know I woke up in the morning and wanted him gone. Even made up a story about having a meeting and said I could drop him at his place down the road. When we get there, he tells me to come inside real quick so he can show me his pad. I protest, but he insists. I don't want to, but I say "okay then" out of fear of being impolite.

How many women have ended up in bad situations merely by not wanting to be impolite?

When we get to his room, he pushes me inside, roughly, onto the bed. I tell him I have to go, and try to leave. I tell him "NO!"

He won't listen. He is also bigger than me, overweight, stronger than me, and despite my struggles, he strips me and fucks me. Again, I go somewhere else in my mind. I had imagined him as this spiritual person because he said he spent time as a monk, but I can't even recall his face now, only the fact that I focused on a single long hair that grew out of his belly. I remember watching that hair as he fucked me, zoning out, dissociating, and willing him to finish, fast.

When I got in the car, I grip the steering wheel and say, "wrong, wrong, wrong" out loud. I didn't cry, I felt numb. I turn the car on and drive away. Later, I told a male friend what happened. He said that it couldn't be rape if I fucked the guy the night before.

It took me weeks, again, to understand that is not true, that saying no should mean no, no matter what. I ran into this guy on the train one day, and was civil to him, but the way I felt afterwards confirmed it. I hated him. I wanted him nowhere near me. He kept showing up at the club, asking for me. I was finally brave enough to speak about it and told the head security and manager what had happened. For the first time, men stood up for me. Good men, who said, "that is not acceptable", who offered to beat him up for me, even if I would never take them up on it. He was told not to come to the club anymore, he protested, sent messages. He did not understand, he would never understand, even after I told him that he raped me. I wanted him to stay very far away from me.

Now, over the next decade of being a nightclub booker and promoter, I had one-night stands. I made a conscious decision at some point in the evening, that I was going to sleep with them. Even if I felt gross and stupid the next morning for the shallowness that had driven me to make those decisions, none of them were rape. Even when I did the walk of shame from some arrogant fuckhead's house in the too hot, too bright morning, I made those choices and I never used the word rape in that time.

Until my recent birthday, when all I wanted was to hang out with friends. I did not want to be in a nightclub, did not want to be around anyone that was not totally loving and only wanted family near me. One of my best friends makes me a cake with her husband and I go to their place, fairy lights twinkle and we drink champagne and celebrate. She calls a boy I kissed a week ago and invites him over. I have misgivings. He is almost a decade younger than me, and something the week before stopped me. A kiss was it. Then I wanted him to leave me alone. He turns up. Drugs are consumed. I kiss him to see what it feels like. I realise while kissing him that it's the drugs making me feel good, not him.

He is awkward, he is arrogant, puts his hands between my thighs when I have not signalled that that is okay. I push him away. A couple hours later, and there is a weird dynamic with the others in the room. Everyone is way more wasted than me. I want to escape. He asks if we can go cuddle. I ignore my instinct, and say he can come with me. I say *very* clearly, "I am not sleeping with you tonight." I drive us home, make us drinks. I do not want him in my bed. He is far from home now with no way to get back. I tell him again, "I'm not feeling sexual at all, I do not want to have sex with you tonight." I tell him this again and again. Tell him *only cuddles,* with emphasis. When I cannot drink anymore, I tell him I'm going to bed.

I race to my room, drag out a long sleeved, shapeless top that hides my figure, and pull it on quickly before he arrives. We get into bed. I'm wasted. He is all over me. I tell him, *"no."* He tries to kiss me. I am repulsed, and tell him, "I'm too wasted, please stop." He pulls my underwear off, not listening to me. He goes down on me. I am not turned on in the slightest, I am almost unconscious, he is relentless, mashing his face on my pussy, it is so unsexy, I want this to end. He is fucking and I'm not here, it feels so wrong. Once again, I go somewhere else in my head. I push him off, curl into a ball, into myself. I fall into a fitful sleep.

When I wake in the morning, he is trying to get close to me. I'm perched on the edge of the bed, I hate the fact that I have no underwear on, the night comes flooding back to me and I am disgusted, feel dirty. I want him to get as far away from me as possible. He doesn't feel the vibe one bit, trying to get me to lean on his arm, trying to kiss me, feel him on me and it's the worst ever. I tell him he has to go. Like, *now.* He doesn't understand as he's leaving. I don't care, I just want him gone.

After all this, even with all my honesty, boldness and command of words, I still can't communicate what I'm thinking which is: *GET THE FUCK OUT OF MY SPACE AND DO NOT FUCKING TOUCH ME,* which is what I have felt about him all night.

When he leaves, I lie in the foetal position for hours. I feel dirty. Sick. Horrible. It is not till much later when my housemate comes in and flops on my bed that we chat and I realise what actually happened. I told him no. Many times. I tried to stop him. He did not listen. He was bigger than me. He did not stop. He forced me. Fucked me when not one part of me wanted it, mind, body or soul. He raped me.

Rape.

He raped me.

Even just saying it, a wave of relief washes over me. I am not dirty, nor am I confused. I am a victim. At any age, strong and independent, it can happen to anyone. It should not, but it does. Again, the boys I live with as housemates say, "that is not okay", and I cry a bit. For it is not. It is okay for me to feel like a victim. It is okay for me to feel abused and hurt and angry.

Yet again, I'm all too aware of my sexuality. Of the fact that I know when I want it and when I do not. That when I say no, I mean it. That so many men can't hear the words for the pulsing of blood in their cock. I am disgusted. I suddenly don't trust men with my body. Don't trust them to listen to me.

Right now, for all the good men in my life, for all my brothers, I feel there are too many who don't care. Who would ignore what they know and take what they want regardless. This is not fair. This must change.

Rape is not a dirty word; we need to use it more.

The men who do it are not men. They are scum, not warriors but cowards. They need to be told that word, tattooed with it, and we need to remove the stigma so they feel ashamed enough to NEVER DO IT TO ANY WOMAN EVER AGAIN. For now, I am celibate.

I make no choice in this matter because my body speaks for itself. I am repulsed. Can't imagine intimacy right now. I'm not even capable of thinking of sex with a man. I do not trust. I am still sexual, still feel things, but it will be a while till I trust anyone with my body again. When I see attractive men and they meet my eyes, I look away.

One saw me ride up on my scooter in the street and said, "You look like you are going to punch someone out."

So, perhaps I am. Perhaps my guard is up, and perhaps, for a while, it fucking well should be.

Rape. Say it with me. Reclaim it. Only then can we move past it together.

CHAPTER 23

I Used to Be a Real Tomboy

I used to be a real tomboy. When I was little, I hated wearing skirts, was happiest in jeans swinging on the monkey bars with all the boys. As I grew older, this didn't change much. I shaved my head for ten years and wore ripped clothes and stuck two fingers up at the world. "You want to judge me, fuckers?" I said. "Then do it!" So they did. Labelled a freak, too loud, too brash, too 'full on', too 'American'. Not many could—or wanted—to see the softness underneath. The vulnerability of a little girl told to grow up too fast. I hung out in graffiti worlds and in the music industry, surrounding myself with men. I was even called 'one of the boys' by some men I respected once, and it crushed me.

I had a couple of amazing lovers who allowed me a safe space to let my guard down. To allow me to find more about the woman I am. To see how wild and intuitive and complex she was, and is, and am. Eventually, I got tired of being stereotyped and standing out so much. The more tattoos and experiences I collected, the more I saw that real people would recognise me for me, no matter how I dressed.

In recent years, I blend in a bit more. I'm not wearing torn overalls; in fact, I only wear skirts and hardly ever wear jeans. My hair is long and feminine. I have become comfortable with my femininity. No longer a tomboy, and I'm not angry anymore. I respect me, past and future. There are still things I have to prove to the world but I care less about the judgements about me based on other's projections and fantasies. Never perfect, always striving for more, but actually content with the person I am. Where I used to live with men, date men and work with mainly men, now there are a growing number of strong women in my chosen family who weren't there before. I know a blonde goddess who has castrated stallions and who fixes things other men have faltered at, all whilst being effortlessly beautiful. I know a tall, well-travelled brunette who is compassionate with relentless optimism and self-awareness.

I know another loyal-as-fuck powerhouse of a woman who I am constantly in awe of who grabs what she wants to make it real and is an amazing mother and wife on top. There are even women around me who only really help me through the internet. One of them, I have known for 20 years, but never met. She lives on the other side of the planet and though some of our values are opposite, she is a sister I have laughed and cried with on forums on Facebook, and been through her divorce and remarriage and the birth of her child with her. I love her dearly. Another I know is a woman who is a powerful priestess, actually a guardian angel perhaps, and even though we have hung out in person only a handful of times, we talk often and I watch her from afar and am empowered by how she lives her life.

I know women who have moved around the world for love, moved mountains for their children, have selflessly, timelessly—again and again—sacrificed so that others may see. So that others may love. I'm well aware that I have manifested these goddesses around me. It's my power they are drawn to also. It is my love and my femininity and my drive and determination and optimism and honesty that they admire that helps them show up and do what's important in their lives. For maybe the first time ever, I feel a multitude of generations of women behind me, around me, supporting me now. The scars we collect, these stories and tattoos, these wrinkles and grey hairs, they all have a reason. These are the stars reflected, our ley lines and history that make us the wise women we are.

I'm so glad my female friendships do not live in a place of jealousy, competition, resentment and feelings of inadequacy. These women allow me to feel exalted when I am in their company. They demand that I value myself as much as they value me. It's a feedback loop of effortless love, encouraging and inspiring self-love that ripples outwards and reflects off everything.

For me, friendship is for life. I am loyal and honest and I will say the tough things from a place of love when I really care about you. The sisters in the sisterhood are even stronger than that. It's actually timeless, ancient knowledge we are channelling and perpetuating in our regular, suburban lives. I feel very lucky to live in a society where women can meet and talk freely about what it means to be strong as well as vulnerable and how we can heal each other.

Whoever is reading this, do not take the amazing women in your life for granted. They might bring chaos and confusion and tears you don't comprehend but they are real. Their hearts are actually open and just waiting to be recognised. I see you amazing goddesses everywhere.

Riding your bikes in vintage summer dresses, making art in the night when everyone sleeps, pumping iron at dawn to feel better about your curves which are actually intended and beautiful, buying your groceries in green bags, staring at your mess of hair and feeling overwhelmed, feeding your kids dried fruit on a street corner and hoping for some sleep soon.

This is a gentle, loving reminder that you have all the knowledge and strength that you need right now. Throughout time, so many things have tried to squish us but still, we prevail. All around, we are prevailing!

All the lies, the abuse and violence, the prejudice, and all the slut-shaming and inequality in the world cannot break us.

Will not break us.

We are powerful and we will continue to roar.

CYBERPUNK ERA, EARLY 2000'S

CHAPTER 24

Sexy Trouble

Far North Queensland

When I first saw him, my friend had one word to describe him: trouble.

Ex-punk in baggy jeans and a band t-shirt with startling blue eyes, baseball cap tilted slightly to one side. Hot. It was instant electricity. That energy we seek and some never find, but which is often also dangerous as hell. After drinking for hours, walking the streets yelling, joking about looking for a bar fight—it's far north Queensland, if you've never been there, you might not understand. Hanging in the street outside the only gay club in town—'The Toy Box'—drunk, disorderly and fuelled by booze, my friend tags the wall outside the club in six-foot letters: DIOR NOT WAR, with a shitty marker. It's obvious we are all generally looking for trouble. Needless to say, he came home with me that night. We make slow love on a mattress on the lounge room floor as the dawn turns to day, where he pulls his shorts on in front of everyone who had gathered in the kitchen, comfortable with his cock and himself.

Trinity Beach, laughing and brushing the sand from each other, eating hotdogs and quietly marvelling at this man who called me 'baby' like it was easy. Nobody had ever called me baby before.

One night, he took me to the beach with a blanket and we scooped out a dent in the sand and made love under the rustle of palm trees, the ocean sucking at the shore as we sucked at each other. It felt endless and natural, same as the tides. With this man, was the best sex of my life so far. We just fit together.

One night we slept together in the 'dollhouse'—a small rickety bungalow built in the tropical yard of my friend's house. All night, he twisted, sweated, shook and turned from detoxing as the rain poured down outside and came under the door, flowing across the floor underneath us. I held him all night long till he finally fell asleep as the birds woke near dawn. However, nothing could get in the way of this love. Not the fact of his two small children, babies really; not even his long history with drug addiction. It was mainly heroin, which I knew too well from previous lovers, even though I would never and have never touched it myself. Nope, not even that could deter me. Here was a man who instantly made me feel sexy, smart, and accepted for exactly who I was. Who was quieter than me, slower in his processes, but gave me room to breathe.

Others who knew him well told me firmly, "Eyes wide open, go into this knowing his past and knowing not much will change." I didn't care. I had found him. The trip ended at a lookout over the ocean, our faces literally glowing in the pink sunset, where we held each other, limbs entwined, and felt like it would be a small death to separate, physically unable to part.

We promised each other that somehow, we would make it work.

CHAPTER 25

Moving North

ROADSIDE HEADING TOWARDS FNQ

The red, red road and the blue, blue sky with cartoon clouds that go on forever. Cows sheltering in the shade of scraggly trees, barren farmland as far as you can see. When a water tank is exciting and we meditate on the road so long that we see sheep and mistake them for baby rhinos.

This country we live in, so harsh, so rugged and unforgiving. Outside, it's over forty degrees, baking like an oven. No phone reception, a broken petrol gauge, our measured water supply and truckies two days awake on speed driving road trains like giant 1000-tonne torpedoes hurtle towards us.

Lumps of roadkill shimmer on the horizon. Crazy mission through the desert like on Mars, a hurtling car becomes a rocket ship and it's a four-day flight to get where we're going. Mining settlements and alcoholic towns where there are bars on the windows of every shop. We share sleepless nights in motels with over-chlorinated swimming pools and dubious grey nomads, eat strange pies in stranger places, and go from car cabin-fever hilarity to long, meditative silences, our thoughts and the road becoming one. It's hard on our bodies sitting so long but it's even harder on my mind, I liken it to doing Vipassana in a car. This land is freaking massive, and it commands respect.

I admire it from my climate-controlled pod, appreciate the vastness of Earth again that I have grasped only a handful of times.

Breathtaking. Precious. Humbling.

We set off on a run of two hundred kilometres without a human or landmark in sight, but for the road. The road. The road. It's been a twelve-hour driving day, making progress on over a thousand kilometres of mostly straight road.

I know that on the other side is a paradise. I'm heading there. To lush waterfalls, friends and hopefully good coffee.

For now, though, it is still a few European countries away. I lose myself in the road, the journey, try to capture the moment by taking photos out of the window but often I drift off, lost in the endless, puffy clouds as the sun shifts around us.

CHAPTER 26

Solar Eclipse of the Heart

Far North Queensland

I had planned to go north with darling Amelia like *Thelma and Louise* across the country. A route I had never done. We were headed to the Eclipse festival to run the Info Tent, another crazy idea that we were making reality in our solo lives. It was 2012 and after Y2K hadn't materialised, we wondered if the Mayan calendar would end, and with it, the world, as the moon eclipsed the sun. One can hope anyways.

Now, it was he and I on the road trip together instead. He had a heroin habit and two small girls, but he also reassured me that I was sexy, smart, and loved. I knew I would do whatever it takes, even and especially if it is scary.

What is this tendency in me? To throw caution to the wind and do it anyways, do the wild, crazy, not cautious thing?

I am usually Miss Autonomous at music festivals. I don't like to feel limited, constrained, or that I have to check with others before moving around. I work hard, I party, and I pass through many circles of friends and acquaintances, often on my own but with everyone. This festival was the first time I can recall in my decade-long career of festivals, when I didn't want to do that.

From the minute I knocked off work and went to make myself look fabulous for you, and saw you walking towards me in the dust, you were mine and I was yours and nothing or nobody else mattered. We danced, we took ecstasy, we flopped on the ground in the dust, intertwined, and talked about everything, and I don't know where I ended and you began. We met friends, talked shit, drank beer, kissed, you twirled me in the dirt and I didn't care who was watching us. We woke before sunrise and dressed up, went with thousands of chasers to sit on the hill and wipe the sleep from our eyes as the moon passed over the sun, and we felt part of the universe. We hooted at the sky and created a feedback-loop with the stars and air and we held hands tightly and not for one second did I wish for anyone else or did I feel you pull away from me. The stars aligned, and we fell in love again.

It was the best time I have ever had at a festival. The best time I have ever had with you. A memory I will cherish until I am old and grey. For you, it was a moment to realise. A moment for the universe to recognise how far you have come, and that you deserved all the happiness in the world. A recalling of your ancient strength, the primal man, the hunter, the provider, the all-seeing, all-dancing, fabulous you that you had forgotten about for so long. For too long. I watched you remember. It meant the world to me. I felt inflated by it, buoyed by your love for yourself, for the universe and for me.

I drove home one day after you, utterly and totally exhausted, having worked long days for a week in the heat. Met with open arms of a man who makes an effort, roast in the oven, children smiling, and that night I sobbed with happiness when I realised that perhaps I do not have to do everything alone anymore. Cried when I saw that you really would look after me if I needed it, when I had never really felt that before. Not since I was a very small girl forgotten in the dramas of my family, not since I was seven years old. In the last few days, there have been hard moments. When the girls are hyper, and we are tired, when the girls are tired, when money and other people and the constant need for chopping wood and carrying water feels like a grind.

I do not *think* we can do this; I *know* we can. I do not *think* I love you; I *know* I do. I have known for many years that when I found the magic, anything else would be possible. Any distances, traversable. Any challenges, surmountable.

The important thing is how we honour our love. How we cry together, laugh together and how we are silly and do things like simulate sex at tourist attractions when they take the photo to sell you. I don't know what the future holds despite my control-freak tendencies trying to work it out. Don't know where we will be or what we will do. But I know I want you. I want to grow old with you. Want to travel with you. I want a series of adventures holding your hands and kissing you in a shower of sparks. Want you to know everything about me, even the gnarly bits.

I want to make a home with you, sweat with you, sex with you, cook with you. Want to give each other endless surprises and trips in our own backyard and every day to feel like Christmas, and relish in this thing called living with you.

Of course it is scary, and it will be tricky and logistical and we need to keep each other talking honestly and workshop all the shit that life throws up.

This is a really true love story. It's ours. I'm up for it. I'm ready. I'm willing.

You know I don't muck around. My prince is six-foot tall with sky-blue eyes and peppered brown hair, he wears baseball hats and drives a Subaru, and I know life is hard and tough and that karma is real.

I hope we prove that living happily ever after isn't just for Disney movies.

CHAPTER 27

Horrible Movie Scenes

Far North Queensland

I put on a dress and took myself to the beach for dinner alone because I am worth it.

The ocean and I break into pieces all over again.

I sob for what I thought I had, what I believed I had found. Cry for the fact that I went forward with an open heart again, gave up everything, moved across the country and took on your two small kids with total honesty, with pure conviction that all the love was returned.

Instead, I have endured the worst week of my life so far. Abuse of so many kinds. A barrage of bullshit, lies, drugs, manipulation and horrible scenes that should only be seen in soap operas and movies. I lost my innocence coming here, lost my joy. You stole thousands of dollars from me. I'm not sure who I am anymore or why I deserved this or where I'm supposed to be.

Even after you hold my dog and my belongings ransom, even after you picked through them one by one and took what you wanted, the abuse hasn't stopped. To the friends involved, I am sorry. I don't know what to do but try to be strong. I have had to ask for my life back shoe by shoe, having to weather more abuse with each garment returned.

I put a dress on and go to the beach and instead of eating dinner, I cry.

Drugs took away the love of my life, and began this month-long horror movie, like a bus crashing over and over, a Groundhog Day of broken-heartedness. I have tried to wait patiently for reality to penetrate but it gets worse every day. The abuse does not stop and I feel afraid.

Is this a reflection of me? Questioning whether I deserved any of this, whether any of the words given to me, beautiful or horrible, were true. Are they true?

I cry, and Yoshi watches me. We are both lost together. I flew him up here in a giant jet plane to start our life with you, and we are in this together. The rain pours down as I say goodbye to the misty mountains, the crazy curlews and jungles that make me so happy.

For I have to leave.

Goodbye Cairns. Goodbye, my first true love the third time around. I hope I'll be okay, not damaged forever. Sometimes, you cannot choose who you love, love chooses you. So I have to walk away. There is no other choice.

I have to walk away.

CHAPTER 28

Broken, Whole

East Coast of Australia

I fell for your kryptonite love. Moved across the continent only to leave a few months later because you went crazy on drugs.

Layers upon layers of lies and twisted manipulations, delusional arguments I did not even engage in. Now, I am broken. Broke and broken, you thief. My soul feels bruised. Am I somehow to blame for this? I leave, driving and crying, driving and crying, back across the country to my family. My illogical and chosen—not biological—who love me, who understand me, and who right now, are very far away.

I devour kilometres and nibble stale crackers on the side of the hot, straight road. Watch the mountains flatten out, the humidity fade, the coast widen. I think and I drive. Question both the declarations of love that seemed too good, too mutual, too easy to be true, and the bitter, venomous abuse of my personality, my actions, my words and everything held true to me that spewed forth from you like someone possessed. I wonder at my own naivety, regret my own unwillingness to be cautious, to have trusted you, to have believed you, when many around me doubted. Every night when I arrive at my destination, once I have secured a place to stay, I cry with the pressure of it all. I walk and pick myself flowers, stick them in a plastic cup next to the bed so I wake up knowing there are things growing outside, that new life is always possible.

New life is always possible.

I eat healthy food and sing along to the stereo, trying to fill myself with all the goodness you have sucked out of me. In the morning, I go for a jog, shower, dress, pack, eat breakfast and then a few hours in, when it's just the road, it overtakes me. The clouds descend and I sob. Moan.

Tears flick on the steering wheel as rain pours down outside. I let go of more of the primal pain that is now tangled with barbs in the tall saplings of love for myself. I feel it. Let it happen. Then I watch it eventually subside with the concrete, with the white, painted lines. Then it's quiet. For now. I have cried every day for a month. When will it end? The only thing that keeps me going is Yoshi dog, patiently loving me, in the backseat, waiting for the beach run we do every day on this mission back 'home' as we drive down the length of the whole country.

Also the knowledge that I am destined for a whole lot more than this. Whereas, I fear you may not be.

You seem destined for a life of personal struggle, with society, with other people, with honesty, with drug addiction, with finding happiness on your own two feet, for yourself, by yourself. I am going to flourish, however; like the giant tree ferns. I will keep holding all of humanity to a very high standard. Will love openly and honestly, without fear. I will keep my expectations at the level of no less than amazing. Will make plans and action, travel wide and make friends everywhere and work on crazy things, because I want a full, abundant life sprinkled with joy, laughter, nature, truth, and integrity.

Next time, I will recognise the men who are dependent, controlling, jealous, paranoid, addicted, needy, desperate, arrogant, financially ruined, emotionally unavailable and doing a whole lot of talking and not a lot of walking. Next time, I'll say: "Nice to know you, buddy!"

However, I've got more important things to be doing with my love, time, money, body, energy, cooking, intelligence, and drive. I'll turn around, smile to myself that I'm brave enough.

I'll cheer in my head, *Yeah, girlfriend!*

I'll walk away, head held high, because who knows who could be watching.

I won't be broken, even if I'm destined to be on my own eternally, I'll be *whole*.

DETERMINED TO GO FORWARDS

CHAPTER 29

Twelve Hours to Make Mistakes

It's dawn and blossoms appear too early on the tree outside, a sign of global warming, which in this end of winter doesn't seem so bad to my frozen bones. The sky changes from black to grey to blue to golden, light seeping around the edges of the blinds like liquid as I turn in my bed like a kebab and try to find some heat by folding my hands between my thighs.

As the day reveals itself, I understand the motivations for a thousand paintings, for viola concertos, for monologues, for wedding proposals and babies pushing towards the light, at sunrise and also sunset. Every day we are given a chance to make a new moment, and a chance to let lie the ones that have gone, a chance to let go and make something new in its place.

Every morning and each night sparkling with stars we can reinvent ourselves, see things or do things differently, choose to move, to stay, to hold tight or push forward with a dream. A choice takes only a second. Yet the planet gives us an hour at each end of the day, where it blasts a spectacular view at us from above.

Clouds swirl into luminous explosions, screaming quietly and loudly at the same time.

I pull over on the highway to breathe in the fading light, feel it on my face as cars and trucks whizz past me, oblivious to what they are missing. Photos, I have taken of these moments all over the globe, a split-second meditation on the skies. I share them online in the hope that even one person might join in my delight, stop what they are doing, look up and witness the change.

It is the hour between sleeping and doing, the hour between clocking on and off, the hour between dark and light where intimacy reigns.

Can you believe there is still a time every day when intimacy reigns?

Today, I allow myself that hour, one whole hour before I do anything that constitutes 'living', before talking, where I simply watch the world and know that I am changing too. Every second. And if I look away, the moment disappears as it drops below the horizon in the blink of an eye, illustrating the impermanence of all things.

Clouds rush past the morning sun as it gains strength, and I get stronger with it. Filling up with breath and ions, light, and juicy energy. Twelve hours now to make mistakes, twelve hours to strive, to try, to laugh and cry.

Then tonight, the light fades, the air cools as the colours tilt towards blues and greys.

We are given a chance to change it all once again.

Tomorrow.

CHAPTER 30

Reality Check

Twenty years or so in the arts and music industries, and I'm ready for a change. At my first festival at Mount Disappointment in 1998, I volunteered for Rave Safe, and sat with a tripping guy taking phone calls on his Lebanese cucumber all night.

It has always been way more preferable for me to have something to do rather than just be at the party.

Skip forward through decor, art department, stage management, bookings, marketing and publicity, running an agency, an art gallery, nightclubs, information tent, community development, recruitment and training, to operations, logistics and coordination of the team, and safety. I have done almost everything in the music industry except play or produce music. Perhaps I should have started off doing that. The only problem is, I can't hold a tune or beatmatch, haha. With a name like Ghetto Kitty, the number of people who thought I was a DJ over the years is ridiculous. I won't lie, I just said yes a few times.

However, my skills really lie in helping talented people reach more audiences.

I was the Publicity and Bookings Manager at Lounge on Swanston Street from 2003-2007, an iconic restaurant/bar/nightclub in the heart of the city with a 24-hour licence. Known for being the late-night spot in the city, sort of the sister venue to Revolver—the 24-hour club on the southside. Lounge had a balcony overlooking the street and the free drink cards were plentiful. The staff felt like a family, dysfunctional and imperfect, but supporting each other as only hospitality people working all night long know how to do. If only that balcony could talk, it would tell some stories about Melbourne in the '90s and early 2000s! If you were there, you know.

After I gave my notice at Lounge, I was headhunted to take on a similar role at another iconic venue, Miss Libertine's—a cutting-edge club in the old bluestone Mac's hotel on Franklin Street, also in the city. The owners were Asian, and they point-blank told me they wanted a tough but friendly woman to do bookings to subvert the 'Asian businessman' stereotype. Fair enough, I was happy to be at the helm of one of Melbourne's newest, hottest locations. I still maintain the reason I was so good at these roles is because I wasn't a DJ or performer, this meant I had no alliances with other promoters or the urge to get booked for gigs anywhere. No nepotism needed. It meant I could book what worked and help the hungriest, bright-eyed, bushy-tailed performers get started.

The boys let me book a range of promoters and acts and gave me pretty much free reign, as long as the bar takings were good. The best night ever was when we had De La Soul show up to our free Wednesday hip hop night for a secret gig I advertised with text messages in the days before social media, and we had the club packed with 500 of Melbourne's coolest people that night.

After a couple years, I opened my own independent art gallery in the unused function room upstairs, and called it 'FOR WALLS'. The gallery was small but amazing. We held over 30 shows in 18 months or so and it gave me a chance to invite all the underground and street-based artists I knew to come into a gallery space with low sales commission, free beer through sponsorship, and free flyers. It was the best deal at any city gallery at the time, and we got a rep for being on the pulse for emerging artists.

However, nightclub life took its toll on me.

I was commuting to the city five days a week, and then 3-4 nights per week, back home to change, eat dinner and walk the dog, then return to the city to network, and schmooze the promoters at the club. I would dress for the event. Hip hop gig? Fat white sneakers and big hoop earrings. Minimal techno? All black. Experimental noise? Something edgy, a pop of colour. For all those years, my eyeshadow matched my outfit perfectly, and I would suck back tall (free) vodka, soda, fresh limes like they were water. Free drinks at every club in town. I would arrive to say hi to people, and the red carpet would roll out. Such is the life of a booker.

Eventually, I burnt out.

There's only so many weekends/weeks/months/years you can back up a 5-day hangover with another one. Near the end of this time around 2011, I bought a baby-blue scooter, and used to lie about what I was drinking, saying it was vodka but actually it was soda water, and rode home at 3am sober, just so I could not hate my life in the morning.

I'd left this heady world to move north, and was happy about it.

When I returned, broke and heartbroken, I had no idea what career move to make next. The arts can be like that, your skills are transferable but unless you work in the same role for big, recognizable brands over years, people don't have context for what you do.

I had worked for K-Swiss shoes doing international graffiti art shows, worked for marketing companies and brands like Cirque

Du Soleil, General Pants and others. Plus, most of the major music festivals in Australia.

But, by happenstance, it was a job at Blender Artist Studios that launched me into my actual calling.

I went for an interview for a Gallery Manager, but they had a load of major activations planned with big brands, and nobody to facilitate. By the end of the interview, I'd created a role for myself there as Project Manager for large-scale murals, and experiential stuff like painting sports cars live in Federation Square. After a few months, the owners went overseas and left me in charge of the artists' studios, where ten or so artists were working on a range of projects and commissions.

It was here that I first really and truly understood that if you're not happy in yourself, or your heart, your work will suffer. There was an extremely talented artist who was much loved, whose relationship had broken down and with it, all of his output. He was stuck. Depressed. Everyone at the studio was worried as he carried a cloud over his head, so one day I declared we were shutting up shop and going to have a beer instead.

About six of us walked down the road to Section 8, a laneway bar much loved by musos, university students and artists right in the centre of the city. We ordered a jug, poured everyone a pot. I pulled out a pad of paper and proceeded to ask the artist questions.

When was the last time he felt happy? He couldn't recall at first.

We talked some more… and after a while he said, "Wait, the last time I was happy was when I was fishing."

This was not what we had expected to hear from this very urban, graffiti-based artist.

I asked him when he had last gone fishing.

He thought about it. Sipped his beer. Said sadly, "Over ten years ago."

I wrote on the list I was making as the first action item: GO FISHING.

Because whatever it is that makes you happy, needs to be a priority.

The other artists thought I was going to give him a business butt kick, set him a creative task or some such, but I had already been doing this process for years with my friends, and with all the creatives who crossed my path in galleries, clubs, festivals and everywhere.

I knew that you don't start with business KPIs, you start with your soul.

I had already helped a queer friend reconcile his sexuality with his Christianity.

Helped hundreds of artists work out how to sell themselves better.

Also helped loads of promoters improve their events, the punter experience, and their bottom lines.

I'd always been someone people confided in, and someone to whom people came for advice. Often, they would say, "I don't know why I'm telling you this stuff."

My answer was always "It's safe with me. Whatever you want to tell me, is safe."

By the end of that jug, we had agreed on a list of 10 things, in order of priority, to do that would help him get his mojo back. I asked him to write it himself because I believe there's magic in writing, scribing. He was already smiling, and excited to begin.

The other artists were speechless.

"What is that thing that you just did?" they said, referring to my rapid-fire, intuitive and compassionate questioning and leading him to his own knowledge of himself with clarity.

"I dunno, this is just what I do," I replied.

"Well, *that* thing you just did, is what *you* should be doing, not all this other stuff," they said, referring to my work at the studio wrangling stakeholders and creatives, procuring art supplies for other people's projects.

They were holding an artist market soon in the small alleyway next to Blender, and they made me promise to offer this service. Over that jug at Section 8, we decided that what I just did, the process, was called a 'Reality Check'.

A week later, I pulled out a card table and set it up in the rickety alleyway with a giant poster that read:

'REALITY CHECK—Love, Career, Happiness, Self Esteem, Biz Marketing, Tricky People—Life is confusing, there is no rule book! But Miss Kitty's tough love, no-bullshit approach will uncover your real priorities. No NLP catch phrases, just personalised strategies for awesome. HELPS CREATIVE PEOPLE GET THEIR SHIT TOGETHER'

I made a bowl of inspirational sayings with 'FREE LOVE' on it, and a sign that said, '$15 for 15 minutes', and did my first ever paid sessions like a strange Tarot reader at the little card table.

I wasn't sure how it would go but by the end of that first market, five people had sat across from me and divulged issues from body-image to business marketing to being brave enough to go after what they really wanted. I doled out my best advice in 15 minutes and gave them a small slip of paper with five actions to take on it.

It was tricky, because people were telling me deep things about themselves in public, and many people walking by didn't even want to take a little slip of 'free love' from me.

BUT IT'S FREE LOVE, I laughed, having fun with it.

I decided I would do one more market to see if the idea had legs.

The next week, one of the clients from the first week showed up.

He had come to find me to tell me that after our session, he had summoned the bravery to tell the woman he worked with how he felt about her. And, his bravery was rewarded, because she felt the same way.

This moment, when a total stranger had sought me out to tell me that the 15 minutes of advice I had given had, in his words, "Changed his life."

Reality Check was born. This thing had legs.

I was going to be a coach, whatever that meant, and I was going to monetise something I had been doing like second nature for most of my life. Supporting and holding people to feel the fear and do it anyway, guiding people towards practical and pragmatic goals they could actually achieve, and cheering them on while they did it.

This was my magnum opus. I found it. I was so lucky because I knew full well that some people *never* find it, their purpose on Earth.

But mine was and still is to help people get real with themselves and their dreams, to take no prisoners and make it happen. I wanted everyone to dream as big as I did. Wanted them to know they were worth it. I wanted to show them how.

It was time to back myself, hard, ten times over, especially because nobody else had.

I was going to help the world as a take-no-shit cheerleader. Was going to build people up and build them teams and help the entire world make its dreams a reality.

Reality Check was born.

FIRST EVER REALITY CHECK, 2013

CHAPTER 31

On Being Tattooed

Being tattooed has been a major part of claiming myself, of working out what I even look like. I've been saying that I'm 'running out of room to be classy' in an offhand way, and yet ideas for new tattoos come like illumination, quickly and randomly.

Such as camping in a field alone, working at a festival, drinking beer and watching the stars. I don't just want to live in my body, I want to really explore its limits and changeability, learn about it and me, and me in relation to it and OWN THAT SHIT. Especially the lumpy parts, scars, and parts I am not comfortable with.

When I was younger, I had a crappy, confused relationship with this mortal vessel. Didn't like it, was embarrassed of it, used to undress in the dark and hide from others, even my sexual partners and from myself.

Becoming tattooed is a process of loving each body part in a new and different way, ritualistic markings to end a cycle or to begin a new one. A rite of passage, a healing process and, afterwards, a better appreciation for each inked part of me. I am on the road to loving myself, loving *all* of me. Then I think I'm done with more ink but here I am, under the gun again. The process of bloodletting, of self-inflicted pain, it's not much different to tribal times.

I have a theory about tattooing. In life, we put ourselves through a lot of emotional pain, by loving people, by taking risks. This pain is visceral, real, and it hurts like hell, yet it's intangible. All we have to remember are our internal scars, our emotional baggage, the lessons learnt. However, getting tattoos is physical pain, on the outside, which you decide to have inflicted upon you. Then, there is art to show, a beautiful scar you have chosen to mark that time. I know which pain I would rather.

PAINTED LADY IN PARK WITH STRATEGICALLY PLACED GRASS
PIC BY NICOLE CLEARY

Especially after emotionally painful times, I often get the urge to force that pain to be real and external. Choose this pain over that one. As I lie here getting my second ever tattoo on my arm covered, it's not from any sort of regret. The art that was there was perfect for me a lifetime ago. Now, I am so different.

I cover it with a new version of me, a new incarnation. That which I am, stronger, getting rapidly covered in tattoos that I haven't seen on anyone else. I want to be different. The fifteen-year relationship with my tattooist comes into play, where I tell him what I went through in the last couple of years, and as he listens and changes my external self, tears roll down my face as I let go of something else.

It's all part of the process, the ink, the rainy grey day and the new forearm I am now going to love in a totally different way. I cry at articles in the paper but I'm fucking tough too.

I am almost a heavily tattooed lady, and I'm not only okay, I'm proud of that. My scars, they are inside and out. You can trace some of them with your fingers. Each has a story, a moment in time. Each is part of me, even the ones covered that are still there.

I might be running out of room to be 'classy' but damn it if classy isn't boring anyways.

> *"Life should not be a journey to the grave with the intention of arriving safely in a pretty and well-preserved body, but rather to skid broadside in a cloud of smoke, thoroughly used up, totally worn out, and loudly proclaiming 'Wow! What a Ride.'"*
>
> Hunter S Thompson

CHAPTER 32

Single Motherhood

Rainy Sunday morning, nursing a very sore and sad Yoshi dog by building us a fort in the lounge room. Waking to his groans in the night, endless cups of tea, *True Blood* episodes and Tramadol the only things providing us relief.

He tore a cruciate ligament when I left him with a housemate who didn't read the instructions and fed him double, made him fat and ran him at the park too hard. Sigh.

I feel useful when he sips water out of a cup like royalty and he refuses food unless it's fed to him morsel by morsel from my fingers. Vow to myself to burn bright and fast and go out before I need handfeeding by anyone.

So, this is single motherhood, the dark times. Not long ago this furry guy was my companion across the country as floods bit at our wheels and he was the only reason I didn't drive off a cliff into the wide, blue ocean. He saved me. Was with me through the heartbreak and never faltered. He was strong for me. Now, it's my turn.

Poor Yoshi has been whining with every breath for 12 hours straight. Canine speak for 'the drugs aren't enough'. It's killing me. He drools with his tongue out and a gaping gash in his leg like a chicken thigh at the butchers.

For the first time in a long time, the reality of mortality becomes apparent. I've lost friends. Lost family. Somehow, there has been a reason behind losing each of them. A strange relief mixed with grief that they exited the building because they were mostly unhappy campers, or battling drug addictions, or dealing with the ailments of old age. None of them have affected me like the idea of losing Yoshi. None of them have relied on me to make the right decisions for them. I can't imagine having children and feeling that way for a lifetime, even after they are grown and you set them free. Stress for weeks and everyone's got the perfect opinion or answer for you. Just like those who kick the tires of cars, but they don't hold back in discussing, it's your life partner they are calling, "just a dog".

I wake in the middle of the night and climb out of the cage in the kitchen to pee. I'm sleeping with him here because he can't move far. Something happens and I'm unable to pilot my body out of the bathroom, my limbs and head lolling as I use every part of me to command my legs to *walk, damn you!* But I ricochet around from the door to the tiles and pass out, askew on the black bathmat. Luckily, my thumping has woken my housemate, who asks if I'm okay and I have enough left in me to say, "no, I'm not okay, please help me." Even just saying those words is a relief because I hardly ever say them.

He helps me up and Yoshi's leg heals and his gait eventually returns to normal.

CHAPTER 33

Eternal Moment

Koh Tao, Thailand

The second I wake there's a moment when I'm suspended in unknowing, where I don't know who or where I am. It's like this every day, tendrils of dreams fade and the world comes flooding in. There have been times recently, where light filters in and my brain remembers. It feels like a car crash and the reality of what happened in far north Queensland smashes me awake. I inhale my first waking breath and exhale with tears.

Lately with you, it's the opposite. I wake, see a foreign ceiling, a chest rising and falling next to me that I am still not used to, and in that instant my entire being is suffused with joy. I now breathe my first waking breath and exhale with optimism, like waking without a hangover on New Year's Day.

I can't believe I found you. After all this searching without trying to search, and doing the right things with the wrong people. Opening my eyes to see your sensuous lips. I feel your arms around me. See the crisp white sheets on a bed, on a tropical island in Thailand, with a view of the wide, blue ocean, and all these things make the picture from so many hours of my secret fantasies. It's real, it's actually happening. It's you and me. Right here right now. It's not a figment of my imagination. Part of me is scared to write this, hesitant to record the feeling. To grasp at it, a dream that pops and is gone the minute you know where you are. Within all the doubt and outward preparation for a life of solitude and independence, part of me knew I'd find you. How else did I hold close the hope, through all these car crashes and train wrecks, if I truly thought I'd never find you?

You are ticklish in the morning and brush me away, already we have had to confront things about ourselves, old patterns, jealousies, methods of protection we have employed. Fears rear up like wild stallions with hooves flashing, terror in their eyes, churn the waters of quiet bliss and soft smiles that abound between us, and for a minute I am afraid to lose you. Like everything, everyone, before.

Somehow, love prevails.

We are brave because we mean that much to each other. We use words, and tears flow, and we hold each other tight and soothe the crazed beasts inside, comfort the scared children we are still hiding. We weather the storm. Are stronger for going through it, like an adhesive bond that strengthens not weakens when it's tested.

All your insecurities are safe with me.

Every way that you have changed and will change, I want to be there. That is why nothing that has gone before matters really, not for either of us. There is only now and the future we can dream up, in our waking reality. I will love you. I will let you love me.

I will let this feedback-loop of what we both have been searching for, waiting, deserving, wash over me like sunshine, and will rise, turn to face it and feel it lift me. Will hear the music between us even when it's silent.

Every step in our lives, every decision and wrong turn, every wasted energy and stolen beauty, has led us to this moment right now. Even though the alarm will go off soon and you will wake too, I won't forget this silent knowing.

I write this for you to the sound of cicadas, to the excitement that is building, at spending another day, another eternity, however long it lasts, in paradise with you.

CHAPTER 34

Eat Me

Let's go on sumptuous, spicy wanderings through hills and alleys, cooking up adventures across oceans and through valleys.

When every taste has a flavour and every moment is one you must savour.

Every delicacy is your beating heart, and every meal a saviour.

Food such a part of the cycle of life, nostalgic smells of baking items or a late-night, greasy, gutter-side feed after a night out drinking that keeps you out of strife.

I'm an American-born bit confused 'strayan' mate, eating Vietnamese rolls made by a German girl on a Thailand beach, drinking wine from New Zealand vines in a glass made in China. Imagining burritos with jalapenos I'll make one day soon with kangaroo on other culinary holidays in my own kitchen.

Where I'll take you with me on a magic ride as long as you are chopping too.

Red-hot chillies mixed with lime, crunchy greens and fresh seafood, cheese and Sicilian olives, ecstatic bites every single time.

Coconut and strawberries, goat feta on pretty much everything, especially avocado creaminess and the pungent smell of fresh basil smeared generously on sourdough rye bread… Mmm, can you taste it?

Don't stop enjoying till your last meal, and even then, while you're eating it, close your eyes and chew slowly because you still aren't dead.

I'm not afraid to tell you, food is one of my greatest loves.

Perhaps forever I'll have this belly to prove it, not hard-bodied or hard-boiled, but soft and delicious, like healthy dough rising at dawn. I'll take an abundance of curves and tasting plates. I'd rather have a sink piled with dishes and sucking the juice out of prawns than some unrealistic diet plan and bones, calorie counting and stone-cold stoves.

My kitchen is both a place and a state of mind, a factory of deliciousness and decadence where you'll find an assembly line of cheese boards and a constant plan for something more.

I refuse to stick with what I know, even if I am the tri-state queen of the healthy Aussie-Tex-Mex burrito.

I want to eat the weird stuff, and live to sweat it, explore other cuisines and possibly regret it.

I do draw the line at beef pizzle soup, however, and other forms of penis and BBQ'd spiders, but most things you can cook up with love for me, I'll be brave, and swallow it down with a smile.

I'm going to eat like I love—messily and with my hands. I'm going to love like I eat—with all my senses engaged and no concern for how I might feel tomorrow.

Perfectly cooked eggs and thick bacon after a big night out, a Mojito full of limes, mint, and sugar sipped as the sun goes down.

Brown, flaky pastry holding steaming surprises inside, fish that melts in your mouth and tastes of the tide.

I'm going to feed my lover ice-cream on planes to far-away places and I'm going to remember all the meals one by one, as if they all had faces.

When I come back, lips still burning from chillies, I'll still savour the memories like hard-boiled lollies, suck them gently and get every last drop of sugary goodness and lick my lips with gusto, for another taste, in another place, anywhere good food calls home.

CHAPTER 35

Gone Again

Just cried on the phone to a stranger at ANZ bank. Whoops. Sorry, dude.

There has been way too much crying in public lately. I feel ripped open, raw to the touch, the smallest trigger a reminder of the love that I'm sure must be out there but keeps eluding me. I cry in cafés, where people waiting for coffees try not to stare, and waiters whisk my cold eggs and mushrooms away, gourmet, expensive and uneaten.

I cry on trams and in trains, pressed up against windows so nobody sees or hears me, but even in the 5pm crush, a small hand parts the crowd as an elderly Chinese lady wordlessly hands me a tissue.

I cry on the couch at home, away from the judgements of society but unable to deny the look Yoshi dog gives me, undoubtedly one of 'Not this again Mom' even when he has no words. I am all cried out, worn thin, like a paper leaf. It's kind of beautiful and raw and real, but I can't cry anymore. Still, I shed a couple more tears.

One tear for myself, for you, for the us that could have been but isn't, for the us that was, that changed. For the pain we keep causing each other, unable to let go. That tear plops on my arm, and slides off, becomes one with the elements again. I wipe my cheek and take a deep breath.

CHAPTER 36

Dance It Out

Yesterday was Valium and crying and trying anything to stop this mess of what has become of our sweet, sweet love. I've been fasting for days, unable to eat the gourmet food I'd bought.

I'm dancing in the kitchen, crying and sobbing and I'm getting over you. I'm inside, alone. The rain hammers outside without a care who sees me or who knows.

I smoke joints and the rain comes down. Start dancing and give it my absolute all as I cry and dance and sob as I move, and something happens.

How I wish I had a video to show you of me losing it in the blonde, fake-wood kitchen of this suburban share house, tear-streaked face, limbs akimbo, joint snuffed out from waving it around in the air with the music blaring. Absolutely cutting sick in the middle, swirling from sink to stove to microwave to fridge.

I dance like I would never dance in nightclubs, completely and utterly in the music, totally one hundred percent free. Through doing this, just through twenty minutes and two songs, somehow the depths of despair, the total lost feeling I had at the start, is different now.

In this life we don't have much time.

Time is precious, you can spend it loving, smiling or dancing and that's it. There's no time for anything else, no time to dwell on the other shit emotions. I've had many adventures in my life, both good and bad. I will say yes to a challenge even if logic and science are leaning towards no. But my experiences are the sum of me. I am only as good as the stories I have to tell.

No matter what happens to me, I will most likely survive. So why not dance around in the fucking kitchen like a lunatic? Why not put all the pain and suffering and dwelling on hold or even delete it altogether?

I think it's possible to do that. There is still that moment when I first wake, of disbelief that I'm alone again, that familiar feeling of surviving disaster I have woken up with many times.

But I'm just going to dance. I'm going to reinvent myself on the dancefloor—right here, right now.

As corny as that sounds, I have made a commitment to myself. And the music still plays.

CHAPTER 37

Compost

I took all the shit you gave me and with it, I grew flowers.

I took the pain you caused me and washed it down the drain in the shower.

You said so many beautiful words, but I gave them too much power.

Full of ego, everyone in town knows. Covering your insecurity with bravado, repeating your name over and over on other people's microphones. Music for music's sake you lost long ago, you are now just looking to be famous and your music shows it.

When it comes to real love, you just got with another ordinary girl because you weren't ready for my amazing world. My approach to life frightened you, forced you to question what you really wanted. You want the easy road—free rent, cheese filled, 'nice' times, and no seeking—boring!

I hope you are happy now, but I know you aren't.

Can see it in your eyes when you post photos online wearing the t-shirts I bought you, your social media posts attempting to be positive yet read like an unhappy baby throwing his toys out the pram.

Not happy in yourself or with yourself. Not happy with your displaced place in the world. I see your fatness holding hands with your unhappiness, bedfellows that take real determination and light to defuse.

You bought the running shoes but have you run a mile in them? Have you done yoga yet? You are in the land of sunshine, are you still in a box making 'choons' twelve hours a day?

Exactly the same waste of space as losing yourself in video games. You say it's about good vibes, but all you have done is denial and lies.

If only I was a bunny boiler, I'd send copies of our porno film to your new girlfriend, I'd write her a really long and eloquent letter.

Good thing I'm not. I'm a beautiful and complex lady trying to be wise, and you squished me down so that I did not rise.

Now, all there is left is goodbye.

Oh, well, I think as I sit at the restaurant where I brought you on our first date, about to have dinner with all your mates.

You fucked me over and left me dry, I acted with love and you threw it in my face.

I tell you what I am over—this story.

It ends now.

CHAPTER 38

On Junigudira Land

Exmouth, Western Australia

BEACHCOMBING

Today, it's raining in a place where it sometimes doesn't rain for three years.

The local Indigenous mob and custodians of the land are the Junigudira, traced back 30,000 years or longer, with a necklace found in the Mandu Mandu Gorge nearby. One of their stories is that Rainbow Serpent came to land here, in a crater made aeons before in another Dreamtime story. Now in Turquoise Bay, an inexplicably large population of sea snakes still churn in the waters. It's the top north-west of Australia, some of the oldest land on Earth.

It looks that way too, feels that way in my bones when I'm here. Hiding in the cliffs somewhere the locals won't reveal in case you steal it, is a Megalodon tooth, from a prehistoric dinosaur shark that could grow up to 15 metres in length. Scraggly grey trees twist into shapes and rocks worn smooth cover the ground in a muted, earthy rainbow as the wind curls and batters them before your eyes. Mother Earth at her most resilient, rugged and unforgiving, hardy and bleak, solid and dependable throughout time. We fly along grey roads cut into red rock as the landscape undulates slightly every couple of kilometres.

Nobody speaks in the car. All of us talked out. Enthusiasm blown out of us with the sand in our lunch and we sat silently as pebbles flick beneath us, and the sun shifts around us. Holes worn into rocks from the eternal winds circling other smaller rocks. These are primitive lands. Fifty million years of evolution and all we have worked out to do here is drill for oil off the blue coast and distract people with whale sharks.

I'm glad in a way. Places like this should be left alone. Moonscape on earth.

No man's or woman's land, not for us anyways.

Who only reveals her tiny translucent crabs and rainbow patterns from the water tide and macro yellow straw flowers surviving somehow in the desolation when you really stop to look. Sit quietly and you'll hear the roar of the surf on the offshore reef, the scraw of galahs and the ever-present, unavoidable soundtrack of a billion flies. You just have to tune them out by humming something else quietly in your head. They get trapped behind your sunglasses, in your drink and in the car with you heading on adventures farther than they've ever gone. Even though we are all bothered by them at times, we smirk a little at the one guy with a head net over his face—we are Aussies, mate, just deal with it.

Curved, white sand beaches with turquoise water leading to the vast blue of the East Indian Ocean beckon, but then batter us with wind and waves, visibility of less than a metre and jellyfish rolling by my elbow. We try to go snorkelling but it's scary and pointless. Not today, says nature.

Everything out here reminds you of your insignificance. The giant, sparkling Milky Way above at night, the fact that it's eighty percent sky here in any direction, the fact that it's no cellular reception and the ocean appears to go on forever.

Ningaloo means 'deep water' to the local Yinigudura tribe and I hope it remains that way, elusive and vast, untameable, wild and free.

We are small and the land is big and once again the sun drops below a horizon that will be here long after we are.

CHAPTER 39

A Bungalow Somewhere

Amed, Bali

He lies next to me in a basic bungalow, air conditioner working overtime to cool the sweat pooled on our bodies. I met him three hours ago talking about tattoos. Next thing, I'm having one too many Bintang beers and dropping my travelling partner at our accommodation to tear down winding island roads on a motorbike, clutching his smooth brown skin, howling at the full moon.

Part of me wonders if I should be doing any of this, the rest of me goes with a flow that only seems to happen when travelling. There is only the moment, right? My white freckled skin in contrast to his, I lick his neck as we ride through villages and it tastes of spices, musky deodorant with an added alluring aroma because of the coconut trees silhouetted above us. Now he is snoring, just a man with a cock. I know this is right here, right now. Tomorrow will bring a new adventure.

Somehow, I'm empowered by the ease of it, the simplicity and lack of games.

We knew within five minutes of seeing each other we would end up here, naked and spent, drunk on cheap beer. His cock rises to me, hands on me in a way that disregards parts of me that I would be trying to hide if he was in my hometown. His feet splayed, toes spread, body covered in dodgy inked moments, other girls' names in other languages—Dutch, Spanish—memories of moments just like this, albeit etched forever on his skin. I am not threatened by any of it.

I know I'll wake him in five minutes when I finish writing this and he will drive me home, kiss me like he means it and ride off into the night, geckos chirping and clouds billowing around the fullness of the moon. She will rise again and again, and I'll collect more stories, some horrible and worth blocking out forever that give me eye twitches until I can forget.

Others are perfect in simplicity, like this one right now with the fan whirring, tide crashing, the four-poster bed I was just hanging onto, merely a lost moment of romance ago in a mosquito-filled room. Before I wake him, before I change the moment back to one of control and knowing, I breathe here, and smile quietly. I don't know how things happen but I know how to let them happen.

I ready myself to lick his pierced nipple, to wake him and feel like Gaia, like Shakti, like Persephone. Like a siren from the sea we just swam in.

I am everything and nothing.

I am woman and goddess, in control of my destiny and yet willing to let it be.

CHAPTER 40

In a Dimly Lit Room

I sit quietly with my mother in a dimly lit room, drinking camomile tea.

She shows me the ring on her little finger—three tiny freshwater pearls and the speck of a diamond. When it was their tenth anniversary, Dad bought it for her, the only diamond he could afford then. I know the size of the diamond doesn't matter. She tells me that you can have all the money in the world but without your health, you have nothing. It is 8pm and Dad has gone to bed already. Couple of wines, some Endone, and he's out.

A moment of normalcy, a glimpse of him, and he's gone.

They retired and planned trips to all the places Mom dreamed of. She wanted to learn to scuba dive but now she waits for an hour when they can go outside, a much bigger challenge than conquering her fear of the ocean.

Him, too proud to talk about it, too staunch to do anything except neck more painkillers, hold his side and pretend everything's fine when it clearly is not.

Mom looks so sad. She says in the marriage now there are three of them. Him, her, and the pain. And the pain is between them. My heart breaks for her, with her, and I would do anything to take it. In the past, things were different.

Dad and I didn't speak for ten years. Even longer. I was young and rebellious, he was old and cynical. His tone of voice changed when he addressed me, closed, clipped, dripping with derision. He was often passive-aggressive, and used to 'joke' about things that weren't funny. When I was in high school I wanted a bra before I really needed one. He threw some oranges at me one day, so I'd have to fumble and catch them. "You'd better put those down your top before you go to school" delivered with a sneer. He never really seemed to accept me. Never told me he loved me, or that I was beautiful. A one-handed slap on the back awkwardly after Mom would plead "Give her a hug, for me for Christmas" which made me want to disappear into the floor, back to the earth. I always waited for approval that never came.

I left to find it elsewhere, in other people and stories. Fought him with all the injustice of youth, the fury of the misunderstood. I yelled, he yelled, and she just watched it happen, failing to make peace between us. Kicked out at sixteen, moved interstate at eighteen and, for a while, never looked back. Shaved my head, stuck my finger up at the world, and fought everything I thought stood in my way.

Till this night.

These nights, when I am older, more mellow, with hair now, and less need to justify myself to him or anyone else. He is a husk of the man I knew, a shadow of the father I hated for so long, for so many reasons. Mother, this beautiful, effervescent powerhouse, this excited, wise woman, was reduced to a place after forty years of marriage where she is only a carer for someone who is sick.

She is married to a man who is married to his pain.

Her love has been left at the bottom of a pill bottle.

Now, it's a year later.

I sit with my mother in a dimly lit room, drinking camomile tea.

Dad sits across from us, reading. He has aged a decade in a year, but he is here. Thinner now, his grey hair turned to silver, but as he lifts his head from the paper, he smiles. The cancer is gone. The pain is gone. I think radiotherapy reinforces the fact that life is, indeed, short.

There is no time for holding onto shit from the past.

I had forgiven him years ago but he held on, which is how cancer grows, and I have been waiting for him. Hoping I would not still be waiting when it was too late. Now, we drink tea together, all three of us. Just humans who have lived and known each other a very long time, my forever. They showed me photos of Thailand where they learnt to scuba dive for the very first time. Dad pale but relaxed, Mom's wild hair blowing in the wind, her smile effusing her whole being, reflecting off the clouds.

I know that sometimes good people do get over bad stuff that happens to them. Cancer can leave a wiser person behind. The banter and light-hearted love that is between them, still golden, still growing, married for a lifetime.

That isn't forever even then, but right now, it fills me with joy and illuminates everything, even when I am sitting with my mother in a dimly lit room.

CHAPTER 41

Never an Easy Choice

I'm pregnant.

Found out today while visiting my folks in Adelaide. Ironic, right?

To the Balinese guy I slept with on my recent adventure to learn freediving. Fuck.

I came back as a mermaid with the added cargo of a little brown-skinned baby fish. The answer to the first question is easy. I would not tell him this; I found out after I left that he was married to a white woman with kids. Which means I would be doing this alone.

Right now, I'm more financially independent, capable and comfortable than I have ever been really. Which are things that a) would allow for an easier mommy life, and b) that I would completely give up by doing so. I am also just at the point of setting up my business and career to do seasonal work and travel in winter, mainly working from home. This has been my dream for a long time.

As well as the fact that it's already hard for me to find lasting relationships, let alone with a baby or child in tow, dictating my lifestyle, limiting my chances to meet someone. However, when it comes down to it, I cannot imagine being pregnant in my current reality.

Truth is, I don't want to be pregnant—physically or emotionally.

When I think about the process of birthing a child and raising a baby and then raising a child into adulthood, the thought of doing it alone doesn't just terrify me, it also doesn't sound like much fun. I love my independence, my spontaneous nature and my financial freedom and I don't know if I want to give any of those things up for anyone, whether to a baby or partner or job. Not for anything.

I'm in the bushland of the Adelaide Hills wearing steel cap boots and a raincoat, walking on the slippery train tracks where I used to eat magic mushrooms and wag school as a teenager. It's cold and grey, the rain swirls in eddies and blasts sideways around me. The sky is black and looks ominous as I write these words to understand. To feel the feelings, to allow the imagination to lead me to the answer I already know.

When the doctor said, "You're pregnant", two immediate thoughts arrive simultaneously: Abortion and Amazing. I have had a healthy sexual life since sixteen, but been pretty dodgy with using protection at times, I'll admit.

Never before have I been pregnant; the chemistry hasn't been right till now I guess.

This is one of those times you never forget, just like losing your virginity.

My birthday was last week and I didn't know this fact then. I spent the night snorting lines of coke, a myriad of booze and other drugs.

Spent the last month feeling incredibly solitary and old. Fat and alone, fat and alone, a crap mantra I couldn't shake.

I pull the raincoat tighter as the rain comes pouring down. Each step carefully on the tracks, because I know that now I take more calculated risks—I don't jump in blindly as much anymore.

With the wind howling in my ears, I say out loud to the forest, the rain and the mist curling through the black, shiny trees like snakes, "I don't want to do this alone."

I know in my heart of hearts that I absolutely do not want to be pregnant and have and raise a child alone.

I know.

CHAPTER 42

All Silent

I sit in a room with five women, each of us wrapped in blankets, all silent.

We are in hospital gowns and paper booties, waiting to be called.

It is an eternity.

The only magazines on offer are *Top Gear* and *Car*. I'm pretty positive a man has never sat in this room before yet they are dog eared, torn, worried, and flicked through. Any distraction from what has happened and what's about to occur is welcome.

But there are no tears, not even a sniffle. I'm sure those moments happened already for the others like they did for me.

None of us speaking or acknowledging each other in any way, lost in thoughts, probably different, but I can hear the same echo: *I can't wait for this to be over.*

It's the opposite of what society wants you to feel, the dark side of fertility, when faced with a situation or a partner or a lack thereof, which means that being pregnant is nothing but a horrifying, imminent plane crash you feel powerless to stop.

There were no protestors outside the clinic today, something I was dreading.

Horror stories of cow hearts being thrown at teenagers raped in the hands of righteous men who will never feel the wonder and fear it is to have a person growing inside you.

I have only known I'm pregnant for four days.

But it's been two months of getting fatter, eating more, feeling inexplicably sad and melancholic. Right when it felt like my limitless joy was returning. In the last four days, my body feels alien to me, craving strange things, reacting instantly to things.

My emotions are only tempered by a steady stream of smoking joints and honesty.

A nurse calls my name.

I accept the end to this chapter, and cut it short because in a few hours I will once again be me, solo, stepping into the world, shining and free.

CHAPTER 43

Exhausted, Dirty and Happy as Fuck

The setting: Stars and a golden moon cut with lasers, only trees for walls.

Watching a sheep paddock turn into a multisensory mini-city, from bugs turning to beats. From the quiet silence to humans feeding back to each other on the dancefloor at a deafening roar.

A community united by something much bigger than just music, because many of us don't even share love for the same genres. I've been working at psychedelic trance festivals for years but I like drum and bass the best. Go figure. Festivals are the vehicle we use to find each other, the place to gather. The TAZ (temporary autonomous zone) where we create a temporary space that eludes formal structures of control. We build a city, then we govern it, even just for a weekend. This is the Aussie festival scene of the 90's through to about 2015 or so. This was where I first found my 'family'.

A place where the default world doesn't matter, nobody cares what you 'do'—they care who you *are*, what excites you. They care more about the stuffed dinosaur you're dragging along behind you in the dirt than where you went to school. What's his name? Is he going to the dancefloor with you?

The flavour of the incredible dish cooked with love for months, years, in the hearts and minds—makes it the best dish ever. The ethics of rave culture and leave no trace, the childlike play, the Monday sprinkler dance-floor looseness, the elders teaching the younger generation how to party with style and grace. The stuff of legends, really. As parties become corporations, as events become mass-marketed, unimaginative, mainstream money-makers, there are still thousands of people preparing all year to brave the harshest Aussie summer in a valley with hundred-knot winds to stomp in the dirt together. It's our Ramadan, our Passover, our Diwali. It's the one week a year that we stop what we are doing and gather, religiously.

I am proud to be a part of this, of the history, my own history that spans scenes, trends, and a core crew of amazing people who are still around. Still making crazy artworks from trash, getting off grid, changing their tiny pockets of the world, little paradigm shifts. I am so proud of all of you, and I remember why we began doing this.

Twenty years ago for me now, my first rave. To everyone who makes the mission, faces the challenge and allows themselves to let go, to fly their freak-flag with a smile—even if only once a year—I salute you.

Thanks for being my weird family. Thanks for leaving your comforts, your jobs, your worries, even if only for a few days. Thanks for feeling like we can create our own reality. Every one of you is important. I've been around long enough to potentially be jaded, and I can be. Bad deals, unkempt promises, egos bigger than personalities, and great opportunities that fall to dust. The creative world is like that.

I still feel the magic, however.

Still, every time, I come back from festivals rejuvenated. Full of smiles, hugs, connection with nature and primal-bass heartbeat. Solid again. After that, the 'real world' just isn't as important.

For each their own experience, like everything in life, it is what you make it.

That is why these festivals feel like another weird kind of home, an island of understanding.

Psy Bus quesadillas, Funktion 1 sound systems, art, sequins and so many things a gnarly, crazy gang of visionary people drive. We are blessed with an ethos, spirituality, technology and a place to call home for those who never quite feel human. A collision of worlds, a smash-jam of psyches wanting to connect with something, anything, everything. Each other. The great cosmic Us.

We are here, there, and everywhere. We take at least a few days a year to remember.

Then we use that experience to fuel the biggest, wildest dreams we can handle for an entire year. Till we try and succeed or try and fail, and regroup again. On the dance floor, under the trees, thanks to my rave family. I worked for a week, danced for twenty-four hours straight, now exhausted, dirty, and happy as fuck.

See you in another sun revolution. Bring your stories here again and prepare to let them go.

WORKING MY BUTT OFF IN THE PADDOCK

CHAPTER 44

Landing

New York, USA

I'm visiting my dear friend Sarah, an artist whose work I exhibited at For Walls Gallery. She brought an entire bed and set it up in the gallery, along with loads of amazing works, technicolour mashups of iconic movies and music from her dreams. She had invited me to stay in her Brooklyn rental loft over summer, where her latest project was based on documenting and illustrating the typography of old-world Coney Island, before it was replaced, removed, upgraded.

For the first time in a really long time, I feel like I'm home.

I've never been to the east coast before, but after two days in New York, I feel like I belong. Deep in my heart, in my soul. I belong like I've never belonged in Oz. I don't feel crazy here, or caged. Every job I have, every relationship, I'm 'too much', too honest, too driven, excited and passionate. Everyone wants me to calm the fuck down. Sigh.

I'm no stranger to the constant tall-poppy chop-chop. It feels like everyone in Australia wants me smaller. Quieter.

Here, it feels like a pulse of energy runs under the concrete. I arrived and Sarah asked me if I wanted sleep or adventure.

"ADVENTURE!" I cry, and off we went to Paul's Daughter on the Coney Island dock for lobster sandwiches, then on every roller coaster on offer, my heart swelling with glee.

Do you know how many people I've seen dancing to their headphones? Lots, really getting into it. I have met life coaches. Entrepreneurs. They scream, "Reality Check, that's amazing, sign me up for one right now!" and take my business card. People who encourage me who don't even know me, while some friends at home hide my Facebook feed because I'm doing things that spark their jealousy.

FUCK. THAT.

Beautiful music everywhere. Dancing in the streets. Gorgeous African-American and Latino men who look you in the eyes, ask questions and genuinely want to hear the answers. Break dancers on trains with friendly faces, smiling people, all the best food in the world and then some.

Here, I don't feel fat or too tattooed, too white, or too bored at any minute. I'm not on social media every five minutes. There's too much actually going on to take in. I have never felt like I'd find love anywhere more than here.

As the train rumbles in, and the buskers sing to me, it's my fucking station.

WITH SARAH AT CONEY ISLAND

CHAPTER 45

Occupy Yourself

New York, USA

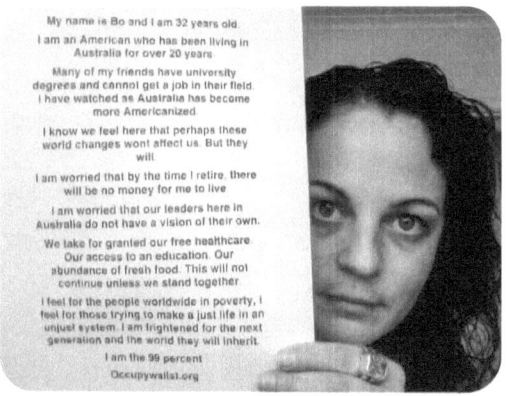

WE ARE THE 99%, 2011

Sitting in Zuccotti Park where the Occupy movement happened, where the world stood up against the fat cats for the first time in my lifetime.

As mangy pigeons scatter seeking morsels, I watch an overweight mother judge me for my tattoos with a frown as her chubby daughter drinks coke. The daughter and I exchange a moment with the pigeons trying to eat my food, she pulls her daughter closer, I meet the young girl's eyes and smile.

I remember being a fat kid, chubby before puberty, when I found solace in stolen Snickers bars and meat pies, hiding all of the wrappers under my bed. There's a theory that when you feel neglected, you eat to give yourself the sweetness you are lacking.

Such was my life that I left my toys, my friends, the life I knew, and my Dad who was still studying there, and moved to Australia where it felt like everyone was racist, the sun burned and the sky was blue and hot every single day. I was a chubby American with a very different accent and my nickname at the new school became 'Yank Tank'.

Fast forward a few years, and I lost weight taking acid and walking everywhere on train tracks in the hills where I went to high school. But the nickname and reflection of myself still haunted me. Smoking weed and taking LSD meant henceforth by the unspoken law of the lunchtime society, I became 'cool'.

It's been a long road from self-hatred, my physical form often inspiring disgust in the past, to the slow growth that is becoming a confident woman comfortable in her own skin. I am now, in my early thirties. Mostly. Can walk tall and proud even in a room of magazine models. I laugh it off when people say mean things, though they hardly ever do, adult political correctness is a good barrier to truth.

I see this mother decide things about me based on my ink. I'm a drug addict, I'm a sex worker, I'm a carnie or a gypsy or just from a scary side of the tracks, a borough she wouldn't ever visit. This judgement doesn't bother me. I know who I am and the light I spread just by being me.

These tattoos didn't come lightly. Each one has been a new discovery, a challenge for me to see myself differently. When you judge me for having them, mother across from me, think twice.

Sometimes, I still see that chubby eleven-year-old in the mirror, just like the one sitting next to you now, a bottle of sugar in her puffy hand.

It's a hard reflection to see. Will appear in the mirror suddenly at moments when my guard is down, throughout my life. It probably will for her too, and my heart breaks a little.

Instead of saying anything—lest we humans reach out and tell each other's stories—I sip my water instead. I hope that other mothers might think about what it's like to be young and not know what wise women know with age, with the time it takes to accept yourself.

Don't do as she does, little girl.

Be free. Be yourself.

CHAPTER 46

Love Story in Two Chapters

New York, USA

Chapter 1

The setting is *Shakespeare in the Park* in South Brooklyn, a hot summer evening.

Sometimes in this life we are presented with opportunities, forks in the road, and it is exactly these challenges I love to face with optimism for serendipity. He kissed my hand only once. We spoke for a matter of minutes yet through the last week and all its adventures, mishaps, moments and wonder, his face had been on my mind. How a simple 'hello' can mess with the grand scheme of things.

I turned up, second night of *Othello*, a community theatre group that trains kids. Sit on the grass and watch timeless themes and battle scenes played out before me, the sun a red globe setting over the ocean as if we are on the savannah in Africa, not the bay in New York lined with tankers.

As the lighting fades, fireflies come out to play and the audiences' faces light up in wonder. He plays Lodovico—gallant, brave and fighting for justice with thunder. Afterwards, we head for a few cherry beers and quesadillas with the cast and I touch him lightly, a brush of the arm here, a glance there, subtle flirting because why not? I am single and free and have nothing to lose.

He is young, Latino, an actor, a model, a sound guy at the Coney Island Freak Show, but it's none of these things that truly impress me. He tells of his reinvention, his dedication to himself, by moving across the country, and I see in him the same drive that's within me. I see his heart bursting out of his shirt because he cares about others.

I can smell it on him like a scent of compassion more attractive than any job or hobby. He wants to move to Los Angeles, to be a firefighter, and if all else fails he said, he will join the marines.

I'll admit my heart clenches when he says that; another brave man wanting to help the world who might become a futile casualty of the military. I sense this man will always selflessly help others.

Here's to all the men with big hearts who give over their own needs to protect the universe, may they stay safe and blessed be.

He leans close and asks me what perfume I'm wearing. I feel the spread of intimacy, adding to the humidity. His lips brush my neck on the train platform, and I hold back the soft groan that wants to escape me.

When we change trains, mine comes suddenly, rushing with a gust of hot air below us, and I touch his face tenderly and plant a kiss, hopefully translated as a promise for more, and run down the stairs with glee.

'Twas a night of Shakespeare, fireflies, and sweet subway goodbyes, and I ran into the night knowing magic is everywhere. Whatever will be, will be.

Chapter 2

The next day is a Monday. After a few disjointed texts that could just be subway or lost in translation, he is three hours late to collect me. At 9pm, I'm standing in a street in Cypress Hills of all places, watching a woman with her pants down gyrating her pussy lips on the stairway underground in front of all the commuting faces.

I am fast letting go of expectations or controlling the story. It's nine-thirty, and he's still coming, apparently. I laugh at the movie scene right now and lean against a doorway in a polka dot dress, giggling at the absurdity. He arrives, kissing me hard in the street, biting my lips but without passion, his version of sweeping me off my feet. We arrive at a black hole of an Irish pub, called The Slaughtered Lamb, with a real dungeon, each table like a prison from the wall on *Game of Thrones* and skeletons in the dining room.

We were handed a burger menu, and I'm surprised because I had said earlier, "Let's eat Mexican." I grab his hand, leave the dungeon and run back down the street, pulling him into a happy, bright place when he says he's already eaten six times today. All I have eaten is a bagel and two bananas. I order, we eat, we talk, it feels like it's going great. He's passionate, agreeable, confident, positive, engaged. I drink two piña coladas and eat most of the three appetisers while he drinks a coke and nibbles calamari. When he goes to the toilet, I pay. He's horrified, feels terrible, I convince him for three blocks that it's totally okay. (I will learn later on the value of just letting men pay, but not yet.)

We pass a guy with his pants down holding his dick pissing and squatting inside a glass bus shelter on a busy corner. Everyone walking past just turns the other way. We go to Washington Park and sit on a bench under the arch around a fountain full of New Yorkers kissing and dodgy dealing in the summer night. For four hours we talk and talk. We kiss too, but that's all. He hardly touches the rest of me. If I'm honest, I'm not feeling the chemistry.

He works out for three hours a day and I notice he shaves his arms and chest. He just works, trains and fucks 'lady friends' he boasts, but he doesn't make me laugh, doesn't seem to have fun or play. He jokes that he was born a girl and I totally believe him, then laugh when he's shocked and say, "In New York, I suspend my judgements extra."

He tells me I'm 'not his usual type', and pulls out a picture of one of these girls—an orange Barbie with fake boobs and ridiculously giant lips who sucks a straw and looks back at me. Suddenly, Lodovico isn't as appealing. He tells me he's so free, sleeps with the burlesque dancers at the freak show where he works yet doesn't make any move on me at all. Just talks. At four in the morning, I ask, "Are you going to take me home?"

To which he just shuffles his feet and says, "I know what I should do, and what I shouldn't."

"I'm only here for a few days, dude. On holiday, y'know?"

In the awkward end we walk to the subway and he demands I kiss his neck till I walk out at my station, utterly deflated, completely frustrated, walking home alone late and over men again for this lifetime.

Well, today.

When telling this story later to people just as frustrated for me, I hear how dates in New York are often late and uncommitted, non-forward and strange. I realise he never grabbed me with lust, and the whole Barbie thing had thrown my perception of him anyway.

So here ends the short tome that is my New York affair, sometimes two chapters are enough, eh?

CHAPTER 47

Struggles

Tikal, Guatemala

The jungle calls to me. Sweat pours from my eyelids as I walk dark pathways quietly in the dawn. Toucans and parrots slice through the air where spider monkeys jump across branches causing leaves to flutter to the ground. The call of howler monkeys sends shivers up my spine, the same sound they used to emulate the

T-Rex in the movie *Jurassic Park*. So primal.

Ancient Mayan ruins tower out of the brushed forest floor, set in grids to cast shadows at equinox and solstice, telling time, creating seasons by the moon's cycles. This primitive sophistication is humbling, built well before Jesus was on the scene. Smart in design and lasting longer than almost anything we erect now. Only twenty percent of the structures are uncovered, the rest lie under layers upon layers of earth and temples built on top of temples where jaguars call long, green corridors their home.

Stolen from my backpack in Antigua by a guy 'helping' me with my bags, I have had no phone for a week. Having no phone has become a beautiful experience. Sitting on the highest temple to wait for the sunrise, everyone else is looking through screens at what I'm seeing and breathing with my own eyes. I leave before the others to walk the paths alone, communing with animals that wake and, as a reward, get the entire Gran Plaza, the crown jewel of Tikal, all to myself.

The Mayan calendar never ended in 2012; it just began again.

I have hope that we can overcome anything, any scourge upon the Earth we have wrecked. I am small and the jungle is big. That's exactly how it's supposed to be.

Later, driving through cornfields in the Guatemalan highlands on a chicken bus, reggae in my ears, I'm feeling incredibly free. Humbled by how lucky I am. We just don't know how good we've got it till we see how others live. Most of the country here survives on thirty cents a day.

Ancient churches rise from the landscape, slums stretch to reach the jungle, small children hold their noses from the pollution as exhaust fumes spew into their faces.

I grip the seat in front of me with my freckled hand, and the elderly woman at my side hangs on with her small fingers, and we smile at each near collision together. The teenagers toting machine guns on street corners smile shyly when I ask for directions.

Humans are not really that different. Music, love, food, weather, and heartbreak unite us. War makes us angry and sad. Everyone has struggles. Best not to get too caught up in them, there is a huge world of possibilities.

We survived the chicken bus ride, and everyone is happy about it.

ANTIGUA, GUATEMALA

CHAPTER 48

Island Politics

Caye Caulker, Belize

Caye Caulker is a tiny island off the coast of mainland Belize in the Caribbean, among thousands of similar islands that spread along the coastline where jungles and jaguars meet the sea. I've headed here to dive the Blue Hole, a giant sinkhole in the ocean that plunges 124 metres deep. It's one of the best dive sites in the world, Unesco Heritage listed and known for how extreme it is, where underwater stalactites grow.

Tropical islands always bring a sense of relief to me, more so than your average person, I think. There is often no way for me to slow down unless I'm forced to ride a bike in forty-degree weather, with nowhere to go but the beach or a bar. Before I catch the boat, a tall woman spies me at the dock and gives me an impromptu massage, her healing hands pulling the tension from me as she tells me, "I saw you, you holding some tightness in those shoulders, girl."

I give her some dollars. Forty-five minutes later I turn up on dock in a fast boat loaded with dishevelled tourists and locals carrying beer coolers through azure water dotted with seaweed patches, to white sand as fine as dust, to a shanty-town version of Club Med full of Rastafarians.

What a scene.

Wind blows through the palm trees as toothless guys with dreadlocks hang off golf carts touting you for a room or a taxi to get to your accommodation. After four modes of transport starting at 4am—including a flat tire on the highway and a border crossing on foot from Guatemala where soldiers with gold-ringed teeth smiled at my AK47 necklace and waved me through—the golf-cart taxi was too appealing to turn down.

I've got some inside tips and a growing sense of relief after leaving Antigua in Guatemala. Central American travel relies on some Spanish, and I had basically none. Fleeing to Belize where English is the second language from Patois, seemed like a good idea.

I'm staying at a place called 'Paws', where a crazy cat lady spays and neuters them and takes them in. She keeps over eighty cats, mostly feral. There are a couple old dogs too, some with BB gun bullets still lodged inside them. Sadly, often mistreated by those who live here.

The room is extremely basic—hard mattress and less than clean pillows, bare sheets hung over the windows as curtains—and the dawn light is hot and blasts me awake. The island suffered a hurricane in the '80s, and half of it was cut off, making a body of water the locals call 'The Split', where the currents run both on top and below the water. There's a ramshackle bar here owned by a coke-head English guy covered in dodgy tattoos, run with just a couple fridges and ice in big chests—famous for being the place to hang. At first, I think the Lazy Lizard is like every other bar in tropical places, full of suntanned, skinny, twenty-somethings—the beautiful people—and it takes me two days to get up the nerve to walk through the throngs of swimming revellers up to the bar and order a beer.

Before I get there, a young guy says to me, "Go on, you can sit right up here." He speaks to me in that blessed way that happens when you travel alone. He's half-Black, half-Spanish, he tells me, a gorgeous smile and that smooth skin which sucks me in every time. I buy him a beer and we talk for hours. As we sit above the crowd on a balcony, I see that the people at the Lazy Lizard are, in fact, a mixed bunch. There are a few St Tropez bikini bodies but even more burnt, hairy people trying to find a groove somewhere in their nine-to-five desk bodies, and mostly failing miserably.

He works on a boat, giving tours to tourists, fishing, diving and finding a new adventure in the perpetually changing crowds. I'm under no illusions about the kind of guy this island breeds, though he is from the much bigger town of San Pedro, bustling with way more temptations and a harder hustle than here.

Two beers down and it's 3pm. I'm hungry, so we walk down North Street to find something to eat. He stops along the way to talk Patois to the guys hanging in front of the supermarket, his lingo switching from good English to "Wah unuh up to? Wah unuh a do lata?"

A dark, old guy with dreaded beard asks about a party at San Pedro that evening, it's like a Miss America pageant for the islands, he tells me, and the one who wins is always light-skinned, the Mexican girls trumping the darker-skinned beauties in bikinis as the locals jeer and drink in the rum-soaked sun.

I'm feeling bold, loose from beer and sunshine, and give him a few cheeky words. His eyes drill into me like stones as he tries to work out this inked woman wearing long earrings who's not afraid of him. We snake through back alleys in the white sand, his feet padding quietly, toes flat and solid on the ground. We find a tiny wooden building called Manya's House, painted bright pink and pastel green, with small tables resting on a porch that's on a decided lean. I peruse the menu and he tells me the local drink here is rum and pineapple juice, aptly named the 'Panty Ripper'. Though I have trouble ordering one because of the name, it's a welcome relief from the beer we've been drinking. We share a burrito, and still haven't touched each other, but the intimacy is spreading as the warmth of the day is fading.

I ask him how old he is, he tells me to guess.

"'31," I say, knowing he's younger.

"I'm 24," he replies. "Men always want to be older and women always want to be younger and here on the island it's no different."

He makes it feel easy, unlike so many Western dating and intimate moments when I don't know what is happening next. I know what is happening here. It feels good.

We stop by my place so I can change out of my sarong. He waits outside because apparently, I'm not allowed to have guests in my room. I pull on a dress, spray some perfume and give my hair a quick smooth.

When I walk outside, he grabs my hand. "Oh, I like your perfume," he says, because he knows it's just for him, and with that grab of my hand, I know too.

We run to the edge of the road where the sun is setting, streaks of pink shooting into the sky as the clouds turn orange and the sky fades to blue. We dangle our feet over the edge of the dock where he kisses me hard, biting my lips. We cruise down the street together, back to the Lazy Lizard where I had left my bike locked, where we have one more drink as the bar closes and the evening wind picks up. The owner is out of his head on coke, muscles straining, eyes crazy, as he yells something unknown and rips his shoes and socks off, throwing them into The Split where his staff jump in to save them, some sort of game he has done before. We laugh and leave, unlock the bike and cruise back down the street where we run into a guy named Dice who gives me one look and declares me "trouble". I guess it takes one to know one, hey?

As we cruise down the road, we buy a giant bottle of coconut rum and some pineapple juice. Well, he selects and I pay. When we leave the supermarket, a golf cart full of blonde English girls scream, "Come party!" waving their half-empty plastic cups of dubious green cocktails in the air.

"Let's go have a drink with them," he says. "I'll help my friend Dice because he wants to know them."

"I have no desire to hang out with those girls," I say.

"Really?"

"Yes. I don't come here to hang out with young, trashed tourists."

But he persuades me to join them for a drink. One drink, he promises, then we will go somewhere else. We walk down a street and up some concrete stairs to a small apartment, and right away the girls start booty dancing when the hip-hop is turned on.

Before the drink is poured, I'm already ready to leave. He pours rum for everyone, and the three other guys there mill around the girls and try not to be too sleazy but can't take their eyes off the long, dorky limbs and only just pubescent bodies of these screeching Pommy girls.

He takes me to the bathroom and gives me a bump of coke. I snake through the bright lights and cups held high in the air to sit on the balcony outside with a guy named Conroy who's tall, dark, and very quiet. He tells me I'm hot, and that the guy I'm with is a player. I watch him work the room and it's like I'm not even there. Conroy asks if I want to go for dinner with him tomorrow, or actually, do I want to take a walk with him right now. For a minute, my radar is off. I don't know who to believe, what to do, but I also know I don't want to be in this apartment.

I find my first guy and take him aside, tell him what Conroy said. He tells me straight up, "You can go with him if you want but if you want to leave, say the word right now and we will go."

So, we leave holding hands, pushing the bike with a basket full of rum, and head around the corner to the 'I & I' reggae bar. A dark dance floor is filled with tourists bumping and grinding in a terrible fashion to ragga remixes under a cheap red and green laser. Sitting at the bar, I watch Conroy enter and cruise through the dance floor. After years of running nightclubs, my radar is a lot better when in this environment. I instantly see him for who he is.

Grabbing at girls' waists, then when they resist, moving two or three people away to do it again, and again. The curvy blonde girl wearing jeans and a tight singlet loves the attention at first, but it's still too much for her after a minute and she moves away. My guy goes to score us some drugs and Conroy comes up to me immediately, "Want to dance with me?"

"Nah, I'm good thanks," I reply.

"Well, I'll be dancing over there but I won't be dancing with you."

My guy returns successful. We leave and head to the beach with

Jones, a quieter, tall dude with thin dreadlocks. We sit on a bench and have bumps of coke off a key while they tell me Patois stuff about Conroy.

"Him nuh respect us, him nuh respect di gyals, wi just look after him 'cause him a human being."

I'm high on the beach with my legs entwined in his, and it feels like the right place to be. We go back to grab the bike full of rum and juice. As we leave, hand in hand, Conroy is outside the club, puffed up, giving one of the young girls a hard time. "You dance with me and then you dun respect me, why you gotta do that?"

She's looking scared and nervous. Dice grabs her and pulls her away, sends her off with her friends; she is leaving the island tomorrow and looks rattled. I had told them not to wear those booty shorts in Guatemala and I hope they heed my advice. My guy is angry, and tells Conroy to shove it, suddenly as they grab each other in an angry embrace, the police turn up on a motorbike, cuff them to each other, and lead them away to jail.

As Dice and I walk past the cop station, he says, "Why you hanging out with children for?" He says he was asked to look after me, so we go down to the Voodoo Bar, another dark place with rickety stools and an empty dance floor pumping loud crap, the lack of red and green lasers the only distinction here between bar and club that I can see.

I buy the booze and smokes and we sit behind a cabana on the beach, having bumps off a key and talking shit. We go to the police station, where Dice talks with the cop outside and I sit quietly inside in my pigtails and polka dot dress, very aware of the bag of coke down my bra.

I be playing a dangerous game tonight.

After much shit talk and even some moments when the key goes away and a cop turns up immediately after, I back up Dice's story and leave his place at 5am, riding my rickety bike down the sandy backstreets to home. He tries in vain to assure me that I can stay with him because "He said it was okay."

Nope. I've learnt my lesson for the evening. Don't want any more island trouble. I go home alone and take a Valium, so high but needing to sleep. I may not see him again but I won't feel bad about my place in the events of the night.

The next day, I have the worst hangover of my life. I'm barely able to get coffee, feeling as if I'll die in the heat, wetting my sarong and laying in front of the fan in my too hot, too bright room, throwing up occasionally from too much rum and wishing I was anywhere but on the island. Finally, I fall into a fitful sleep around 10pm.

At 2am, I hear, "Hey!" outside my door. I stumble awake and don the sarong, open the door fuzzy-haired and bleary-eyed to him, just released from jail. He's wearing clean shorts and a singlet and we grab each other in the hot night air. We kiss and he asks if I'm angry.

"No, I was worried about you, but it was stupid, I should have grabbed your hand and dragged you away."

"Yeah, you should have," he said. "You were the boss!"

I laugh—as if I was.

When it suits them, I'm the boss, otherwise I'm at the mercy of local politics and small island mentality I don't understand. We rode on bikes to the only place open for food, a tiny burger shack on the beach down from Voodoo club. Then back to my place via a dark house where he asks me for five dollars Belize and we grab a bud to smoke. We eat burgers on my back steps and he rolls a joint with one big tobacco leaf as the paper, breaking the weed up in his palm. We start giggling.

"Let's go down to the ocean," I say.

"No, we gotta keep it on the down low. This time of night if we are out, they will give us trouble but if we stay here, we can just watch the cops ride past."

He has to go to court on Monday. Buy a shirt and wear long pants, shave. We lie down on the hot, hard bed and switch the light off. His skin holds the heat differently to mine, where I am clammy, he is just warm. He kisses me, and rolls on top of me, it's 4am and I want him bad. A skilled lover, he moves like a fish, sucking at me like the tides and the pull of the ocean under the almost full moon outside. We make love, it's fucking but it feels different, his body hard and sinewy pushing against my curves and thighs. I want him, I want him, I want him. He knows how to tease me, how to make me hot for him, his hands, mouth and legs around me till I want him so bad, even more than I have him, if that's possible.

The events of last night only made me want him more. I had left not knowing if I would see him again or if he would come find me at all. He makes me cum; I moan loudly and we dissolve in fits of giggles.

"Why are you laughing?" he says.

"I'm laughing because you are laughing."

We giggle in the night again, stuck together with the fan blasting warm air onto us. We fuck twice—hard and soft, deep and slow—with his perfect cock and condoms I produce. I suck him but stop him after the third time, nearly dawn and exhausted, sated.

"Are you happy?" he asks.

"Middle of the night, yummy boy turns up, food and smoke, you have my heart," I joke.

"Do you want mine?"

"For tonight," I reply, then add, "Maybe tomorrow too."

It is just that, and it feels right.

"You can write about it," he says, and I laugh, because it's true. There is a story waiting to happen around every corner, just like there's a new moment for him with each boat of tourists that disembark at the water dock. He wakes in the dawn, and jumps the fence. The skies open with rain, the first tropical storm since I've been here, and I sleep a bit longer, the palm trees whipping around and the drops leaving patterns in the sand outside.

The next day, and I have no phone nor any idea where to find him but he knows where I am because I'm not like the other girls. I'm a woman who knows what she wants and how to make it known.

I sit on the beach and plan to ride my bike down the street again, hoping for more of him before my own boat leaves the dock in a couple of days.

YOU BETTER BELIZE IT, CAYE CAULKER

CHAPTER 49

Glow Sticks

San Diego, USA

My baby sister sits across from me with hair frizzed from too much bleach, and translucent skin in this southern-Californian retirement town of palm trees, brown stucco buildings, and military bases.

She says, "I tell them they better make it rain, not sprinkle, or I'm leaving." About her job stripping at private parties in town.

We pass by a dollar store and she waves at the skinny Latino guy behind the counter, where he tells her, "we just got 'em in", and points to the rear of the store.

She beelines for the glow sticks, and as I'm heading to Burning Man, I naively think 'rave' while she tells me they are for a game she plays at work.

"How many people do you know that can say they do anal ring toss for a living?" She laughs.

I have to think about the logistics of that for a second.

How I wish we connected and understood each other more. With no other close family except parents, I long for a complementary mirror in which to see my reflection, but am met with a different entity, polarised and separate to me in almost every way. I tell myself, that's okay.

We are just different.

We hang out on the balcony; she drinks beer and I smoke weed as we paint our nails.

Perhaps this is what sisterhood is, sharing the simplest things even if everything else in our lives is different. She's lived here for two and a half years, arrived on a plane from Canada to meet a guy she'd only spoken to online, only for him to never show up or call. She has stayed in this town of tourists, hustlers, and more homeless people than I've seen in any city in America. She is twenty-five and already saying things like, "I'm single forever, the next guy I date has to pay for *everything*." When being objectified for so long turns the tables and men become objects, it is just a means to an end.

At her apartment, the furniture is a set, the vases match the rugs and fashion magazines lay fanned uniformly across the table. There isn't much that illustrates the personality of those who live here, and I wonder how many people spend their days and nights in someone else's idea of what a living reality is, how it should look. I peek into the other bedrooms and it's the same. However, my sister's room has leopard-print bedding and UV artwork on the walls, along with a giant picture of lips.

She's very independent, strong in her opinions, good with money, and determined to be herself, but that's pretty much where our similarities end.

I was kicked out of home at sixteen—when she was six—and then I moved interstate two years later.

Occasionally, she says something like, "I whip a guy if he touches me without asking", and I still see her in fairy wings, strawberry-blonde hair falling about her in waves, hiding behind the couch watching cartoons, humping the nose of her teddy, huffing quietly thinking we don't notice.

Actually, wait. Perhaps it began there. I don't know.

Now, she walks with me in the heat of the noon sun and meets with a big guy in a shirt and jeans who seems nervous. She buys two grams of 'snow' from right across the border for a hundred bucks. Then tells me she is thinking every minute about the second it gets dark so she can have a line. I remind myself we all draw our own lines in the sand, or on the cistern.

It's a small city and she says hello to people she knows on the street as she clutches keys with a barrel of mace attached to them, ready to strike, though she tells me it won't work on the military guys "because they are trained to resist it". The town is full of war veterans with amputated limbs.

We go shopping at a sterile mall full of families in shorts and flip-flops, and buy a rope light to put up in her room. She stays up all night drinking sake playing card games with her housemates and snorts coke in the bathroom, then moans and doesn't talk the next day when we head to the beach with a friend of mine.

She tells me she lets guys suck her feet and give her money for it, and I wonder what she's not telling me if this is the stuff she is willing to offer.

For all her self-assurance, I sense a deep sadness.

She doesn't seem to get close to people easily, whereas I am almost too full of love for too many people and at times it weighs me down. Her friend is a chick named Whisper who downs shots as she drives us around in her convertible Jeep, messy hair extensions flapping in the wind. When we are left alone, Whisper tells me my sister is stand-offish, that she gives attitude when it's not needed—even in job interviews—and that when they are out partying, she often storms off in a huff. That she tells guys on the first date that she's worked in porn. I ask my sister about the porn and she says, "no comment" with a smirk. It really hurts when she starts berating me for being 'boring' because I don't want to get 'turned up' after we were out doing lines and drinking till dawn.

"I wanted to hang out with you," she says angrily as we eat food and drink daiquiris. "That wasn't partying, just having drugs."

I twist my fingers under the table and remind myself she's still young. I start counting the seconds till I'm back in my own life.

"Being sober is boring," she says later on, after I've shown her Cosplay, fetish models, Instagram, Tumblr, hashtags, prosthetic makeup, and tried to convince her to open a Facebook account.

I can't help replying, "Maybe it's you that is boring, darling."

We eat salad on the balcony with the hum of air-conditioners accompanying the fairy lights where no stars are visible through the apartment buildings that tower over us. We swap stories of growing up ten years apart. It's almost like bonding till she whines at me, throws a tantrum and leaves the room, two minutes into the movie we are supposed to be watching.

Again, the gap between us feels insurmountable.

I sleep on the couch, badly, and the next day she's sullen. She stays home on my last day while I make a mission to the beach, suddenly feeling free and talking with strangers on the street like I have been all over the country. When I return, she's silent except for the ping on her phone—another message from a baby-faced bodybuilder guy on *Plenty Of Fish* who's standing her up again.

It's my last night and there are no words exchanged between us. I'm left feeling depleted, criticised, like trying is futile.

She is wordless in the morning, and when I try one last time to speak to her, she tells me to leave.

Again, I am left with my bags, alone, on a hot road I'd never be on by choice, feeling as if my blood family have a pattern of walking away from each other.

You can't choose your family, but you can choose your FAMILY, and I choose to give my energy to those who at least meet me in the middle. Self-preservation and a need to be surrounded by people who make me feel good are so important in my life these days.

For now, little sister, please try and be happy.

I love you, and will always love you, but for now.

I set you free.

CHAPTER 50

Burning Man

Nevada, USA

Day 1

Burning Man is about six hours' drive west from San Francisco in the Nevada desert.

It's been three days since we left the city and we are still not there.

It's 2014 and it took me ten years, or a lifetime, to finally get here.

A week of pre-organising, stressing, and last-minute plan changes with a sleepless night in a Reno hotel room, and more supplies, re-packing, then climbing slowly through the mountains the next day. Overtired already; this is going to be an epic mission.

Along the road, hippies on bikes with 'NEED TICKET, HAVE CASH' signs look hopefully at every passing vehicle. Breakdowns are pulled off the road, ourselves included, gunmetal Chevy van 'Gigi' protesting the tonne of bikes, coolers, carpet and plastic bins full of sandwich-bagged clothing we are towing. For a few minutes, it's a stressful highway moment, stuck on the mountain range with no reception or idea of what help we need, even if we could get some. All the cars are going one way, and there's no tow truck. I pass my hands over the searing engine as the pink sunset streaks across the sky, knowing she is just too hot but also sending her mechanic-Reiki, asking for her to just please deliver us safely.

After half an hour of frowning and trying to be patient, she gurgles to life to whoops from us.

We have been in the line since 3pm yesterday, pulsing along the highway in an endless snake of RVs, trucks, art cars and vans as far as the eye can see. Six hours on a single-lane road, travelling one mile, then stopping for twenty minutes, then one mile more. We reach the event site—a giant, dry lakebed known as the 'Playa'.

It's another three hours of stop, start, stop until we are parked miles from anyone by frazzled parking attendants, to collect our tickets at the box office. It's the middle of the night when we reach the line, a dark mass of thousands of people huddled together like emperor penguins to keep each other warm as whiteouts of dust pass over us, blinding all visibility. It's 1am, and we discover it's a six-hour wait standing in line for pre-purchased tickets.

It's this moment when we exchange looks and I realise…This. Is. Insanity.

We take it in shifts. I collapsed into a hard sleep in the back of the van, and was shaken awake.

Our time in the line had come. The line was full of hugs, exhausted and overtired people being friendly to each other. We got to the front and cheered, whoops from the whole crowd each time another soldier got their pass. Rode back to the van on bikes through the dawn flashing with lightning as the black sky turned shades of blue and pink with the rising sun.

We jump in the van as the rain starts, and quickly realise this is a very bad sign. The dust of the Playa becomes alkaline mud, sticking to itself, turning shoes and tyres into giant stilts of thick, crusted goo. We have travelled a few metres from the box office and suddenly all movement onsite halts. Vehicles and humans. We are not going anywhere. The thunder rocks us awake with a start and the rain pours, turning the ground quickly back into the lake it once was.

For the week it operates, the seventy thousand people that build Black Rock City make it the third largest city in Nevada. Alas, right now it glimmers on the distant horizon, man standing tall above the metropolis, and we are not there.

It's six hours later, and the party has already begun. The city shimmers in the distance but out here, we have friends united in stasis. There's bacon frying, rum being shared, ukuleles playing, break beat blasting and people hugging in the mud. Everyone offers what they have, everyone approaches each other. My shoes weigh ten pounds and I'm drinking whiskey and cherry juice in someone's shade.

The mission for survival has already begun as we share wasabi peas and face wipes and turns at being optimistic. Now and then someone is out for the count, too tired, headachy or hot to be happy, and that's okay too. We have not passed through the gates and I'm already in the right state of mind. Even though it's day three of travel, I'm calling this day one of festival.

Only eight days to go.

The reprogramming has begun.

Day 2

After twelve hours of being stuck in one spot we finally arrive before sunset and set up camp. Eat some much-needed, hearty lentil soup, and jump on our bikes to explore. Around a few street corners, and a giant fish playing bass tunes rolls past glowing green and blue. Ahead, a neon city skyline and pirate ship from last century pass by each other on the road ahead.

As we make our way to the centre of the Playa, the lights brighten, the energy increases, dings and whizzes of hyper-lit humans as they fly past us on bikes, increases. We reach the esplanade and the giant man standing tall at one point of the circle, and I realise how incredibly magic this city is.

I'm breathless. Hundreds of intimately-themed dance floors, self-created and people powered, every person lit up, whooping, bikes and crazy art cars the only vehicles that pass on the roads with no rules. It's a wonderland. It's the best dream you've ever had.

It's friendly people who don't judge you for being yourself because everyone's a freak out here. It is however drunken, fun, hilarious, sexy, or strange as you want to make it. It's the most amazing playground in the world. With everyone pitching in and few paid workers, the scale of this event is mind blowing. The stage we set up at our camp looks welcoming and inviting, the sound from the self-built speakers, warm. It's just like any city, with a post office, radio station, rangers and a grid of streets mapped out in the middle of the giant, dry lake.

It's loose and serious, politics and playfulness, sex and innocence, with everything neon, everyone sparkling with giant beams of light shooting into the sky as we make an alien city in the desert.

The food passing around today is ridiculous. Waffles and fried chicken you are forced to eat at the same time by someone yelling into a megaphone, French toast with berry cream cheese compote and crispy bacon, chicken tortilla soup with fresh coriander and avocado, and this is just at our camp. Beverages consist of either booze or water, and everyone takes a siesta in the afternoon waiting for the cool of night to descend.

When you need something here, it's given freely. When you even just want something to make your moment that little bit better, it manifests. You hug hellos out here, real hugs too. I walk the night streets alone like a flashing tank girl in candy land with a huge grin on my face in the dark. I understand now why everyone greets you with 'welcome home'.

Day 3

The temple rises out of the dust, intricate lattice pieces slotted together that form a magical, circular spire with wooden panels throughout.

As we dismount our bikes, silence overtakes us. I have never experienced a place with the energy of the temple at a festival or, in fact, anywhere. I've visited other temples, mosques, churches, giant buddhas and sacred spaces all over the planet and nowhere has ever felt as reverent as walking around this elaborate temple constructed with intent to burn with the elements in a few days. The wooden structure is covered with messages and altars.

Framed portraits sit next to wedding dresses from the fiancé who died in the war, bras from breast cancer victims, homages for loved pets, grandparents passed, and special friends taken too soon. There is even an Indian wedding dress with a sign on it that says 'Never Again'. Everyone enters and is immediately overcome by emotion.

Burly queer men hold each other as gang members wearing colours light incense for a lost brother, next to naked hippy girls splayed on the ground, sobbing. All allowing each other to be totally vulnerable and letting go in the dust. There's a giant altar in the middle, piled with mementoes. Robin Williams, recently departed, is featured, looking young and happy, along with so many parents, friends and lovers. There are messages to people in the afterlife about lessons learnt too late.

I leave a note for some friends who lost someone dear in a plane crash recently, and a couple messages from me. Different each time I visit, letting go of the fear, letting go of the soul of my aborted baby, allowing the letting go.

My friend places his father's ashes in a little baggy there, and we all meet silently outside, to cry, to hug. All who pass by are doing the same, feeling the same. It's humbling. Powerful.

It makes all of us realise what each other has lost. Everyone has experienced so much loss.

People sit under eaves and write messages, quiet sniffs the only sound, temples of one praying, meditating, sobbing, reading, writing and reflecting. I wish there was somewhere like this for all of us to go. Somewhere in every metropolis that felt like this, no matter your beliefs, for us to retreat when we need to.

A place where the others accept, understand and support each other through any loss, wordlessly, and allow it to be let go. To burn it to the ground at the end, when the suffering is done. We mount our bikes and ride in silence across the Playa, a troop of souls seeking. *Mad Max* bike crew of spiritual warriors who want desperately to let everything go with the wind.

I visited the temple multiple times, leaking tears from the bottom of me.

It draws me in a way no dance floor can. I come back to hang onto the feeling. Come back to let it all go.

Day whatever...

Whirlwinds of dust that rise in a minute to choke you are gone in twenty minutes to reveal blue skies. Attempting to ride 'deep Playa' and we get only a hundred metres, blinded, the dust rushing above us covering the sky.

All week there has been incredible freedom here. Booze is cheap, drugs are both cheap and plentiful, food is gourmet and abundant, and the element of giving is constantly evident. People run up to you to give you presents, day and night. Everyone gets trashed, dances and kisses strangers like other parties, but everyone collects their own MOOP (matter out of place) and encourages others to do the same. It's the largest leave-no-trace event in the world, amazing to witness.

Saturday night we trek out to see the man burn. It's the most fiery, most beautiful spectacle ever, watching a giant, wooden effigy burn with tens of thousands of others whooping all at once. Similar to watching an eclipse, there's a feedback-loop between nature, sky, earth and humans. It's a heaving mass of all the craziest, sparkly people on Earth.

Afterwards, everyone is high and ambles back to camp for a lovely, mushy gathering of forty of us. We head out in a big group after many false starts for torches and toilet and another beverage, still managing to lose each other quickly. There are so many varied sound systems playing different music, it's a smorgasbord. If you get bored you just move on to the next one.

Art cars everywhere, a giant set of glowing teeth race past as we see a small porch with a house facade, just a porch on both sides. Electric Mayan gods, cloud buses, pirate ships, a roller skate, a giant Pac Man ghost streaking across the Playa. People just walk into camps here, and say, "Hey". Everyone shares so much booze, has booze left over, has a selection of booze, the bars run out of mixers before booze and serve you a half-cup of straight vodka or gin, then give you more booze instead of a mixer. As the camps disperse over the next couple of days, someone comes to say goodbye to us, and a line of dancing people forms, waiting to hug him goodbye.

Punters help fill the toilets with rolls of paper as a guy from our camp known as 'Evil Brian' (there's another guy, Good Brian, too) hides in vacant porta-potties in a giant penis costume, freaking out punters desperately needing to pee. There's heckling with megaphones on every street corner where the signs are stolen rapidly. People run up to you to give you jewellery or a piece of paper that folds into a one-use cup if you forget yours and pass by a bar. Rowdy ladies with stop signs tell us to "halt or drink!" and when I tell them I'm sick from too much gin yesterday, they run off to get tummy pills and essential oils for me. It's fucking beautiful.

We walk around in a little group, high and silly, dancing for a bit at each stage, then moving when bored or when something twinkly catches our eyes. Stand in front of a giant wall of bass bins dancing hard to trap, my boots kicking up sand around me, the beat circling in my head for days afterwards. We lay under a giant tree made of glowing boxes with sequenced lightning playing in time with classical music. Magical. Like out of a Disney movie but real, with the night sky above it and new friends clutching each other in glee. Arrive back to lie on the giant trampoline as the sun rises, heckling those ten metres away at camp with a walkie-talkie to deliver us nitrous balloons and cuddle under a blanket as the sun rises.

I don't care if 'drugs are bad', being high can actually be super fun, often works to clear your mind from random worrying about regular-life crap and allows interactions other-than-the-norm to occur. Extra connections sprout, people you might not otherwise connect with.

DEEP PLAYA DUST STORM, 2014

Like all these new friends who add me on social media the second we get back into mobile range. It's the craziest mission these people make each year and it's totally worth it, even and especially with the moments of this-is-total-insanity-and-I'm-doing-it-anyway. Now, I'm back in the city. Default world.

Somehow, things feel different.

I feel at home in myself, with myself.

There is love sprouting, growing and evolving.

I am changing and everything is fluid, even more than before.

CHAPTER 51

In Transit

Fiji

Day four of transit again and I am now stranded in Fiji, the solo star of what will now be known as the *'National Lampoons Transpacific Nightmare.'*

Airport authorities threw out my toothpaste because I didn't have a dollar Fijian for a Ziploc baggie for my liquids. The airport food appears fossilised and dangerous, as if it was lovingly baked in 1986, and my supplies of optimism, water and starburst are running drastically low.

I'm contemplating Bear Grylls' idea of using pigeon guano as an enema to get moisture into me, but have not yet seen any pigeons arrive at this gate.

To avoid the onset of spina bifida and incurable insanity, I am doing yoga, trying to sleep on the dirtiest carpet ever in a fluorescent corner decorated with stained seats and chips all over the floor, the lights randomly flickering on and off.

Zen is very, *very* far away from here.

There is a lone potted palm somehow surviving in this Petri dish of grime, humidity, and no natural air.

I focus on that, imagining myself back to the pure white beach in Belize perhaps, or the park in Brooklyn or the ghettos of Oakland, even Guatemalan slums ringed by volcanoes would be better than this hellish prison of duty-free shit, tacky souvenirs and tired, grumpy children.

Have started to go mildly crazy, muttering "cunts" over and over as I do downward dog and don't give a shit if anyone sees my underpants. This may be my last diary entry as the distant shores of Australia seem like a mythical fable conjured by a hopeful explorer—too good to actually be true.

My friends, this life has been a grand one.

I regret nothing but trying to buy cheap flights and spending over four thousand dollars on changing them instead, leaving me now stranded without a flagon of wine to drink or a man, dog or pillow to cuddle. Drifting alone in a sea of crappy carpet and endless security checks.

Then the dreaded final announcement: fight cancelled.

I'm destined to spend another day at least unmoored and lost in a country full of gated resorts and twenty-dollar 'salads'. I may come down with scurvy, unless starburst has vital greens I am not aware of. My final words before I turn into a machete-wielding psycho are: "NEVER EVER *EVER* FLY FIJI AIRWAYS!"

CHAPTER 52

KFC Island Style

Tasmania

MY OVARIES ARE CRYING, FLINDERS ISLAND

The tiny plane rattles and dips as we descend towards the Furneaux Islands where fifty-two rocky outcroppings poke from grey buffeting seas in the Bass Strait right under Melbourne.

The largest one is Flinders Island, "the same size as Hong Kong" locals tell me, but instead of neon-studded skyscrapers, it's sheep, cows, and scraggly trees as far as the eye can see.

I've never heard of it before but AJ lives here now and has got me a week of work on the island. He's an old friend, a production and lighting tech who used to play techno in my club 'The Sandpit' when it was in the basement of a gothic club in Adelaide and the policy was vinyl records only, just before 2000. Now, he lives on a farm with a woman named Sarah and their two kids, with chickens and pigs they serve up for dinner.

He runs school holiday programs, and I'm here to facilitate. Usually, they get twenty-five kids to art classes here during holidays, but over eighty places have been filled for the three days. That's ten percent of the island coming to learn stencil art from me. The kids are great, the classroom quaint, and each night we drive home content, picking coloured boogers from our noses from spray paint as the sun streaks purple and orange across the mountains.

It's a weird kind of peace. Big skies above us move with layers of grey clouds that shroud the top of Strzelecki Range like something out of *Lord of the Rings*. They call it paradise, and everyone raises a hello finger to each other as dirty utility trucks pass each other on empty, unsealed tracks riddled with corrugation and the sinkholes where wombat burrows have fallen through.

We drive to the beach where farmers have holiday shacks half an hour from their farms in the south, and BBQ fatty chops by lantern light as I sip cheap wine and think about not drinking but drink anyway. Others exchange stories of lead in the groundwater, and defensively argue that the permanent population is definitely more than 370, which some guy has been telling tourists around town.

We drive home at night, the stars a luminous smear above us, the darkness absolute. Wildlife scurries across the road like an intersecting highway. AJ drives slowly for my benefit but we still hit a couple. The thump of wombats being killed under the twin cab tyres sends an electric pulse of horror up my spine and through every pore and hair follicle. Here, they pull baby mutton birds from the nests of global migratory parents who have just come home, to smack them on rocks and break their necks to eat them, and call it 'the KFC of the island'. The kids love it, apparently, and have small arms to reach further into the nests. I get invited on the first day of the season, and decline.

I feel like a morally inferior, supermarket-frequenting city person, despite all my healthy, ethical, mom-and-pop consumer choices. At night, I retreat to my room, not used to the endless chatter of kids, and Google some history to find that allegedly the last Tasmanian Indigenous people were exiled here, only to die from lack of shelter and new diseases.

Outside having a smoke, I look up from my phone and the darkness seeps in like ink. Even the stars blotted out. Wind rushes through the trees and I flash the torch into the darkness in a defensive move.

Ghosts lurk here.

At times, the wind is still and the clouds part for a blessed moment. It does seem like paradise but it's a utopian dream to call it the 'hub of the universe', which is printed—not ironically—on t-shirts in the general store at Lady Barron.

The next night I eat freshly caught crayfish and gummy shark, freshly killed mutton-bird. We eat wallaby shot nearby and pork raised in the backyard, fed nothing but milk powder the last month of its life. It's delicious and rich but way too many animals, too much meat for me in one meal. The roquette salad? It does nothing. My diet has become healthier lately, mainly vegetables and fruit, small portions of meat, bread and some cheese.

I walk outside with a full, aching belly, to smoke. Tonight, the stars are out, a giant network of fairy lights. I take it all in. Breathe deeply and feel the darkness envelop me, and tonight it's not scary.

It's only the sky, the silence, and the shadows of trees.

The same quiet the world over.

CHAPTER 53

Microdosing Diary

Day 1 – Dose 1 – Paper acid 1/16th

The clouds streaking purples and blues across the mountain ranges as I read articles about James Fadiman and the microdosing movement in America.

I'm pretty sure a new dawn is coming: microdosing lysergic acid diethylamide (LSD) in a medicinal way for performance and mood enhancement rather than recreational 'tripping out'.

We are going to try it.

We'll go about our daily lives—work, eat, exercise, sleep a full night, observe and discuss.

Nat and I are not a couple, and live together with others. Nat occasionally takes acid recreationally but I don't, really. Maybe once every couple of years.

This morning, at our kitchen island at around 10:30 am, we placed a tab of acid onto a plate and cut it into 16 tiny pieces with a Stanley knife. I had already gone for a morning dog walk and had my second coffee of the day.

I don't know if it's a placebo effect, but I'm in a great mood today. We have both been home all day, the mood around here has generally been-up.

Not manic, or worrying about later things, just dealing with things as they come up. Productive. Making phone calls, typing emails and invoices, things feel direct somehow, as if there is clarity of action.

Also, today I'm not emotional. Not dwelling on anything. Potential dates have communicated with me, I have responded and let go, and gone on with my day. Perhaps I am less attached to outcomes? I feel positive, optimistic.

I've eaten well, walked Yoshi in the afternoon, and feel my wit is super sharp. Made the tradie laugh when he was here to fix the front door. Played on kids equipment at the park, whizzing around when I usually might have just stood there.

Felt sexy.

When that cute guy on the street wearing overalls talked to Yoshi, I felt his eyes, a palpable energy. I don't feel as much need to consume food, smoke, or anything. Well it's day one… on what could be a long and interesting journey.

Day 2 – No Dose

Levels of anxiety and irritation seem high today. Bubbling under the surface. Feeling as if everyone wants a piece of me. Triggered by messages from some underage kid who thinks they are invited to our party tomorrow. I'm feeling nervous about my date today and my party tomorrow, rather than glee at having some male attention and gathering with all my friends to get loose. Heading out there, will shake this off. Report back later.

Report: Shook it off. Had a good date. Left makeup on his face when we met, whoops! Went to work, it dragged. Came home tired, went to bed at 1am and slept well.

Day 3 – Dose 2

Good morning grey Melbourne rain. I won't deny we were excited for day two of dosing. Took it at 10:30am again, with coffee after breakfast.

Spent the day doing chores for our housewarming party tonight, more giggles and less irritation than yesterday. Loving the weather though it makes our firewood wet so the fire drum idea is redundant. Optimistic about the party tonight. Got dressed in a great outfit today without thinking about it, all greys, pinks and purples with pearls and silver earrings that tinkle.

Productive once again. Without feeling guilty or nervous I'm not addressing all that *'needs addressing'* or whatever. I have let go somehow.

Do I really think like that?

Weird.

I felt removed from the manic-ness, or like it's just a handy part of me that gets things done.

Okay, time for a shower and the donning of the sequins. Time to turn on the sparkly lights and pour a glass of wine. Not drinking much lately, bored of drinking for the sake of it, and now it's only for special occasions. I have earned whatever I want tonight.

Also more typos and dyslexic swaps of letters in this as I type it, but possibly impatient (no change there, haha). Over and out.

Day 4 – No Dose

Recovering from our house party, hardly any sleep. Totally and utterly hate booze and how it makes me feel. Felt sick last night and wiped-out emotionally today. Cleaned the house, sticky bottles and cigarette butts everywhere, but no broken glasses. Quite civilised, really.

Spent the afternoon eating junk food, streaming endless Netflix episodes and answering the door to people who forgot things or are picking up music equipment.

Bed early, where I had vivid dreams that I promptly forgot in the morning.

Day 5 – Dose 3

Still recovering, obviously. Woke feeling irritated with the world and my housemates. Left them a note and came back from a morning walk with a friend at the river to a flurry of activity at the house. We made it nice together. Spent the day hanging in the backyard even though it was too cold, talking shit with others, doing sweet fuck all, and feeling okay about it. Had a cry moment but it passed like clouds over the sun, internally telling myself, *it's only today, Bo, let it all be today.*

Day 6 – No Dose

Woke feeling as if things should be better today, regardless.

It really does take two days to recover from a night of partying when in your mid-thirties. Slight anxiety at going to the dentist, and shock at the coldness of the air, but both were dealt with fine. By midday, I was back at the computer trying to find 'wins' and sense and meaning in a world of freelancing. Tuesday fun, right?

Tradie came over to replace the oven, only the 5567th thing wrong with the majestic-as-fuck palace we are so blessed with. We moved in a month ago and it has been a constant list of things to get fixed. I still feel blessed, and will not let the constant flow of tradies leaving muddy footprints on the rugs and uncovering gross, ugly, dingy parts of the house that haven't seen the light of day in ten years, break me. It ain't my house or mess, guys! I'm just the new tenant! Helped him change the oven over, all good.

But still a growing level of anxiety and hopelessness today, as if nothing I'm doing is right and working out. This feeling is not associated with any one thing—not a man, not a situation—just a bubbling of extra nervous energy, frustration that comes.

Nat calls at 3pm, freaking out on the phone. Feels the same way, sucked of energy by vampires in the street and manic as hell trying to work it out. He arrives home, upset at the world. We talk for a few minutes and realise the heater isn't working, go outside to find it off. We try in vain, but have no idea how to light the pilot, and have had problems with the heater since we moved in. No heating again!

I lose it, kicking it, walk inside in a huff directed at heater, tradies, universe, everything, and Nat asks, "Do you want a hug?:

"No, I'm actually wanting to go ARGGHHH right now," I say with a controlled outburst, mimicking that feeling.

He stares right at me. "Let's do it then."

Both of us instantly SCREEAAAAMMM and grunt and yell and stamp our feet with all our might for about 15 seconds, completely let RIP, then break it simultaneously to grab each other in a tight hug and laugh really hard for twice as long, our bellies contracting against each other. I had a headache from it, my throat hurt, my body was briefly yet highly tensed... then released. It was a complete reset.

A reboot button for our own realities; the story we were each perpetuating all day long. Afterwards, something has been released. I am exhausted, all screamed out. So is he. We both calm down. (I call this 'rage therapy' and later on, will help other people, clients and families through this process in a controlled and intentional way.)

We proceed to talk in the loungeroom about processes, letting go, outside influences, everything. I take him through some pros and cons lists and drawings of the important areas in his life. He appreciated the free coaching, and it's a reminder of what I'm good at.

The world calms. The sun sets on another day.

But something is different.

I have never been able to do that sort of 'crazy' with another person. Well, I have, but it has never had a good ending. 'Crazy banshee' has had to come out directed at people; for example, men who won't leave my house, who are threatening or manipulating me. It has never just burst free in someone's company, and been allowed.

And it has never been accepted. It certainly has never been met in the middle, and then worked through BY ME.

I have, in the past, been at the mercy of these feelings. Fight or flight styles, my nervous system reacting.

Perhaps that is the work that happens now. Not the external stuff like business logos and packages and coaching and browsing for random arts jobs I don't even want. But the internal self-talk/limiting-belief/self-clearing courses everyone seems to be attending... I am doing it now. In my new house, with dog and cat as witness, and Nat often as a mirror.

I won't deny—I'm looking forward to the dose tomorrow.

Day 7 – Dose 4

Today, something has shifted. Lifted. Walked Yoshi and did thirty rounds of boxing and plyometrics in the shed. Freezing morning but the sun comes out and I allow myself an hour in its rays, flicking through my phone and enjoying the warmth on my face.

Had lunch with a friend on Sydney Road, fortuitous encounter with the date from Friday—we are meeting tomorrow night for dinner. After I walk through Barkley Square, having good interactions with JB Hi-Fi staff and feeling as if people are looking at me differently. Crowned with purple hair, I'm in a suit jacket and combat boots, striding around looking others in the face. Perhaps that's why.

I feel hot today. Sexy. Purposeful.

Today, there is no work on the horizon, and while usually that brings a sense of unease, it is more about enjoying this down time and knowing that it's around the corner. I buy some things for the house, a heater for my room, and don't worry about the money going out today.

Day 8 – No Dose

Sick, sick, sick. I have a cold from all the rushing and the doing of things. Walk the dog with a friend and spend the rest of the day on the couch, dosing with ginger and honey and lemon and olive leaf extract instead. I'm ok with this, strangely enough.

Day 9 – Dose 5

Walked the dog with a friend, still sick. Head feels full of heaviness and I resign myself to another day at home, in the sun, on the couch, in the backyard.

Feeling less attached to outcomes again. Date cancelled last night and didn't respond when I said I was feeling unwell. I am worth texting, calling, visiting, making second dates with, I know this.

Like, actually *know* it. Not just intellectually but at a cellular level. Had a moment this morning where I felt so *lucky* that I'm not currently with the wrong guy. Better to be alone and safe and confident in my abundant life than let anyone wreck that. Feeling a deep contentment the last two days with my own thoughts. With my own company.

Since not drinking much, my food guilt is pretty much gone. Did a Facebook post about being over nightclubs and got a huge response. Seems I'm not the only one looking for different ways to connect with people now.

Nat and I meet in the afternoon to discuss how we are less attached to outcomes. We agree we can tune into the acid energy, consciously tap into that trippy place during the day if we so choose. We agree our emotional state is more level, less attachment to future and past, living in the moment more.

Doing things one step at a time. A widening of peripheral vision, being able to see forward but not have to focus on it. Extreme blissful gratitude and satisfaction moments for both of us, perhaps from focusing more on the now instead of the outcome.

Also experiencing vivid dreams but with hardly any recollection of them. This happens on a few of the nights—we know they are vivid but can't recall them.

We discuss the cumulative effect of acid, so we have had around 1/3 of a tab each over a nine-day period, and that on 'no dose' days we seem to have a different way of doing things. Or, it has an effect on our decision making.

For those of us who are too determined to do *everything* (like me), it might allow room to stay home instead of going into the city to a protest rally when you are sick, because you need to rest. And for those of us who have trouble with routine (like Nat), it might allow for enough discipline to clean your room and do washing and dishes before you lounge on the couch all night. So it works both ways. Amazing!

The ripple effect… because things are generally better, and easier. So, I am manifesting more easier, better, positive things in the world around me, in my reality, increasing the vibration of pretty much everything. Makes it easier to tap into the divine positive now, which means we reprogram the way we process Things That Happen To Us. Feels as if we are on the edge of a breakthrough, we are discovering more about ourselves and the fact that your REALITY is everything, there is no point worrying about outcomes.

This feels big today, and important, and as if I'm poised on a precipice of understanding. This work is exciting.

Day 10 – No Dose

Spent the day at home alone again. Still sick and trying to be ok with that. Went to the farmers market with Yoshi in the morning, bought a loaf of bread the size of my head, and punnets of strawberries. Made seriously medicinal pumpkin soup, so much ginger, chilli, garlic and turmeric, I nearly couldn't eat it—burned a trail down my throat. Soak it up with bread to combat the heat. I am quite content with my company today, which is good because it's all me, baby!

Day 11 – Dose 6

Day 4 of being sick in the house alone. It's Sunday and I fight a growing feeling of boredom and dissatisfaction, creeping edges of depression and sadness till I invite Jamie over and we sit in the backyard in the sunshine with our dogs and a colouring book. Really tired of not being able to breathe well and wondering if this experiment is having any effect at all. And it's a dose day!

Day 12 – No Dose

Woke today feeling better. I can breathe! Yay! Nat came home and injured his arm working, so the day is filled with doctors' appointments and getting things at the house in order.

Finally filmed myself doing spoken word and uploaded, it feels good to put it out there. Letting my expression go out into the world and making it happen, is something I have put off for a while. It ends up being easy. Why didn't I do this sooner?

I go to bed early tonight after a searing hot bath with Epsom salts. Everyone in our house is locked away in dark rooms by 10pm and we sleep to the sound of rain hitting the roof.

Day 13 – Dose 7

Today we took the last pieces of one single tab that has seen us through the last two weeks. One thing I am sure of, I have enjoyed taking one trip over two weeks more than had I taken it all at once. Today, I double dose, and Nat single doses. It's grey and whooshy outside. There's a lot to do today but gladly, my energy levels are back at reasonably high again after days of being sick.

The rain comes in sideways, and I decide to try and find James Fadiman on Facebook. He features in any article about microdosing, and was literally poised to begin conducting clinical trials when 'they' outlawed LSD as a Class A drug back in the '60s. He has been talking about microdosing ever since.

Every person is only a click away now, and he responds to my friend request and we immediately begin a discourse that ends in him reading all the other words on my blog and telling me they are 'powerful' and that he's 'already a fan'! I proceeded to email him this diary, which he is delighted with. James is collecting them to write a book. In just a few days, it's gone from reading articles about this guy to buying his book from Amazon, to emails from him to join his study and being a fan of me?

That's some *Matrix* -style learning. Learning to fast track the regular ways of doing things.

I love this shit! I want to learn this way all the time.

It's been two weeks of microdosing and my conclusions are thus:

- Life should be lived in the moment, and it's much more pleasurable when we focus on that rather than five minutes from now or what happened yesterday.
- My body is an integrated machine capable of many things, and now and then it will fall sick. It is my job to allow it time-out, even if that means staying home alone for five days eating horrible soup.
- I am a sexy, spunky individual and I project that vibe when I'm feeling good.

- There are glorious moments in everyday life, in every reality, it is up to us to acknowledge them.
- We are the product of our own thoughts. We have the ability to create our own world and the way we see things is ALL subjective.
- The 'crazy banshee' energy is NOT BAD. She has a place, and she is part of me. The right people to work with, and be in relationships with, will not only recognise this but help me to embrace it. They will not run away in fear when she raises her head. I realised last year she gets things done, moving faster when perhaps things are stagnant, she DEMANDS change. This energy is USEFUL and not to be ashamed of, just harnessed and channelled.
- I believe there are benefits worth exploring from microdosing for those of us who are able to do it in a controlled manner. There are many other methods and tools at our disposal that are more effective and worth experimenting with than the ones we are permitted to play with. It is up to us to go where big pharma and Western medicine is unwilling to go, and to give it a voice. I am not stopping anytime soon and would be willing to talk, speak, share, write and explore all of these concepts more with others coming from an inquisitive yet serious and self-exploratory angle.

> *"In the scientific world, 'fear' is usually called 'scepticism'."*
>
> James Fadiman

CHAPTER 54

It's Real

I met him. The most beautiful, generous, and loving man. After the first date, we simultaneously delete the dating app on which we met. He lives in Brunswick in a shabby house with a Staffy called Tonko.

Totally upfront about his feelings, we both agree it's the best relationship we've ever had.

Yet only a few months in, he seems to drag the past of his life with him, unable to detach even for a moment. He's forty years old and still at the mercy of his family's needs every day. A messed-up brother who he says he hates but I see the pain in his eyes because he really wishes it wasn't so. A mother who has done 'everything' for them but also enables them like sixteen-year-olds who weren't told it's not okay to drink booze alone all day.

Since he met me, he has wanted to change his life. I see it.

Everything he watches me do, or asks for advice, he embraces and does tenfold. From diet to his dog, to language; he is morphing into his best self - right before my eyes.

He said he "never believed in Chinese medicine" but takes herbs and then tells everyone how they are fixing him. He likes my friends and even if a little intimidated by our honesty, felt like one of us instantly. I see him reaching out, still unsure of the levels of relating allowed. Want him to know that he has an army around him just as I do. These people are around us for a reason right now... right now when the universe has delivered us each other.

He drinks more than me, is pretty unhealthy and often seems easily depressed. I know the changes he wants to make are not going to be easy. Still, I have no doubt he will succeed at anything he decides to do.

This is why I love him.

I truly feel like he is capable, smart and resourceful to create the life we both desire together. Am willing to stand by him and hold his hand but I also cannot help him alone. I need him to be strong for me too. Hope he stands up to his family sometimes and demands his own happiness at any cost.

The real work and joy in life is supporting each other through this stuff; not just the eating, drinking, travelling, working and fucking. When we penetrate the surface, the real magic begins.

He's the strong, calm rock I need to really fly without worry. Sometimes, he feels like a refuge—where I can relax and forget the hum around us.

I feel safe in his arms, so safe that my baggage comes up and is gone.

Keep a running list of all the ways we love each other.

I won't lie, I've thought about reading it to him as wedding vows one day. Have never thought about that with any other man. Seriously. I hope he is willing to do the hard work that is necessary.

He says he doesn't want to work, and I worry that that means work on everything. Even us.

But I stand before him with an open heart and knowledge that I have done a lot of the work and I am ready.

The next part is where we help each other do all the things we've been scared to do.

CHAPTER 55

Love Is

Love is learning to bake gluten-free, banana-coconut bread when it's raining outside.

Love is driving for three hours through the city to collect your partner from a shit job.

Love is driving to Hanging Rock to pick up your partner from working a gig at midnight.

Love is helping your partner 'Reality Check' their entire house, because they are brave.

Love is visiting your parents together and making it awesome even when it's hard.

Love is compromising the climate control of every room we sleep together in, ever.

Love is missing someone five minutes after they've left.

Love is wearing earplugs every night instead of kicking your snoring lover.

Love is a man who stands up for you and takes over when necessary.

Love is also allowing him to do so.

Love is driving past and stopping with clients still in the car to give me a hug.

Love is good morning texts and sweet dreams messages.

Love is a gluten-free guy delivering tarts he can't even eat.

Love is getting a little thrill every time he 'likes' something of yours online.

Love is systematically working through triggers together without taking it personally.

Love is travelling together and having an amazing time, even when injured or sick.

Love is holding hands while diving in the ocean at night.

Love is tears of happiness for no reason at all.

Love is being able to say anything to each other.

Love is changeable and complex.

CHAPTER 56

Alcoholism

Once more after a great day together, he pours a drink alone. For no reason I can see.

That's four tonight. I can't help counting and my heart sinks when I arrive, kiss him, and taste the sweet, sickly aroma of Baileys.

His mother is there on the couch. Perhaps that's why he needs a drink, but he doesn't talk about it with me. I just assume, and hope he'll open up one day soon. Don't say anything to keep the peace. We go out for dinner, he's happy and it feels romantic.

In solidarity, I order a cocktail with him that I don't really want. It makes me buzzed then tired in the space of twenty minutes, and I can't imagine that feeling four to seven times every day.

We get home and he makes himself a huge tumbler of Baileys and ice mixed with whiskey. I have to ask for a drink and he pours me a glass of warm tap water, no ice. When I ask why the whiskey and Baileys, he replies, "it's sweet" when we have just talked about the incredible dessert we'll have.

It's addiction talking again.

It's addiction rushing to talk about anything else, trying to make it light between us.

I'm heavy as fuck now. All the weight of all the addictive personalities I have known, all the hoping, waiting, and denial. The trauma and abuse that leads to him drinking alone every day is not even up for discussion yet. I don't know what to do, but at that moment I want to be anywhere but there. So, I leave. Quietly. Calmly.

I leave him with his giant sweet drink with the melting cubes, and go home alone and mourn the dessert we didn't have together.

I feel disconnected from him, and it sucks.

Want him to know I love him but can't send a text message.

I wake alone in the grey, rainy morning and wish for him in my arms. But I cannot lose myself to someone else's addictions again.

I retreat, and wait.

Love him from afar anyway, hoping he'll grab what he wants and never let go.

CHAPTER 57

Missing You When You Are Right Here

Tomorrow is six months in the best relationship I've had so far. Today, you yelled at me and I leapt out of the car far from home, triggered and disgusted with the way you have treated me lately.

I'm not going to argue with you, sorry.

To cut me off and energetically break up with me, to shut me out, and say nothing is wrong, for weeks, allowing me to doubt myself because you can't tell me. Then to admit it, acknowledge it, own it and say you actually want me, want it to work, and then not show up.

Not being present is the worst. I would rather have a fight, thanks. Quick and hot and not dragging out for weeks, dulling the glow of the love I thought we shared.

I know your family is a priority. Know Monday dinner is a priority. I know the two hundred-thousand-dollar car you drive is a priority. But you haven't stayed with me in a week. We haven't had sex in a month. Instead, you whisk me to some expensive dinner and pay for it, not talking to me. It's horrible.

I'd rather eat cheese sandwiches together on the couch in sweatpants and be real.

We don't cook together anymore and our travel plans are not discussed. You asked me to move in to your place twice and when I suggested that perhaps we could get somewhere new together, talk of that ceased.

Today, I was silly enough to think you would be on my steps when I got home tonight, with fried chicken and flowers, and maybe I would feel loved again.

But you aren't, and I don't.

I know I'm not a priority anymore.

I take Yoshi—who has some mysterious illness—to the vet alone and know I can't call you to ask for help. When you turn up these days, you are rarely delighted to see me.

It feels like I'm a burden. Another stress. Another person harassing you when all you want is to be alone in a dark cave numbing your head with whatever works. Endless repeats of *Seinfeld* turned up loud. So you don't have to think, you keep saying.

I know what this depleting love, this waiting for love that doesn't come, feels like.

When I see it coming, I'll jump out of the car again, whether you are doing a hundred and forty in a fifty zone or not. As you often do, yelling at those concerned for their children's safety.

You said it yourself, it's safer and easier for you to stay single, mildly unhappy and fuck an occasional chick from Tinder. Stay embroiled in the drama of your family's lives rather than seek to define your own. That's cool, but if you can't call it, I will.

I'll miss you. But I've already missed you for months now, every single day.

CHAPTER 58

Ode To Yoshi

MY GREATEST LOVE, YOSHI

You can't be gone.

You were just here a few hours ago, huffing and puffing at five o'clock on the dot so I'd feed you.

How can you be gone?

These tissues I'm filling with snot as I sob for you, I realise they are safe on the ground now because you aren't here to chew them, and it makes me cry even more.

How can you be gone? I wasn't ready.

Not now. Please don't go now. We had more things to do.

I wanted you to grow old and grey with me.

Today, I vacuumed for a house inspection and all I could think about is your precious hairs, and how there are no more of them to come.

You ate the wrong thing, my love. Food was always your weakness and it freaked me out how you would inhale anything that crossed your path.

You ate entire wheels of artisan cheese, you ate 'lady snacks' (dirty tampons and pads stolen from bathroom bins), which was embarrassing and hilarious. You secretly ate party foods of guacamole and chips and lamb chops off our dinner plates so fast we weren't sure if we had eaten them ourselves. You stole lunches from the bags of workers onsite at events, you even ate special, 40th birthday bacon that you somehow stole from a zipped-up bag inside a tipi in the forest. You had sneaky tricks going with most of the guys we lived with, stealing burgers from under drunk sleeping heads, and pizzas from under our noses. You would remember the rotting chicken carcass in an alley four blocks ahead before I could, and be neck deep in it by the time I got there. To our disgust, you ate human poop. Caught popcorn like a pro to our delight.

Stan taught you to beg and that became your cuteness-overload trademark. Food was your greatest obsession. You ate strawberries, loved mandarins and knew the sounds of cheese being cut from the other end of the house. Even when I got you a slow-eat bowl you still gobbled it like you hadn't eaten in a week.

I could never stop you and it was always too late. It's too late now. Why is guilt a pet owner's lingering feeling? Is it because they can't talk to us? Is it because we make the most choices for them?

I didn't make all his choices.

Yoshi had friends at barbecues I had never met, in all scenes, friends all over the city, because we went everywhere together. We didn't use a leash, both of us were too independent. He waited at street corners to the delight of grandmas. He raided composts in front yards for bones on the regular.

He came to nightclubs, and he was a great babysitter. He modelled for me without complaint. Our holiday cards have been on fridges and in the hands of loved ones for years. He was at dubstep gigs in the park with a sign around his neck warning others of his penchant for spilled beers, after spilling them himself.

He was a quiet partner to friends going through divorces, illness.

He always just knew when you just needed him. He was part of our community, in love with the children, gentle and friendly with every animal he ever lived with, from neurotic dogs to cats with psychosis to kittens found at festivals to rats to human party animals all over the country.

It's 6am and the birds are calling.

Who will walk me now?

Who will make sure I do ten thousand steps and don't just drink coffee in front of the computer for ten hours straight?

Who will sniff loudly and indignantly at parties when it's time to go home?

Who will cuddle me to sleep and match my breathing with theirs so my mind can quiet?

Who will draw me back from tropical destinations with love, when I could leave everything else behind?

Who will demand routine, this house with a backyard, this suburban life in Australia?

Who will save me again if I make the wrong choice with my heart?

Who will unconditionally love me, just because I'm me?

You were the rock that moored me, our walks bookend each day that I took for granted, I see now.

The house is still.

No more chasing bunnies at dusk screaming for you to come back. Not ever again.

You weren't 'just a dog' to me, not ever.

You were my life partner in the true meaning of the word, the being who stuck around for all the hairy bits, unwavering.

You thought you were human and I encouraged you, collecting bandanas from all over the world, sitting up on benches next to me because you wanted to. At bars you got away with eating snacks right from the table because you were so cute. Ageing gracefully, you didn't have much energy for puppies, would rather scout the perimeter with your nose to the ground. That nose was your blessing and your curse. My favourite model, I think I have about fifty thousand photos of you, but now there'll be no more, and there's still not enough. Not enough of us together walking side by side, me on my phone and your nose in some garbage.

We traversed the whole country where you encountered cane toads, curlews, snakes and lizards.

You flew in a plane because I followed my heart, naturally you took it in your stride and sniffed the tropical wind and I swear you actually smiled. You discovered your primal self in the jungles up there and became a tougher, wiser, more streetwise dog than the sheltered puppy you were before.

It was after this that you began barking, definitely. Protectively.

I'll never forget your face when we were separated and then reunited, and I swore I'd never leave you with an abusive man again.

I didn't.

We drove back across the country together being chased by

storms, and you were the only reason I kept going, the only reason I didn't drive off a bridge. We went camping and swimming, we chased bunnies down the coast and I pulled leeches from between your toes and out of your butthole because that's what you do when you look after each other.

We made it home and camped out, then sorted our life and each potential housemate you would lean on and stare at me if you didn't like them. Each new date you would assess and deem either worthy or not by his energy, and my bed would cover him in hair as a reminder of who was boss.

We swam in reservoirs in summer, and we walked the icy moors in the middle of winter.

I covered you in a million kisses and you knew the words 'I love you' as part of your hundred-word repertoire.

You were the Zen master waiting quietly till you could steal all the food and still be ready for dinner.

You won everyone over, and you filled me with love in a way I'd never before felt.

We did have the best life ever; I know because I was constantly striving to have adventures in nature and you encouraged me to do both those things.

I'm happy for you, but sad for me.

I'm not ready to be alone.

I want you with me.

Is that where grief comes from? Just selfish need?

All I know is you were, and always will be, my true love.

You are my main man, and I'm not sure if anyone will ever come close.

Yoshi, Zoozy, Bubbaloo, my Puppaloo, who I told all along 'you're for cuddles'.

Thank you for all you gave me.

Thank you for choosing me and melting my heart the first day we met.

It's 8am and half of Melbourne is mourning you.

I called your dad Stan, and we cried down the phone together, the love you and he shared was different to ours and so special.

This is just death. We all face it.

We lose people, dogs, and things that make our heart hurt physically like mine has all morning.

When you don't have much family, your pets become your family.

I'll walk myself for a while, in memory of you. I probably won't vacuum for ages.

This is an ode to Yoshi dog, you helped me learn to not take myself so seriously, to love myself at all costs, and to smell the flowers at all times. Even, and especially, when they are rotten.

Goodbye, precious soul in Beaglier form. May you fly and be free of that pain.

I'll never forget you.

Anyhow, I have your paw print inked on my arm in case dementia sets in.

Forever and ever till eternity my brumby bunny hunter stuffed animal panda booga-loo.

Love, your Mama.

PIC BY MARK BURBAN

CHAPTER 59

Thirty Ways to Mend a Broken Heart

1. Let go gracefully, especially when it's scary.
2. Try not to stay in a place of blame or regret.
3. Get angry, be sad. But don't forget the beauty.
4. Gather your friends for adventures.
5. Book a trip somewhere else.
6. Feel the shitty parts; self-medication is a band-aid.
7. Have baths often, and walk in nature.
8. Reignite your inner power and peace.
9. Remember all the benefits to being single.
10. Watch sad movies, then pull yourself up.
11. Read books, drink tea till it doesn't hurt so much.
12. Pamper yourself with all you've got.
13. Cuddle every animal you can.
14. Tell your parents you love them.
15. Tell your friends you need them.
16. Tell yourself you are worth it.
17. Make a fort and don't leave till you are smiling.
18. Give yourself a break. Give them a break.
19. Believe this ending is leaving space for a beginning.
20. Break up as a compassionate adult; be present.
21. Remember how much you love your own company.

22. Get a haircut and shed stuff along with the hair.
23. Send beams of love to your ex, even remotely. (It's for your healing, not theirs.)
24. Love yourself first, always.
25. Declutter your bedroom and move things around.
26. Write, sing, dance, thrash, and get it out.
27. When you are ready, go on a date with someone.
28. You started this journey alone; you'll end it alone.
29. Howl at the moon.
30. Remember, this too shall pass.

CHAPTER 60

Mom Arrives

Mom arrives tomorrow to help me pack up my life.

Everything has fallen apart.

My beautiful dog died, the man I thought I would marry is gone, and my final share house is over.

The festival I was about to run, the pinnacle of my career, lost its permit at the last minute.

Mom is very house-proud and tidies her place to within an inch of its life whenever visitors come over, including me. I asked her to come help me pack up this giant, 5-bedroom share house while I go on the road, crashing with friends before I try to buy a home.

Of course, even though I am a mess, I will be spending the day preparing my house for her.

She always threatens to bring 'white gloves' to check for dust on the windowsills, but she actually doesn't give a shit, will smoke a joint giggling and sit among the rubble and eat peanut butter sourdough toast cooked golden-brown crunchy, just the same way I like it. Also, cleaning is a good distraction from everything.

Losing Yoshi feels like losing my child. There's a big hole in my life no lover or friend will ever fill.

I feel like I'm at the bottom of a very deep well, and I can't work out how to climb out.

Can't wait for a bit of Momma loving, because as old as we get and as wise as we are, sometimes you just need a hug from your mom. Sending love to all whose moms are not here anymore. To all who have mothered and lost babies or dogs or chickens or anyone who looks at you with that adoration of 'you made me'—there is just no love on Earth like it.

Mom will come, and she will make everything okay because that's what Mom's do, right?

CHAPTER 61

The Biggest Secret Ever

When she arrives, we drink a glass of wine.

For an hour, we catch up, and she sees a constant stream of people in my life—at my door, on my phone—whom I exchange with, that I am vulnerable with. Those in this crazy family I've created.

They are consoling me, lifting me up, supporting me, through the shitstorm of grief I've been living for the last few months.

Two glasses in, out of nowhere, she reveals a secret jewel she's been keeping for 36 years. She tells me...

I'm not who I think I am. My dad isn't my dad.

I'm not German nor French after all.

I'm half Italian, and neither Dad knows the truth. I'm actually HALF ITALIAN!

At first, I think she's kidding and laughed it off, but she quietly says, "I'm sorry for lying to you and Dad for all these years."

From disbelief to shock to wonder, I probe her with all the questions. It takes a lot more wine. Perhaps more than all the wine in the world.

Did you have an affair?

– Yes.

Does Dad know?

– No. But he asked me three times throughout your life, 'Is she really mine?' and I said yes.

Does my biological father know?

– No. But I took you to see him when you were little and he said, 'She has big eyes like my kids'.

Who else knows?

– I told your grandmother when she asked me on her deathbed, and a few close friends.

Is he alive?

– I don't know.

Are there others who look like me?

– Two of them, yes.

Is this why you have suggested I visit Italy so many times?

– Yes. I kept this secret for thirty-six years. I'm sorry.

My whole life I've been seeking the answer to a question I never thought to pose. I'm terrified, liberated, angry, sad, lost, confused, hurt, joyful, filled with wonderment, and like you could have proposed any curveball to me and I would have believed it.

Although not this one. Not ever. And I am shocked.

Utterly. Totally. Completely. Shocked.

You could have told me a million things and I would have believed you, but not this.

So many layers of unpacking and rediscovering.

This process may never end.

CHAPTER 62

Identity

HIGH SCHOOL PHOTO OF ITALIAN GIRL

On becoming Italian halfway through your life.

On somehow owning a giant mystery that has been filled with lies and guilt and shame and turning it into something empowering—because that's my aim.

It's not pretty but this is the story I'm currently living.

Bear with me if it's a bit wobbly in the feeling and telling.

When your family neglects you when you are small because you are different, because you feel too much too deeply, because you aren't afraid to cry, yell, weep truths and leave endless essays on their beds. When you have always been told you are too messy, too real, too dirty.

It's raw, unresolved, and digs up painful things they have worked so hard to bury in layers of intellectualism in an ivory castle. They don't want to talk about it. They never did.

They abandoned you then and you worked and worked to fill your life with others and lovers so it didn't matter so much. You move to a different city and change your name and ink your skin and reinvent yourself and you are happy.

You are you and you are content.

Then it happens again.

I used to say I 'couldn't be shocked', and that meant everywhere. Everyone.

Oh, the government is exploiting us? Oh, that friend was only around for self-serving reasons? Oh, that man has issues that mean you can't love him? Tell me your drug addictions, your fears, your darkest moments, they are safe with me. I can handle it. I've seen, heard, witnessed worse and lived to tell the tale—nothing is sacred. Nothing is taboo.

I was ready to hear it all. Nothing scared me except fear itself.

Makes for a great coach, doesn't it?

I'd see my own fear, shadows creeping, and smash the walls down in front. I'd sledgehammer my way to the other side and often it was just grass that was painted green but I'd go back educated regardless.

I knew what desires I held. Had goals and all the ways to reach them, not just the theory I'd tell others in the hope they could join me in living with total power and total responsibility.

Right now, however, I don't even know what to wear. I walk aimlessly through a mall where the items are literally all beige and I don't fit the young demographic and I'm sure I am not quite matronly and middle-aged just yet.

I'm thirty-seven but I feel sad, little and seven, when they discarded me. I'm as tired as a ninety-year-old because the weight of this secret and all the shame that's not mine, is only mine to deal with.

Psychic baggage I was born with carried in my veins. This mystery began before I was even alive and now it's mine to decode. There's no trail to follow. No help. No loving arms to hold me through this one. Not except for those I've manifested myself.

All the good in me, in my life, is only down to me. The rest of my family couldn't deal with it then and they can't deal with it now. They couldn't offer it then, and they certainly can't now.

I just do each day one at a time. Work towards little wins, seek only to eat well and make enough money to survive. Is this living? A state of fear. Fear at who I am, what I was before, what will I become?

Fear at homelessness, at rejection, at being single in a world where 'love' of the romantic kind is often the only kind validated, even if it's shitty. Fear at my lofty ideals, my business goals helping others—who the fuck do I think I am? I can barely help myself to smile these days. Here we are now.

A grey Sunday in June when I had the worst birthday I can recall, sobbing in the street unable to eat anything, friends unable to light me from the sodden mess that was my internal flame. It's snuffed out, not even a spark smouldering. I don't know if it can be relit again.

My biological father is dead. He died five years ago, in Melbourne.

I pay thirty dollars and get his obituary from a newspaper—three tiny lines of text that mean an end to the story that just began.

Meanwhile, the man who raised me asked my mother three times in my life: "is she really mine?"

She lied to his face every time.

No wonder he resented me.

No wonder I was the butt of jokes, put down repeatedly, still now, waiting to hear the words, 'I love you, you are special and beautiful'.

But those words have never come.

He hasn't called.

He won't call.

His pride too much, shame too deep to permit him a humble moment of "I knew in my DNA you weren't mine, it coloured my love for you with hatred and, my darling, I'm so, so sorry".

Instead, I hear from Mom more justifications about when I was sixteen and lonely and didn't understand what I'd done wrong and the reason for everything that was heaped upon me is: "Well, you yelled at him too."

I was sixteen! I was half-Italian, full of fire and passion and a personality, genes, goals and dreams disconnected to my upbringing. Shipped off to counselling for being 'too angry' but it's almost forty years of bullshit you are now uncovering, and there's not been one psychologist's session attended between you.

Baby Boomer parents often seem to be above self-work. Instead gardening the world away, eating Endone to deal with their emotional, self-inflicted pain. "I'm sorry, I messed up and I could have done better" isn't in their vocabulary.

Well, I'm sorry, family, but that isn't even my last name.

This isn't my fucking shame.

I'm the only one willing to face this and perhaps that's how it must be.

Maybe I'm the only one brave enough, or so it seems.

As I said… I can't tell this story gracefully yet.

It's not elegant, it's not romantic. It's ugly and messy and weird and too big for me to comprehend.

Bear with me, it's the chaos after the revelation before the sweet relief and beautiful lesson has occurred.

It's so uncomfortable here.

Where all I knew isn't right, and things I felt but didn't know were so real.

Where I can't see a single thing of what the future holds and it seems as if all that glitters was never gold.

It's the middle of the dark night of my soul.

It's the biggest thing I'll ever have to face.

It's the scariest story to tell.

CHAPTER 63

What Happens and What You Do With It

What Happened

In the last six months, my beloved dog, Yoshi, died suddenly.

My boyfriend, the first man I ever thought I would marry, left me hanging—repeatedly—and I had to say goodbye.

Two huge contracts of mine that bookmarked my summer and filled my cup in every way, fell through.

Twenty years of mostly sustainable shared housing, where I have lived across many houses and warehouses with over three hundred people who felt like family, turned into being threatened by strangers, locking myself in my room at night, and paying thousands of dollars to keep it going.

My home had become a boarding house for broke, angry men, and I was terrified.

I had a rift with my father (now stepfather) again, and was stranded in the Adelaide hills without wheels or food, reliving teenage woes.

I began the process of moving out of a five-bedroom house on my own, throwing out and giving away thousands of dollars of things. I'd leave them on the road out front and they would be picked clean, broken, then finally taken, which is how the rest of these events had made me feel. Trashed. Discarded.

As I was going through this process, my mother came to help me pack when I pleaded for her help, her presence, on the phone across state lines. Two glasses in, she revealed I'm not who I think I am. My dad isn't my dad.

I'm actually half-Italian, and neither man knows the truth.

What You Do With It

I had a funeral for Yoshi, a gathering of twenty people and five dogs in the amphitheatre at Fairfield Boathouse. That day, I was terrified and wanted to stay in bed but I put on a long black dress with his bandana around my neck, and went to the park anyway.

I read my piece—*Ode To Yoshi*—and we went through pictures of him and stuck them in a book where people wrote him messages. We laughed about how we could never have had the BBQ spread on the step if he was still here. We walked down to the river. Poured some whiskey on the ground for him. We all had a shot too. I handed out kibbles and we threw them into the river saying, "YAY!" and then we licked our fingers and raised them to check the wind.

None of us had ever poured anyone's ashes anywhere.

When I leaned over the cliff toward the water and the ash flowed from the bag in my hands, I felt part of me, of him, of the eternal bond between us, poured out with it.

My heart broke even more, sobbing.

Everyone understood. Everyone felt it.

He's now the river.

We walked back in procession and some told me later, it was the most beautiful funeral they had ever been to. I miss him like hell and wear his ashes in a vial sometimes, have his paw inked on my arm, and basically still sob randomly when I feel his presence, or don't, and miss him. But that's grief, isn't it?

It hurts like forever and gets a tiny bit less every day even if it never disappears.

When it comes to my boyfriend, well you just can't force love and partnership. He even answered a phone call during Yoshi's obituary, and everyone turned shocked and horrified in his direction. His body was there but he had already left me. If someone pulls away and their actions betray their words, you have to be the smart one and let them go with love. That also hurts like hell. When you still love someone, to actively walk away when they don't have the guts to do so.

Relationships take work and are supposed to be full of joy too, but both of you have to choose it, see it through. I moved out of my place, packed a small house full of awesome stuff into a storage unit, set up my caravan in a friend's driveway, and decided to sublet at another friend's house because winter is cold and caravans like mine don't fit enough stuff in them for city life.

I'm warm and eating well, loved and safe.

I cannot rent and share a house again, too traumatised. I am in the process of selling my investment property in Brisbane, bought as I left salary-life in nightclub land. Then I will again, borrow a whole lot of money, and buy somewhere to live. An actual home. In fact, this has been my biggest dream ever, apart from the ones already fulfilled or in progress. This process is exciting, exhausting, terrifying, nerve wracking, intimidating, liberating, exhilarating, and totally taking way too long for the usual dream-activation pace I like to run at. Baby steps towards the big dream is what I'm doing now. Each day a couple more things on the path.

Eat well, sleep well, drink less booze, research, do life admin, tie up loose ends, find out more options. Seeking loopholes, different ways of doing things, and possibilities. Finances, brokers and driving around suburbs every spare minute you have. Managing your expectations with everybody and nobody as your counsel. Learning so much, imagining, exploring and making progress every day, today's news is: Watsonia is out!

Amongst all this, the repeated phrase, "I'm half-Italian, my dad isn't my dad" as a quiet soundtrack to everything. Again, it's taking too long.

Waiting for the paternity test to arrive in the mail every day, fantasising about some big, warm, verbose family I might meet and who might not reject me and who might even learn to love me.

Even just seeing *one* person who looks like me apart from my mother. Wow. Mind blown.

No wonder I have inked myself all over with tattoos and often said, "I don't know what I even look like." It's true.

Then there's my 'dad', the guy who raised me.

Well, I still haven't heard from him.

Last night, I emailed him.

I'm waiting, not that patiently, for his response.

Then I find my half-siblings on Facebook and THEY DO LOOK LIKE ME. However, despite my best intentions, they don't message me back ever and I squash the quiet expectations I had for a soul-affirming family reunion.

I booked a trip to Bali to heal, to re-set, and to recall myself.

I'm done trying to sugar-coat things.

That doesn't work for me.

That is what happened and what I am doing with it.

What are you going to do with what happens to you?

CHAPTER 64

Parasites

Canggu, Bali

I spent two days projectile vomiting like Regan from The Exorcist.

Not sure if it was something I ate or what. One whiff of cigarette smoke and I walked briskly to the toilets at Old Mans, the most popular beach bar in Canggu, where I unloaded my stomach so hard it splashed back in my face. Elegant, right?

After beating it out of there, I got a burrito on the way home and ate it ravenously. Only to projectile spew it up twenty minutes later, along with the valium that was supposed to make me relax. This happens four more times throughout the night.

In Koh Phangan in Thailand in my twenties, I once had a parasite that floored me for three days straight. I could feel every pore on my body, every hair on my head as I purged everything in my body from both ends. I hallucinated, my own personal Apocalypse Now scene, as I told my friend, "please tell everyone back home that I love them", and she leaned over me and said with certainty I didn't share, "You are not gonna die". She took me on the scooter to the tiny hospital where I pooped in a cup and they diagnosed: "Something inside you is eating you."

Um yeah, I know. Thanks for that, please get rid of it!

So, having been this sick before, I knew I probably wasn't going to die. I lay still and rub my own back, and wonder if I did die, how long it would take someone to find me. At midnight, I'm waiting on the road outside, naked except for clutching a towel around me, vomiting into the gutter. My phone has only eight percent battery as I flick the torch on and off as bikes ride past, willing the guy with a delivery of activated charcoal to find me on the back streets. Not my finest travelling moment.

Two days later I was meant to fly out on the red eye, my stomach still protesting everything I ate, I blamed volcanoes and changed my flights. I've been here another ten days.

This morning I ate a dragon-fruit smoothie bowl that's pink and frozen, full of Goji berries and beautiful colours, and cried into my coconut-milk coffee for a minute. Fuck, I'm overwhelmed.

It's all been so big lately. So much to think about, process, move on from and move on with.

My heart hurts at the bigness of it all, at the pressure that's only coming from myself. I made a live video online yesterday about friendships and saw that two years ago today, I was alone travelling in America, also missing everyone.

I'm reminded that people are my life. People make me happy. Not just places. Not just adventures. Not just unknowns, but those who love me and accept me for all my faults and wondrous things.

Again, I miss them. 'Them.' All of them. Even when they change and it's only ever about ten close people in a sea of acquaintances, they ebb and flow, and often grow to 20 or more, and back to the core again. This is how it feels without a blood family. You're never guaranteed they will stay with you. You'll still travel alone most of the time.

I cry in paradise. Maybe seven or eight times when I was sick, or when I felt lonely, or when I realised you take your head with you wherever you go.

However, it does get better.

Better than before.

A little better every day.

CHAPTER 65

Homecoming

I sit at a table surrounded by a family I share no blood with, but they are mine. Chosen family. I don't take this phrase lightly.

They talk of resemblances, of bad teenage behaviours, of exploits and similarities. There is an easy familiarity echoed in their lips and noses and curly hair. Meanwhile, Mom struggles to keep her marriage alive to a man who I simply don't have to own anymore if I don't want to.

I'm making the choice to un-own him. I call him Jimmy now. For all the years of being made to feel I am less-than, I take back my role and title of 'daughter'. I'm not angry anymore. All that energy was used up in my twenties and burned hotter than it should have.

I'm just done. Done with taking the blame for an inability to love me because of things I said at sixteen that I still pay for now. I'm done with taking on the shame from their love, which I have held on a pedestal my entire waking life, for it seemed so perfect and true.

This 'father' I thought was mine, he won't speak to me, maybe ever, and Mother won't come visit me now, riddled with guilt. I'm an inconvenient blip in their lifelong love affair, and I never expected this. For a minute, I'm heartbroken again. Who is my tribe? Will others ever speak of me in this way? If my story ends with me on my own with no kids and no guy, is that enough? Can I borrow all these other families? Will they love me when I'm old and grey or do I have to be continually, perpetually amazing for them? I'm not sure if I can. I'm sure, actually, that I can't.

I'm only human. Flaws and all. Missteps and all. I am just on my own road dodging traffic trying not to get run over. Where my family once stood is now a gaping hole of lies. Cavernous. The wind whistling. Everyone is peering inside but it's just too intense, so they navigate around me.

I tell strangers my story because I can't bear the weight of it on my own. Been popping out with it unprompted when I first meet people. Even shopkeepers who ask me innocently, "where are you from?"

"I'm an Italian-American-Aussie mermaid. Yeah, my dad's not my dad, I just found out. Crazy, huh?"

I used to make up stories about my life when I was sixteen and got kicked out of home because I dropped out of university. "The only way you can live here is if you get an education," he said. I left university and the abuse at home in one move.

I thought my life wasn't interesting enough so I fabricated exotic boyfriends who hadn't turned up yet, terrified of a mediocre story being mine. Now, I'm a holistic business and empowerment coach, and I encourage people daily to reach for their dreams. I'm a writer who will risk political correctness for a story, who will be objective and a gonzo anthropologist whenever I can. It's exhilarating and I'm finally comfortable with admitting that I'm good at it.

I'm a dear friend to many, a dog mother, a lover, a creator, a modern, practical psychic who always knows who's calling when the phone rings. I have a massive global family I've chosen based on shared experiences, including brothers who have my back and help me put car stereos in. I have sisters I cherish, and I'm Aunty to a load of children, really, and I nurture and encourage wherever I go, making new friends endlessly. Use whatever vehicles necessary, a 4WD, a keyboard, the internet, a camera, radical honesty and integrity, or even speaking absolute truth while hoping they are brave enough to hear it and not run away.

I am using every single thing I know to feel and find 'home' in a world that has constantly told me that I don't really belong.

There's only one choice: to keep creating myself, on my own terms.

Find love and support in those around me who don't make me feel like a naughty child. Well, unless I'm doing something naughty and fun and they want to join in. We are equals and we know we have flaws, secrets and fallacies. We navigate them, encourage them to come into the light, protect each other and help each other be brave, so we can grow. And, well, my parents… those people who raised me. I'm not sure you are in this club anymore.

Perhaps you weren't ever and I thought you got automatic membership because you made such a being as *me*! You didn't shape me, and you still don't make me. To the little girl inside who still feels deserted and not good enough, I love you but you don't control me. It's time to set these feelings free. It's time to run and scream with joy. You aren't owned anymore. You are your own divine crystal of light refracting rainbows moment by moment forever fantasy.

You are both a mermaid and a fucking unicorn. You are whatever you want to be.

CHAPTER 66

Invocation About Not Settling

It's hard in your thirties when everyone is holding babies aloft like status symbols and you are alone on the couch wondering what to download next.

Just like the illusion of some sort of career ladder to climb with a pot of gold at the end that will magically make all the trials worth it, this feeling of inadequacy because I am not part of a partnership, because I don't feel any clocks ticking apart from the one that urges me to keep pursuing adventures at any cost, is purely an illusion.

I'll admit it's very tempting to settle. All around, people offer themselves to you in different ways, often lacking. But I'm tired of sharing my life-force with people that only take from me. Some tell me my standards are too high because I often reject the co-dependent, the depressed and anxious, the victim mentality and the almost-forty and still-don't-really-know-who-I-am-or-what-I-want-to-do-with-my-life types.

If you did a line-up of all the lovers I've had, you would not see a typecast. All races, all sizes, all kinds of faces. For all my talk about not settling, if I'm truly honest with myself, I have made it far too easy for some of the wrong people to get close to me.

I'm saying the words right now. Am about to ask the universe what I secretly think twenty times a day inside my head.

Dear universe, stars and all the goddess power that is available, all the technology and all the pure hope that I carry inside me, to you I pray. I have done the work on all the wrecks of my past and while some lessons will always continue to teach me, I have cried, I have felt and I have been real. I have also acknowledged the joy and I will not forget either side.

However, for now I'm going into the future. I allow these parts of my past to just be part of me, not the definition of me.

I acknowledge all the choices I have made as my own. I relinquish the need to control the outcomes of the things that I manifest with intent. I tell you now with whoever hears this as my witness that I'm ready for an evolved love to be met head-on and heart-on by a brave man who is actually up for it. Who's willing and able to walk his talk and chooses his own growth.

Many people get caught up in my enthusiasm and make promises they have no intent on delivering. I am sorry universe but I will not stop being myself. Will just forge onwards, secure in the knowledge that perhaps somewhere he is out there speaking into his phone similar words, asking for a blessing from the powers that be.

I know that when I meet him, I will not have to encourage him to be amazing. Whoever he is and whatever he looks like, he will be making plans and doing them towards his happiness. He will not be financially dependent on me in any way. He will have a group of friends and family as support for him in anything he chooses to pursue. He will know how to make people laugh and he will tell great stories even if he is a bit quieter about it than I am. He will bring to the table some amazing things, ideas and pursuits that I have not yet considered. He will also join me on some of my adventures just because they give me joy.

He will be passionate, considerate, humble, and content in himself. Will make me feel great just by being around him. He will have his own baggage, I am sure, but it will not dictate his behaviour all the time. He'll be able to communicate with honesty and bravery even when there are tricky things on the table. I don't care how old he is or what his background is or what he does for a living as long as he is relatively happy with his lot in life.

For the sake of magic and the need for being specific, I will also state that he needs to be single, willing to have a relationship with me and live in my city or be willing to travel. Dear powers that be, I do not think this is too much to ask. I guarantee that I will bring the same amounts of enthusiasm, love, positivity, honesty and communication to whatever relationship eventuates.

I also maintain that I will not settle for the next 'nice guy' who comes along or the next 'bad boy' who says the sweet words. This is my responsibility to the universe.

I know love comes when you least expect it, and I also know that being in love is part chemistry and part a choice two people make. I've felt love in my life before and I will not settle for anything less. I also know that I am an amazing, beautiful person whether I'm in love or not and I will be incredible on my own regardless.

So, I release all doubt that a man with these traits is not out there. Release all feelings that I may not be worthy of such love, back into the cosmos.

With these words and whenever they are spoken, the people who hear them will attest that I know I am worth it. I'm using this invocation as a modern-day prayer, a call to the Galaxy to not settle for anything less than amazing.

May every person who hears this and may all the forces out there witness the fact that I am perfectly imperfect and am ready for a real love.

As above, so below, and it is done.

CHAPTER 67

When a House Becomes a Home

BRUNO MAKING SURE HE'S NOT LEFT BEHIND

In the last six months I've lived in four houses, a caravan in a driveway, two villas in Bali, and spare rooms across the state. One of my best friends, Aria, took me in to live with her entire family—a place to rest and to be. I will never forget it. We cooked together every night and it felt like her husband was also my husband, I was integrated into the family. I will always be grateful for this.

I've workshopped, watched TV, and partied with many lovely people, cooked for them and with them, done the dishes, played with their kids and animals, folded laundry, helped renovate a house, made my business mobile and adulted the shit out of life. Been both patient and not patient, adaptable and determined, optimistic and frustrated in equal measures. Had about half my clothes, a box of elixirs, technology and some bling. Gotta travel with bling.

I bounced around every few months in my early-20s when I moved to Melbourne but in the last 15 years I've lived in two share-houses, each time moved on, farther out, for redevelopment. One in Northcote and one in Thornbury, and every place I've rented I've made a home. A sanctuary. I've made palaces from shitboxes and covered wonky walls with artworks, but it's clear to me that the rental market is fucked. I am a victim of gentrification and now a perpetrator of it.

Jumped through hoops and dealt with discrimination to get finance as a single, female freelancer, but today it's time. The keys to my kingdom, a lifetime of dreaming. If you have ever been displaced, evicted or homeless in any way, you will empathise.

I'm never going to be homeless again.

So much of my energy has been devoted to sustainable housing. Seeking eternal flat mates, agents, moving, carrying around boxes. Seeking a place to call 'home'. Not anymore. I'm finally sitting on my couch with my new puppy, in my *home*, for the first time ever. Nobody will ever kick me out of here, nobody will ever leave me on a hot road in the sun with all my belongings again. Is that even real? The idea of that never happening to me again lands deeply.

I'm feeling serene. Serene is not a word usually prescribed to me in any way, I'm more kickboxing than meditation, more adventure than knitting. But today, all is quiet.

This house, my home, is an ex-commission house in Reservoir, known as 'the hood' by me and many others. My street is across from a swathe of neglected parkland that has Darebin Creek running through it—a small tributary more north than the much better-known Merri Creek trail. There's a path that winds for miles in both directions along industrial estates and behind malls. But it's a huge green corridor, and each day I'm woken to the sounds of galahs, the warble of magpies and caw of crows. On warm nights, the crickets and frogs dominate. I walk the puppy there every day, even when he wants to be carried for most of the time.

I named him 'Bruno' after the father I never got to meet, so that saying that name repeatedly would mean joy and not regret. He looks up at me with those big eyes and wants to be carried. I pick him up because I know what it's like when the world is too big and you need arms to hold you.

There are gorgeous willow trees dangling into the water, rushing this morning because of the constant rain. The clouds are a symphony above me and there aren't many people walking this trail, perfect for my need to think and process. The humans can have me all day after this.

When I worked in nightclubs, regular river walks became necessary medication to counter all the booze and sweat, dark corners and screaming over loud sound systems. I loved that world for a while but the expansive space of nature, the wind rushing, creek flowing, legs beating a rhythmic pattern below me, was a huge reset. I've been walking in nature every day for years, often getting in the car at dawn to drive to the nearest place the green slashes through the suburbs to greet the coming day, frozen grass crunching underfoot the only sound.

I seek this morning walk wherever I am in the world. Whoever I'm with is often dragged along, and I made myself continue after Yoshi died even if I howled in the streets for months, the sobbing, tattooed woman in active wear carrying poop bags for nobody, missing him by my side.

Now, I live in a sprawling suburb 13 kilometres from one of the best cities in the world, but today it feels like I live in the country. The only sound is the staccato beat of rain on roofs, bird calls, and the silence between.

At the end of my street, sheep graze along the creek, and early in the morning, we surprise mobs of wallabies, their pointy ears frozen for a moment in our direction till they hop away together.

Honestly, I'm serene as fuck now. I'm content. Happy even. I've overcome the curveballs and am quietly confident that I'm inches away from total, blissful happiness. Peace. Contentedness, and mastering the ability to be still and grateful. I am so grateful.

I'll never take these walls with a kitchen that's mine, for granted. Ever. I'll never take nature for granted because it's right across the road. It's in my every day without having to go anywhere.

I'm having my city life, freelance business rocket ship and my calm, nature-reflective, mellow country life too. I have lived with hundreds of people and done my best to create this feeling wherever I've landed. But now I'm here, *we* are here.

I have arrived, and I'm not leaving.

This is home.

OUR PLACE

CHAPTER 68

Alessandro

Today, I met a man called Alessandro. He was cooking pasta like his nonna taught him outside a delicatessen at Northcote Plaza as I happened to walk past.

He saw me pause to watch and called me closer, piled me up a huge plate of spaghetti with pancetta, chilli and olives, then demanded more parmesan so he could give me three scoops. I was on my way to a lunch meeting but stopped here to marvel over the pasta with a growing crowd. How can you say no to pasta like that? You can't.

An elderly woman paused in her pasta-to-mouth shovelling to share a smile with me. After a minute of discussing pancetta fat and always adding red wine, I told her, "I'm half Italian, only known for a few months." Still unable to keep this to myself.

Alessandro overheard me, and came around to the front for a hug. "Welcome to the family."

Suddenly, I'm crying into a plate of pasta in the shabby plaza mall, feeling like I'm in some strange '80's family-drama movie scene.

He asks, "Where is your family from?"

"Don't know," I reply.

"Doesn't matter," he says, "because I'm here to treat you like a queen."

I walk into the meeting with wet eyes and get asked if it's the chilli. "Nope, it's the feels."

Deep, heritage, visceral, unknown, new, strange feelings about pasta and pancetta connecting me to some new part of me— the smells, the language, somehow feeling like a strange home I always had but never visited.

CHAPTER 69

Happily Ever After

My life may not be the fairytale we can blame Disney for—of me and one prince forever more.

It might be a bunch of dear friends and my dog, perhaps some kids that aren't mine and lovers throughout time but, ultimately, single. Unattached. Solo. Walking alone. Is this really so bad?

It could be me cuddling on the couch watching Netflix with whomever I decide is worthy at that moment. Sharing parts of life, choosing them. Sex may be separate from that intimacy. Or not.

Who is the world to tell us how to love? Why should we quest and be continually seeking, hedging bets, keeping expectations low. Loving yourself while waiting but not waiting for the person who may or may not show up and be brave enough. For the other half to a 'whole' that may not be reality. Why should I feel like half anyhow? I think I'm more than half. In fact, I might be double.

My 'other' better pack some heat!

In the past, I would've been whispered about-thirty-eight and no husband, no kids.

Do what I want when I want, how selfish, how free. But luckily, now I'm 'independent'. One of a growing league of strong, beautiful women with opinions, drive, and plans. Sometimes we are called 'too powerful'.

This shits me to no end. Too powerful for what? Do you men have motors that burn out?

I'm tired of trying to be smaller to fit your required size for me.

I'm glad you have found love, all the couples, partners and polyamorous unions out there. Really, truly, I am. It's been my holy grail and I'm not even fucking religious.

But questing after people who can't have an honest conversation is a waste of my precious energy. Apart from that, my life is bloody amazing. So, I'm rewriting the story.

The happily ever after is when YOU DECIDE THAT YOU ARE WHOLE AND ONE WITH EVERYTHING AND HAPPY RIGHT HERE, RIGHT NOW.

Then the birds sing, the sun fades, and all the people rejoice. Because it's your personal movie, you can decide how every scene plays out.

CHAPTER 70

Uluru

Northern Territory, Australia

We call this 'remote Australia' but the local Indigenous mobs will tell you this is the centre of the universe and everywhere else is remote. Still referred to as 'Ayers Rock' even though we all know better now.

A sign at the lodge reads: 'The Anangu people prefer that you don't climb', right next to the prices to climb it. I can only sigh, for humans are basically stupid and need to feel like they conquer everything. Stick a flag in it, like that means something.

As we arrive, seeing the metal poles and chain walkway stuck into the crest literally makes my heart hurt. We joined the tour and within five minutes, I split off. I don't want to be here with tourists and their fancy cameras, shuffling loudly on the soft, red dirt. As I walk, I read the information boards and avoid other people. Before even a few minutes alone, I have the absolute knowing that we should not be here at all, deep in my gut like white-mongrel ancestral knowledge.

This isn't my place.

Areas where boys went through initiation, sometimes for months, till they learnt the skills and stories needed to become men. Still used two months a year for ceremonies from December to January. This land is still alive. The men's camp—a giant incredible wave in the rock, concave like a rolling ocean tide, somehow formed when the ocean drained over millennia and left this desert, left this monolith that isn't otherworldly but actually more of the earth than anything we've built. 850 million years ago, a timeline we can't even comprehend. There are so many spirits here visible in the rocks and whispering in the trees.

People still sing this land, and its stories are strong. Not so much in some parts of the country, covered in concrete. There's a history of bloodshed here. I feel ashamed of this. Deep shame I cannot erase with my own life or actions or feelings. It will carry for generations.

I cry quietly, tears rolling for what we have done to such an ancient culture, that we should honour deeply as 65,000 years of history we will never fully understand. My friend and I whisper to each other, awed and quiet and wanting to be away from others. Signs ask for quiet contemplation but a guy answers his phone and starts chatting about last night to someone on the other end. Luckily, his buddy notices us stiffening and leads him away.

I can't help but feel we should not be here. White fellas don't deserve to be here. This is not our sacred place. We are trespassing. Everything screams to me: *not your place.*

Way too much knowledge, lineage, lore and laws I'll never understand, way too much for a small, metal plate with text on it. Doesn't even come close. It is haunted with spirits whose descendants need to be here. The caves with blackened overhangs from fires are eerie.

I imagine the First Nations from here, walking and discovering this giant vision, how it must have felt. We 'gave' the land back to the Anangu in 1985. Perhaps another moment in politics that is more symbolic than actual, like the day Kevin Rudd said "Sorry". There is a sign that says, 'No climbing due to...'. Another hung underneath reads: 'strong winds' but I want to graffiti it and change it to 'RESPECT'. No sharpie on hand, though.

Later, we drive past and there are humans dotted up the chain walkway who have jumped the fence, ignoring the sign and the multiple messages throughout the cultural centre asking—almost pleading—them not to. The Pitjantjatjara call them 'Minga'—tiny ants. There's been a decision to stop people climbing Uluru, but it won't take effect for two years. Things happen in their own way and time in the Territory. I feel it can't come soon enough.

There is a saying about visiting nature: 'take only photos, leave only footprints' but I can't help feeling that here, in this special place, even that is too much. I stand quietly and listen, feel.

Today is exactly two years since I found out my blood wasn't as I thought, but Italian. I call it my Truth Anniversary. It wasn't planned, but it's fitting that I'm here today. I wish so much for the history, lineage and community etched in the rocks here.

More tears fall, this time for my lost history, which I may never find. Then I turn to see my friends coming up the path, and I know with the same certainty as before, that I'm making my own stories.

My own community is also strong.

I belong.

CHAPTER 71

The Letter

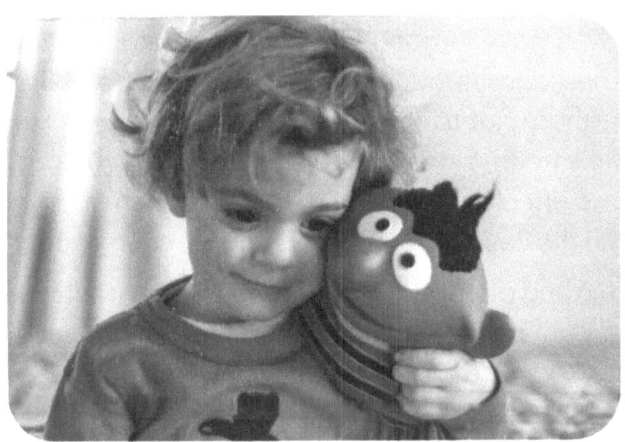

2 YEARS OLD WITH ERNIE, MY FIRST LOVE, CALIFORNIA

It's been two weeks since my mother disowned me in a letter. After she lied to everyone for 36 years about who I was, and how I was conceived.

When the letter came, I did not cry.

I cried enough to fill the Mekong River in the last two years. I cried every single day for a year. That's feeling it. Processing. As if I want to suppress this shit any longer. I want it gone. To feel it deeply, then let it the fuck go.

Today, I had a sob while drinking coffee in bed.

Little me, dragged across the globe and told to wait in the background while other things happened. Still told at nearly forty years of age and even in the letter that just arrived, to be quieter, feel less, talk softly, lose weight, take up less space. Stop being serious, stop being loud. Stop feeling so much, would you?

Stop being who you are because it reminds us that *you aren't ours*.

Ours.

The great parental love story that has been the reason behind all this deceit. But they met as hippies in the sixties and it obviously wasn't the free love set, or this would have been tabled.

"I had an affair and I'm pregnant" are seven words that would have changed my whole life. Yet they were not uttered.

'Dad' often asked if I was his and she said yes. She looked into his face that she loved and lied. Because honesty was more frightening than anything. She let him treat me as 'less than' and used a nasty tone of voice while he piled judgement on me, and she has admitted this in a moment of clarity.

But then it's gone. She oscillates between a subjugated '50s' housewife and some sort of liberated woman that actually reads the spiritual books on her bookshelf. It's exhausting to keep up.

I don't cry for her or for the loss of him. I cry because I am a strong, amazing and powerful, beautiful woman. Unfortunately, I have no lineage I wish to own. No history. No roots.

The letter she wrote was thought about while international travel was happening, then when she got home, it was typed with intent and printed and signed. A legal document telling me I'm not worthy of this shit family dynamic.

But guess what? This is my story now, and it's my life and I will put it online or in a book or tattoo on my chest whatever chapters I feel the need to.

All I feel right now is pity and anger towards you.

All I feel is pity towards 'Dad'. If he really did love me, he would have stopped you from sending that letter. If he really did love me, he would have called me up within the last two years and said, "even though you're not mine you're still my daughter".

This letter tells me that you are completely wrapped up in your own selfish world. That absolutely no reality will be able to penetrate this story you are telling yourself. I don't know whether you are a united force in this or whether all the lies are between you as well. Nobody knows what goes on within other relationships, all we know is how it feels.

And dear blood family, my entire life it has felt toxic being around you.

A friend of mine nursed her mother over to the other side last week. As her mother was taking her last breaths, she put a photo of her grandma next to the bed and said, "she's coming for you, Mumma", then she asked her mum if, when it was her turn, she would come back for her.

This has caused me to cry more than any bullshit in that letter.

I keep thinking about this moment by my friend's mother's bed, and the tears come. Maybe there is no one coming for me at the end. Maybe there is no one from beyond the grave who wants to know me. However, I'm pretty sure I am going to have some fabulous people at the end of my bed when I do decide to leave.

So, I am keeping this letter forever.

Keeping it as proof that this is not my shit—not one bit.

I'm going to show people what reinventing yourself truly looks like. Going to prove that it's not where you came from or what happens to you, it's what you do with it. This is my lifelong legacy, not all these other things I've created.

I guess I have to say thank you at this point. A mediocre life was never going to be mine.

I'm standing in the middle of it, curvy with a Mediterranean body covered in tattoos with a name I created and reinvented before I even knew the truth.

I am Italian and my history starts right here, right now.

With me.

CHAPTER 72

Things Mother Said

1 YEAR OLD ME, CALIFORNIA

Things Mother said:

You eat too much.

Stop buttering your bread.

You'd be beautiful if you lost that belly.

Don't be so dramatic.

You feel too much.

You'd be pretty if you lost some weight.

The discord in our family is all your fault.

Why are you so angry/emotional/loud/intense? Stop crying, it's no big deal.

Don't be ridiculous. (Said a lot.)

And... *I probably should have aborted you.*

Also, your dad's not your dad and I lied to you and him for 36 years. And I think he knew and I let him abuse you out of my own guilt.

These things were all said to me.

Some phrases I thought were normal, and then, in adulthood, with assistance from psychologists and self-work, realising that actually those things were abusive. Even if not intended that way. Shame around food has been a tough pattern to unlearn. Along with all the rest.

Unwinding and living with family trauma is always hardest during the holiday season. Being around families who delight in each other's company, who share stories about knowing each other a very long time, forever… and the familiarity that comes with other faces that look like yours and knowing, I fit here.

I belong here. They know me. I come from here.

When you don't have that, it's hard not to wonder: why didn't I get that?

Don't I deserve that too?

Reminding yourself that it's not your fault, over and over, like the kid whose parents divorce and thinks it's their fault, these are tough cycles to break.

So how do we break them?

How do we reinvent the stories told to us by parents who couldn't face their own trauma? Who weren't brave enough to show emotions or have difficult conversations.

By doing the 'work'. By learning about trauma. By learning about attachment styles.

By going back, even if we have disassociated the memories. Finding the feeling, and identifying it for what it was so you can rewrite that into your adult life. And do it differently.

We can make it different. We can set loving boundaries. We can know intuitively what we want and need. We can learn to speak up and ask for that too.

We can.

We do not have to live life as a victim to anything and everything we were told and taught. Discard programs we are still running as adults, which came from parents not ready to parent us. Change patterns of relating by learning new tools and ways to talk about things. So many of us were not raised with the language around:

- Asking for what we need.
- Honestly talking about feelings.
- Conveying when we are hurt.

Anyhow. I'm determined to help my little kid inside, and everyone else's kids inside, and your actual kids too, become better at this stuff.

We can change these paradigms. Just have to know where to begin. Please just let your kid butter the bread, ok? Life is too short for dry bread and this work is tough.

And tell your kids they can do or be anything they put their mind to.

CHAPTER 73

When It Hurts

This is when it hurts:

Easter. Mother's Day. Father's Day. My birthday. Their birthdays. Christmas. New Year's. When you get a new job. Meet a new lover. When a relationship ends. Something exciting happens. Something tragic occurs. When you are bored with your own problems and wish to hear about someone else's. When you want to share a win. You want someone to be proud of you. When you need reassurance. Need reminding who you are. When you need to remember where you come from.

I tell random stories from my life, and strangers identify them as 'abuse'. So bizarre to own. I still feel like I'm a naughty child who will be reprimanded if I speak the truth.

Dread all of these holidays now. I work straight through, so there is no rest.

Rest is when your mind wanders.

I avoid social media and gatherings of other families lest I burst into tears and bring everyone down. I'm sorry in advance for all the feels that are yet to come. I'm sorry.

Often, I cry because beautiful families exist, and I can't help wishing I had one.

I'm not writing much at the moment. Except, occasionally, like sitting in the car in the supermarket car park right now, unable to go shopping.

Until this comes out. Until the words pour out.

These words that I don't know where to put anymore.

You know… you can walk around crying in this society and nobody stops to see if you're ok.

I would stop and ask if you are ok. Have done it before.

All I'm certain of is… I walk through the fire with people. I'm not scared of what is messy. Painful. Dark. Hidden. Terrifying.

I am loyal.

Not everyone can walk through the flames that burn them. It's a choice. But I'll promise to hold you till your feet heal over.

They sent every photo that existed of my childhood. Erased me. They took me off the walls so they didn't have to be reminded.

I cannot burn these pictures... they are full of pain, but it's still my history. I burnt everything else though.

They are not 'Mother' and 'Father'. Then again, they never wanted to be.

I don't know if I could have done anything differently. Can't be anyone except who I am. I tried. It's exhausting.

I am sure it is enough. Just not for them. And there is no pretty bow on this package. All I know is how to be honest.

Any small talk and false ways of operating have been razed to the ground. Burnt. Scorched. And all I can be is real.

CHAPTER 74

A New Family

Tonight I am going for dinner with my new-found family, after I discovered a sister on Ancestry DNA.

I wrote a message to her: 'I think you are my half-sister.'

A minute later, my phone rings and a voice says, "Yes I am."

The whole thing played out like a crazy episode of some drama. Within two hours we were talking on the phone, swearing like sailors and laughing. It turns out she lives two suburbs away from me, and we used to frequent the same fruit and veg shop in Thornbury—Cozella Brothers—for seven years. We probably stood next to each other and picked through beans together. There is a whole fucking world and she lives down the street. Perhaps this is the glory to come from this shitstorm I'm living in.

I'm going to meet my nieces in their thirties for the very first time, as well as the rest of her family.

At first, I was going to dress all conservative and try to hide my tattoos because she is 20 years older than me. As I'm getting ready, I think about how I have tried to be 'less than' for my other family, have tried to be less colourful, less loud, less outspoken and less emotional. None of that worked anyway. I'm tired of masking to be more palatable to others.

Instead, I pull out a pair of leggings with clouds on them, giant mirrored earrings, and I put Bruno in a diamanté collar and a denim jacket covered in Anarchy patches that I sewed for him myself. I have to tell my new sister that I named my beaglier after our dad.

No, this time—whatever family this is, they will have to accept me for me. I've got a bottle of Prosecco chilling in the fridge because I figure that is what you take to a first dinner with your long-lost Italian family you never knew existed.

Sounds about right, huh?

It feels like this trainwreck and rubble has unfolded to create a golden path out of this shit. There is finally a pot of gold at the end of all this crying and crying.

There just might be redemption in this story.

We spent hours telling stories. She is a take-no-shit, very smart, self-made Italian woman who was born in Northcote... We both have the same infectious cackly laugh.

I am still digesting everything but basically there isn't much family to find in Italy and in fact they are mostly in the northern suburbs of Melbourne—where I moved without a real reason twenty years ago and have called home ever since. Drawn by unseen forces for sure.

She takes me to visit my long-gone relatives, we swore like sailors as we got stuck on one way roads in her car that I joke makes her look like a Mafioso wife. (She's not one). Randomly she's wearing black and gold too. We are straight shooters and don't waste time with idiots. Who knows how much of this is genetics and how much of it is coincidence. Or perhaps ancestral lineage.

Nonna's grave in Templestowe, sleeting rain and no flowers to be seen. A yellowed photograph that doesn't stir anything in me. I wore a long black dress and a gold jacket. That's what you visit grandma in, makeup and everything. Then to Carlton, where my "dad" is buried. The office is closed today of all days, and the sparkling sun comes out. So we drive around looking, and I randomly spot his face staring out from a slab of granite. It feels surreal, I've only seen two photographs of him but there he is, staring at me. Unmistakeable. No tears. There is no life here and no familiarity. Cemeteries are strange places. Please don't ever bury me in a box.

Then we went to Brunetti's to eat calzone. The beauty in all of this is.... The world is smaller again. And I have a sister who I never expected to find. Who is becoming more a part of my life with every passing month.

If the last while has proven anything to me it's that your family - are simply the ones who show up. And keep showing up. Even when it's hard and strange.

If we have one person who does that for us then we are truly privileged. I get to call Deanna among my family now, by blood AND choice. For that I am truly grateful.

Since then, we have had a typical sister relationship, where we call each other randomly for updates and to complain and support each other through the regular things life is. To do errands or have lunch together. There is no obligation, no demands, and no bullshit. I give her shit for the mafioso car and she tells me to fuck off. It takes two to form and maintain a relationship at this age, and we both put in the effort to make it real. It's beautiful. It's simple. So glad I found her.

I was renting giant, cream-brick, wog palaces with lemon trees out the back and cooking for many hungry mouths wearing a Virgin

Mary apron in the north of Melbourne—I was so freaking Italian and I didn't even know it.

And so here we are.

Literally, the story is writing itself, I am just at the mercy of it. Or in the glory of it.

It's like the story is an ocean and I am just the waves.

Just the sand and the sea and everything and the story is me.

CHAPTER 75

At The Airport

When you've never been to Europe, and you find out you're half Italian, it moves up the priority list of destinations. Sometimes, the universe decides where you go, there is no other choice.

This is my first time to the motherland. It's ironic that a few years ago, I went to the United States for a three-month pilgrimage because I thought *that* was the motherland. I cried walking the streets because it felt like home.

To find out that the only American in me is ten years of childhood memories, a passport, and the funny accent that survives, has been an interesting shift of self-identity. I'm not a loudmouth American, I'm a loudmouth Italian, and with that declaration, it makes so much sense.

It is not bloodlines that make our homes.

It's not even culture anymore.

It is belonging, and we find it everywhere. In cities on the other side of the globe, in the living rooms of strangers, on idyllic beaches, at the top of mountains, and in dingy dive bars.

This is the first time I have ever planned a trip in advance; trains and accommodation, all booked.

I'm a fancy adult and shit. I'm not going to seek 'family' per se, I'm going to find ancestral, visceral roots.

Going to eat the cheese and drink the wine and have a spiritual experience... right?

Wish me luck, famiglia!

CHAPTER 76

The Most Arrogant Man on Earth

Rome, Italy

I touched down in Italy. Finally.

I cried when the plane hit the runway. Fuck. It's been a 40-year journey to get here. What if I'd never made it? I took two trains from the airport and met my Airbnb host where he showed me my very cute, very white apartment with a view of the Vatican.

Even though I've been awake for nearly 24 hours in transit, I just had to get out there.

Fast forward a few hours where I ate delicious paninis and bought beautiful black-lace bras that fit me so well, but felt allergic to all the other tourists buying plastic trinkets and Rome fridge magnets. I decided to switch on Tinder after six months of not dating at all back home. Within 10 minutes of swiping, there were multiple Italian men chatting to me. Some downright sleazy and pushy. Others seemed ok, from what I could tell. A guy named Daniele, says, "let's go for a drive to the ocean and then we can party here." When I asked how far it was to the ocean, he replied, "oh, you want to go to the ocean?"

Ummm.

Then he says that he wants photos of me because he can't open the ones on Tinder. My Spidey senses are tingling that this is a massive line of bullshit. Who swipes yes to people with no photos?

I sent him a photo on WhatsApp and said this was today.

He asks how tall I am, then says, 'I hope you are not too tall.'

I'm already completely taken aback by his bluntness but, of course, chalk it up to cultural differences.

We agreed to meet at 8pm for dinner.

Then he texts me to ask if I'm alone, and can he come to my apartment for a drink first?

I replied, 'no, let's meet at the station and go for a drink after that.'

It is three minutes before our scheduled meeting time, and I get a text asking where I am.

When I turn up, I spot him in the car and he does not acknowledge me.

I wave. Get in his leather-interior Alfa Romeo, and he hoons off, texting the entire time.

When I tell him this is a nice car, he says, "no, it isn't."

Pretty much everything I say, he says no.

This guy is not even looking at me.

I understand that he's driving and texting but he still hasn't acknowledged me.

Within five minutes of being in the car, he tells me Australians don't know what food is. He brags about how in Italy, we bake bread every day for the day—we don't eat it for weeks, like you. He tells me how the food is seasonal and comes from farms. He tells me how his Australian friend is from Cairns and she has told him everything.

I explain that Cairns is not really a good representation of Australia, and that in the south we do bake bread every day in bakeries. Our food does come from farmers if you know where to find it.

He simply said no.

Tells me he has to go to a meeting for dinner in about an hour, but he's not sure yet. I smell bullshit again; it sounds like a Tinder excuse.

We drive along the river to a place called Trastevere, which is a beautiful area of cobblestone alleyways and ivy waterfalling from the windows above. He still hasn't asked me a single question or looked at me at all; keeps telling me how tourists are such assholes, and that we don't know food or life like Italians.

He is going on a tour to Thailand next month, but he said he won't eat any of the food, will just buy bottled milk and drink that because he's scared of getting sick. He used to go freediving but burst his eardrums once and will never dive again, not even with oxygen. I tell him the diving in Thailand is some of the best in the world. His reply? –"No, it isn't."

He's never been there before.

Then he proceeds to tell me for half an hour how sick paprika makes him feel. He also tells me that he drank wine once and it made him 'have a coma'. And, he can't eat any chilli of any kind. I tell him that he better be careful in Thailand, and he says, "I am not eating Thai food. Ever."

When I tell him there is plenty of pizza in Thailand, he says, "no there isn't."

I told him the best pizza I've had in my life so far was in Hong Kong. He says... "no, it isn't."

He tells me pizza was invented in Naples, which I know. I tell him about diving the underwater cities in Naples and how I want to do that. Then he tells me Australians have no food or culture of their own, which is why they think Thai food is exciting. I just don't respond to this one.

We are not even out of the car yet and I'm wondering how the fuck I get out of this.

Over the next hour we hang out, I hear a lot about this dude's stomach. He is completely horrified that you can't drink the water in Thailand and must buy it bottled. Goes on to explain he bought some tablets to put in the water, and I said be careful of that. He said, "no".

I get flustered when we exit the car, and put my water bottle in my bag, 10 minutes later it's leaking all over my phone and cigarettes and everything else. That shit never happens to me, so I think it's a sign he's a dick.

He is about five centimetres taller than me but is a tiny slip of a guy, so I guess that's why he was asking how tall I was. If I'm honest, I'm not really into tiny slips of guys. We have one drink together and we spend an hour together, the only question he asks me is what I do for work. He doesn't appear to listen to my answer.

He tells me about a place that has locally brewed beer on all its taps, and says, "yeah, we don't drink that shit you drink in Australia like Fosters."

"Nobody drinks Fosters in Australia," I say.

"What about that one with the kangaroo on it?"

"I have no clue what that is, but we drink and make real beer and IPAs and have microbreweries all over the town where I'm from too."

He does not give a shit. Doesn't believe me and he's not listening anyway.

Someone nearby is smoking a joint, and he tells me how they're fucking idiots.

"Is it very illegal here?" I ask.

"No, not really. They are just idiots."

He's a lawyer who works for Trenitalia, the biggest train company here. Fuck, I'm accidentally dating a lawyer for an hour! When I sit, he just stands over me and tells me how Italians will often say, 'yes, no problem' but then give you a reason why they can't do what you're asking them.

Then, he proceeds to tell me to be careful of the €50 I have in my wallet because someone might rob me; this, right after he told me I'm safe everywhere in Rome at night. Next, he tells me the colour of every single note, and by that point I don't even tell him that we have different coloured notes in Australia as well.

And wouldn't you know it, his dinner is conveniently back on. He doesn't offer to drive me home. Says it is a short walk back. I look at the map and it is nearly an hour of walking and it's extremely hot. I've already walked 12 kms today.

As we part, he says that if I need anything or am getting any trouble, just call him, he will answer. I can absolutely tell this is complete bullshit as well. We do the double-kiss, European-style on the cheek thing, and in an effort to get away faster, tell him I'm walking on a different side of the road.

When I'm a few steps away from him, I mutter "fuckwit" under my breath. This becomes my mantra as I walk many more kilometres in the heat to get home. It's only when I arrive home, nearly dead and pouring with sweat at 11pm, that I say out loud to my quiet apartment, "he was the biggest asshole I have ever met."

Don't get me wrong, I've met a lot of assholes, and I have probably been on over 100 Tinder first dates that ended pretty promptly. But Daniele, who drives a black Alfa Romeo, the lawyer who lives in Rome, was literally the most arrogant man I have ever met on Earth.

When I got home, I sent him a message telling him what I thought of him, then blocked him. It felt great.

Side note: He also said that today it would be 45 degrees. A guy standing next to us showed us the weather app, which said it would be 30.

Daniele said, "no."

It's currently 28 degrees.

CHAPTER 77

When in Rome, Date a Roman

Italy

On the hellish walk home from the most arrogant man on Earth, another man on Tinder is messaging me. He says that he is working at a cannabis shop the next day, and I decide that dropping in to check him out before committing to a date is a wise move.

The next morning, I walked for half an hour uphill to get there.

When I arrived at the tiny hole-in-the-wall shop, I'm greeted by the cutest smile behind the counter. His name is Simone and he is 34, my height, and straight away we see each other for who we really are. I chatted with him for half an hour about the fact that weed is legal here but only if it has CBD and low percentages of THC. However, he grows high THC weed at home to smoke himself.

He says my freckles are beautiful, and while we are chatting another woman comes in with tattoos and buys some CBD-only weed. When she leaves, he says she is nice but doesn't have a pretty face like me.

This is already going 500% better than last night.

We agree that I will meet him again later on before he closes the shop at 8pm.

He invites me back to his place to help him set up a new grow tent, and meet his two cats—Jamal and Larusa. Nothing about this sounds threatening or bad, all the right vibes are there.

When I arrive, he says he made the most money he has made in a week. Rectifies the till, and we leave. He tells me we are going to the 'Bronx of Rome'. I can't wait.

Rome has a giant ring road around it like many other major cities, and Simone's neighbourhood is just on the inside edge. Torre

Maura does feel like the Bronx, groups of different people hanging out on small crates chatting in the street. I don't recognise the language and when I ask, he says there are many Romani here.

We stop at a small corner shop and grab fresh tomatoes for him to cook dinner. Tomatoes here are unlike anywhere else in the world; they are sweet and succulent, deep-red, juicy fruits like they're supposed to be. We went back to his place, which has beautiful old trees all around it, and took six flights of marble stairs to his apartment, which is a tiny place with no balcony but all the essentials.

He gave me the first joint I've had in three weeks.

He really loves growing good marijuana, and I'm suddenly more relaxed than I have been for the last few days of transit and travel. Funny that.

In one small room, he has his woodworking area, giant logs waiting to be made into something, a double bed, a desk covered in computer and other tech and weed smoking paraphernalia, and a grow tent in the corner with three healthy looking plants inside. He notices that Jamal has kicked out his baby seeds, and laughs and builds the new tent and puts them inside.

Then he heads off to the kitchen and cooks spaghetti with garlic, chilli, olive oil and tomatoes. I realise that in the West, we often overcomplicate flavours. Also, we add tomatoes that are shit, white and flowery, so they don't taste like these, so perhaps we have to. Tomato paste is nowhere to be seen in this kitchen.

We eat sitting on the bed in our underwear twirling forkfuls of spaghetti into our mouths, starving. It's roasting hot inside, and the lights in the grow tent don't help this fact.

When we make love, it is passionate. He kisses every inch of me, and when I respond, he tells me he can tell I am half-Italian because I am also passionate. He kisses my belly, which most Western men shy away from, and it feels so good. We cum together in an explosion, the tiny fan from the weed tent is pointed at us instead of the plants.

Afterwards, my feet and legs are so tired and I have still only slept seven hours in the last three days. We crash in the middle of the night as thunder rumbles and lightning flashes. We wake and roll together, the rain pouring down. Banging the windows and dampening the extreme heat and humidity, which has preceded it. It's epic.

In the morning, we rise and I feel like I've had a proper sleep. Jet lag is over, I'm refreshed. He goes down to the street and grabs custard croissants, peaches and plums, and we climb up the ladder to the roof to eat because it is breezy up there and the rain has brought stifling humidity.

What's funny about being in the 'Bronx of Rome', is that it looks like every other Bronx in the world. Tiny concrete alleyways, a slew of TV antennas and satellite dishes on every rooftop, and every balcony an extra room of the house with people eating and lounging on banana chairs and drying laundry and growing herbs.

However, I can tell that I'm in Europe. The air smells different.

The few trees are different, but there is hot-pink bougainvillaea spilling across houses and somehow that also feels like home.

We head into the city, and I asked if we can visit some nature today because it's his day off. So, we spend the day wandering the ancient parklands of Villa Borghese. The rain comes in tropical drifts and the umbrella goes up. We hold hands and kiss in the street, and today feels different to yesterday because I don't feel like a tourist. I let him lead, and it's easy. Non-threatening in every way.

Suddenly, I needed to get a tattoo today in Rome. I don't even care what it is, I'm just living for every moment of this moment. We head to a tattoo shop and within an hour my forearm is being inked with a geometric rose by an apprentice named Michele.

We spent three hours hanging out in the tattoo shop where there are six apprentices huddled around us, watching like an audience of student doctors. It's hilarious. When we leave, I am full of adrenaline and not enough food.

We eat and walk through the city, head back to my place where we drink some beer. He keeps telling me that I'm making him so horny for sex and I tell him the meaning of the word sleazy. It's always great till someone's dick gets hard at the inappropriate moment, isn't it? LOL

By now, I'm exhausted from the intense intimacy of a person I met twenty-four hours ago and this boyfriend dynamic. I make it clear that my friend is arriving soon from the airport.

There is a sun shower on the Vatican, and a rainbow spreads overhead as we kiss goodbye.

He heads off into the sunset.

It couldn't be a more perfect Roman romance.

Farewell, Simone, maybe see you again somewhere on the planet someday.

I am happy that I don't feel the need or the urge to make this anything other than what it was.

Everything is just as it should be.

LEGAL WEED AND FRESH INK IN ROME

CHAPTER 78

Not Quite Yet

Firenze, Italy

Tonight in Florence, there is flute playing through the streets. Roses. Romance.

I shed a tear into my pasta, for all these years of not knowing who I was. So much lost time. I feel cheated. Robbed. Of an identity I wish I could own that still feels so foreign.

I knew this would happen. That visceral knowing, the air, the land, the leylines of heritage. They mean so much to a witch like me. I'm on borrowed time, so much to learn. So much to let go of. So much to integrate. There is no other way, just have to let it come. And go.

And tomorrow is a new chance to explore even more, what this being human thing is.

Firenze, where the streets are winding, cobblestone alleys and there is art on every corner.

We spent the day exploring graffiti instead of Jesus art, and winding our bikes through the throngs of tourists on walking tours trailing snotty kids, well-heeled tourists... not travellers.

Grey-moustached chefs with giant, comical, floppy hats and booming voices standing in doorways chatting. Beautiful, thin women with long cigarettes and impeccable make up. Sudanese street sellers who approach and are super friendly when we say, "no thanks" and some give us a trinket or a bracelet anyways. That's never happened to me in other places.

Seek out graffiti artists' studios instead of waiting in three-hour lines to see highbrow art, head along the river and into quiet back streets where artisans work on crafting their masterpieces. Jewellers, woodworkers, Basquiat-style painters. We take photos of paste-ups, on giant mediaeval doors and eat pizza sitting in the gutter, juicy tomatoes rolling off with a hearty 'plop' on the concrete where dogs look at them longingly.

We want to go out somewhere tonight, so I swipe yes to a few men on Tinder to see what's out there. It's 90% 'no' to the men on the app here, super slick and with the pouty arrogance I experienced in date number one staring back at me. Just nope. Not again.

A man named Giovanni messages me, and we have some back and forth about possibly meeting up later on. After drinking sour beer at a dive bar, then eating our body weight in burrata, prosciutto, steak and salad, we head along the river to a beach bar playing loud salsa music.

He meets us, and has a warm smile. Buys us all a jug of mojitos and we talk on the beach, while my friend joins the Zumba crew on the dancefloor. Then he says, "do you want to go somewhere really special?"

… Yes.

We are near Piazza Ferrucci, on the border of the city centre of Firenze, Oltrarno—literally the 'other side of the river'.

A half-kilometre down a back street, we find a tiny door where he rings the buzzer. The door opens a crack and there are 'No' sounds… but then the owner sees who it is and it's flung open, hugs and grins all around.

Mauro has been the owner for decades, and he never drinks when he's here till all hours of the morning, hosting his guests. This is a members'-only club, where you have to go every week for a year to get a membership card. You can't be a young, drunk dick, and you can't bring outsiders in. Somehow, though, we are here.

It's been a secret club since the '80s and almost forty years of yellowed photos and marker graffiti cover the walls that surround tiny booths with lifeguard umbrellas sticking out of the tables. It's dark, dingy, and you can tell so much has happened here that isn't spoken about in regular life.

Giovanni says, "you don't have a drink here, you have an experience."

We are served half-watermelons scooped out and filled with peach vodka... While he drinks a short glass full of blackberries and fire-water, blueberry grappa or something. Half a teaspoon of his drink blows my face off. These are not quick drinks. It takes us an hour to finish one, scooping out peach drenched watermelon and talking.

About our countries, about his event business, and mine, about culture and drinking and jokes with each other. He tells me the club is called 'Surf Ventura' and I nearly fall off my bench seat. That's my father's name. That's why I'm even here. Ventura...Ventura... My eyes prick with tears. How is this possible? But also, I'm just not surprised anymore at this story that is weaving, it's out of my hands.

"It's not a common name," he says.

We leave at 2am, stumbling into the street but trying to whisper because it's residential around us. The alleyways are silent.

My friend jumps in a cab to go home and we head on his vespa back to his 'office'—a car garage with three huge, shiny, black 4WDs in it. He has an events company and a company with luxury cars and drivers, but as we sit on a broken couch in the dark... I realise, this is where it's happening.

He gives me some water but goes straight for the hand between my legs. We had kissed on the street but this feels weird. A few minutes into fucking on the broken couch in the dark, the smell of engine oil and the low rumble of a nearby train the only soundtrack, and my whole body is screaming NO. Not now, not here, not like this. I need to voice my feelings, but am nervous to do so.

I'm in a garage in Florence with a man I just met, who is twice the size of me, and I'm about to tell him to stop no matter what. My friend has gone home and is probably sleeping, and doesn't have his number or know where I am. Fuck. I breathe out slowly, prepared for anything, and tell him, "please stop, I can't do this. Not here, not now, it's not right for me."

He stops immediately, asks if I'm okay, clocks my vibe. "I think you didn't need sex tonight, you needed cuddles maybe?" he says, and pulls me on top of his giant chest… and strokes my hair.

Tells me he didn't want to meet up to have sex, that I'm an amazing lady, so beautiful, and smart as hell. That I can have any man I want, when I'm ready. That he cares about me, that he would like to be my friend, that he is sorry it went too fast too quick and made me feel sad. He also tells me he has a son—six years old—whose mother died four years ago, and this is why he didn't take me home. The entire story changes how everything feels.

His strength, his certainty, his offer of pure intimacy should reassure me… But it somehow doesn't. I can't look him in the eye; I'm not ready. Not ready to be this intimate with someone I've just met.

I realise now that the Roman boy was a safe bet for me. He didn't make himself a priority, his dreams were small. He was a lot younger than me—in years and life experiences. He was fuzzy around the edges; not quite yet a fully-formed human.

These are the types of men I have often gone for because it feels safe. To be with them, I don't have to risk anything. I can lead. Do lead. Though I let them think they are. It's a mutual agreement, unspoken.

However, a man like this who's holding me in his arms… I have to risk everything and let myself be laid bare. This is the work I am yet to do. This is the work I'm doing now by being on this adventure on my own with no family back home checking on me. This is a real man. Solid, both in body and mind. He knows who he is.

The realisation is terrifying and some tears drop from my eyes and he totally understands. He says all of the beautiful things. Asks me to kiss him properly and I do but something inside of me holds back still.

He drives me home through the quiet 3am-streets of Firenze. His hand clutching my knee on the back of the scooter reassuringly. His fingers find mine when he doesn't have them on the handlebars. I drape my arms over his shoulders and press my hand to his chest; I hope he feels my gratitude. I am so comfortable on the back of a bike, but I am also often only comfortable when I am in control. As soon as I am in uncharted waters, I become avoidant and scared and can't even admit it.

All of this is due to these layers of childhood trauma I'm only now peeling back. I have made the wrong choices for a long time but I just didn't have the correct information to make the right ones. Everything in my body, every fibre of my being wishes and hopes I can overcome this. It really feels like my magnum opus on Earth. Friendships, businesses, making money, navigating the world and being myself all feels easy…

Surrendering my control to a man who can meet me feels almost impossible. I need intimacy to grow and move gently. Not startle me like a snake in the bushes.

This is my journey into myself, and I say goodbye on a street corner as the dawn light begins.

CHAPTER 79

Pandemic Blues

Today is day 189 of lockdown.

My heart aches for the forests, the mountains and the ocean.

Humans aren't meant to be solo in their houses for so long.

This is a reminder that even though we are optimistic, even though we are positive…

Through being polite to each other…

This shit is really hard.

But also…

This too will pass.
It always does.

Anyone who has felt grief,
who has lived through pain,
knows that eventually one day,
It will pass.

One day you look around,
and the train wreck is over.
We will reminisce about this.

We have lived through a war together.
So this is just a reminder,
That I love you.
That we are still connected.
That we will feel limitless joy again.

We will feel love.
Collective love.
It will come.
This is what I hang on to.

I miss you all,
With your imperfections and your sweaty, gleeful faces.

I don't think humans are idiots.
I am not scared of everybody.
Look at how humanity is looking after each other.
Humans are actually pretty amazing.

We will live through this,
And we will learn.
We WILL change.
We have to.

There is no other option. ♥

CHAPTER 80

Small Wins

I keep reading about post-pandemic things but we are not out of the woods yet.

Nine months into a lockdown in Melbourne that seems to ebb and flow and never end and maybe not have an end in sight.

I started with sparkly earrings on, gonzo broadcasting developments on Facebook live videos as they came to hand. Now my eyes are puffy from random tears that come at random times about random things that we no longer have, which I am grieving.

It's been a step in, hands-in connection time for some, and extremely alienating for others.

I've spent entire days on the phone pacing through the house sharing revelations, supporting people and feeling held by my community.

Spent other days in silence, not even music playing, scrolling, scrolling, scrolling endlessly looking for something I can call truth. Some piece of certainty to hang on to. Certainty has been very elusive this year. Dwelling in liminal spaces for so long that I forget where the story ends and I begin.

It's strange that I know I am so loved in my own city but I have spent moments wondering—irrationally—if everybody hates me. This is why isolation sucks.

When your sense of civic duty bumps up against your desire for personal freedom.

When asking really smart questions turns very quickly into 'us and them' and division and separatism and anger. Too easy to do in isolation as well.

Lately, it's been focusing on small wins and small pleasures.

I had my first shower yesterday in the outdoor shower we built, my face bathed in sunshine.

I've been extremely grateful this year about my choice to not have children and I feel so deeply for all my parent friends. Sorry to say that out loud but it's the truth.

Everyone cups their soy lattes with their mask pulled down and for a minute it feels normal.

Isn't it interesting how we lose our sense of self when we don't have other people reflecting back to us? Even the hermits I know have had enough of being alone right now.

My darling community, we are in the shittest bit of what might be the shittest year of our lives for some.

Personally, no year will ever come close to some of mine in the past, not even this. I've walked through some fires already. But you have to raze things to the ground before you build again. It's alchemical and it is never comfortable or easy.

I have hope that we are going to have a Renaissance after this.

I hope the retail slums that pop up are taken over by artists and squatters. I don't have much hope for any government to hold us. To be honest, they never really have. Time and again they prove they don't represent me.

So, it's hands-in, hands-in, hands-in.

Energy together, connect, communicate.

Try to love each other through the shitstorm and hold on tight.

I dip in and out of political conjecture and rhetoric and theory.

Take small breaks to ride the bike and say hello to random strangers and finally bake my first loaf of sourdough for 2020. Small wins, small moments, and one small step at a time. Breathing in and out love. Every single breath.

It's spring now and there are blossoms everywhere falling like snow.

All we can do is put one foot in front of the other, take one tiny moment at a time.

Be grateful, be grateful, be grateful.

We are living through a pandemic for the very first time in our lifetimes, there is no rule book.

We must write it together.

In the future, it will be just another chapter in our stories.

Let's try and write a good ending.

PARK PHOTOSHOOTS, 2020

CHAPTER 81

Fraying

This week my edges are fraying.

Every morning alone, every evening alone.

Days of solitude with no marker on the horizon for when they will end.

I have cried on and off all day. It's been the longest lockdown anywhere and they haven't called me, to see if I'm surviving. To ask if I'm thriving.

This morning I cried because I want some hope from our government rather than being scolded like children.

Then, at 10am, I cried because international borders might open. But I don't have anyone to visit especially.

Then I cried at 1pm, when my friend talked about being a mother. Because I really wish I had a mother who loved me.

Then I cried at 3pm because I got home to the empty house and unloaded the shopping. The food I can't even be bothered cooking. So, I eat crackers again for dinner and veggies go all slimy in the fridge, and I feel guilty and shameful that I let them go to waste. It's a really small failure but it gets me every time.

I cry at 4pm because the government has not handled much in the last two years well. From bushfires to quarantine to Robodebt. Just unaccountable at every turn, corrupt as fuck, and have lined each other's pockets throughout this scourge. We have been misled by the media—poisonous and a behemoth—I feel powerless to take on. And it feels like the bastards always win, time and time again.

I know that I'm super mentally resilient, enough so that I can support so many people. Sometimes, I feel like I hold the whole community in my heart and can be a heavy load. But I'm allowing these feelings today. We are in the longest lockdown of the entire world. There are no promises or guarantees of when it will end... still. So, today, I grieve. Let myself feel all of these things, and the passing of time. Allowing grief is an art.

If I've learnt anything from the last few years, it's that grief is powerful. It doesn't actually ever really go away. And if you have really grieved, perhaps you have really lived. Because it takes a risk to love. It takes shedding whatever masks you show the outside world, to admit when you've lost something important to you.

I don't think I'm going to be one of those people whose life flashes before them when I'm about to die. Been on the funeral pyre already, sifting through broken glass to glue something beautiful together.

It's hard to share these things because we like nice, tidy packages. We like nice, easy narratives. We like it when the broken bits are swept into a corner and we present a shiny new thing instead. Ta-daaa!

But grief *is* a shiny thing. It's a beautiful crystal of many facets. It makes laughing till you cry and your belly hurts even more worth it.

So, here is a reminder that sadness at what has happened is allowed. Your grieving doesn't have to look like anybody else's. Those tears of yours are absolutely beautiful, and we should never be ashamed of crying.

CHAPTER 82

Lockdown Ends

I could write a lot about what we all went through this year. Our collective trauma. Our collective fight.

And all the things that didn't make it a collective but drew us further apart from each other.

Like privilege. Like politics. Like the thought police, and the conspiracies that took over.

But I think this was a year not to be upset at what we didn't have.

Rather, 'twas a year to be grateful for what we did have.

Usually, I write a big laundry list of achievements at the end of a year, an annual reflection and reminder that I'm doing things and it's worth it.

But I didn't 'achieve' much this year. Except community service.

I feel like all I did this year was help other people, and in turn, they helped me.

This year was a reminder that nurturing networks and community is everything, especially when shit hits the fan. So, here are some small moments I'd like to remember:

- When my friend Monkey came over and dropped a plastic sandwich-baggie full of fresh ramen noodles at my door. I'd never made proper ramen before, but I found a recipe and made the best fucking ramen ever and probably wouldn't have done it if he didn't bring noodles. Also, we met in the graffiti scene like 20 years ago and I love how people keep showing up in my life.

- The two times I had to be isolated, and within 30 minutes, someone was at my house to walk Bruno and bring things for head colds.

- That time a lovely man walked into my house and there was a connection and we became isolation buddies, lockdown lovers, made gourmet food, improved the garden and painted the house. And then when the world started to open up, he became really negative, and our relationship came to its natural end because humans in lockdown are not humans in the world. In the world we were so, so different.

- The time I got in my car and drove across the border to stay with a friend who was also living alone, before it was shut, but we didn't even know if you could do that. I did a live video on

Facebook saying there was nothing to be scared of, well just a virus, but that to get through this we just might need to break some laws and break them well and safely. I copped abuse from both sides for that, but it was worth it for the people who kept telling me I was giving them rational hope that we would get through this. Together.

- My regular live video broadcasts, which would prompt me in solo isolation to at least do my hair and put on some makeup to speak to you, asked me to formulate my thoughts into something that would be useful for everybody else. And then I would stop doing them, and I would get multiple messages that I had become the 'news' and that I must start again. So I did. Tried to be funny sometimes, tried to welcome baby activists into the bigger-picture fight some of us have been fighting for a very long time. I tried to share collective stories so we didn't just get lost in bypassing and making sourdough. Tried to highlight what other people were going through and how this would affect our society if we didn't band together.

- This was the year Joe Blow had to face the shit the rest of us deal with often. Like the overreach of authority whenever they feel like it. Like our substandard mental health, welfare, and government messaging systems. Like a different set of rules for wealthy people. I hope this was the biggest lesson for Australia this year as a whole.

- And last week, when my travel plans were thwarted. The state border was just not as forgiving this time, and it slammed shut just as I was reaching Sydney, and I had to turn around and come home. When I arrived to an empty house for Christmas. My phone did not stop ringing with genuine concern, invites to various places, and lots of people excited that I was back in the state again. After an intruder to my property, that night I had three pairs of men's boots on the front porch. The community again. At that moment, I knew I would not leave this neighbourhood because my support outweighs any threats.

The end of the year has been pretty validating, I have to say. All my years of coaching and preaching about diversified income streams, and having work that doesn't rely on an employer, have come to fruition this year. I can say it now with a little hindsight and perspective—I have not just survived but I have thrived this year. Not just with businesses, but with my own healing, my own solitude, and my purpose on the planet. I coached the world and I coached some more, and it felt worth it.

I did a lot of rational thinking about whether there were any big moves to be made this year. Should I sell the house, should I leave Victoria, should I move to a farm in the country and go totally off grid?

As many times as I turned around this crystal of possibilities, the resounding answer that kept coming back was:

STAY RIGHT WHERE YOU ARE AND DO EXACTLY WHAT YOU'RE DOING.

So I did. I am.

But I truly feel like we gained something this year that we had lost.

And that is connection.

Collective experience.

Empathy for each other.

My dear people, those are going to go a very long way in the uncertain future we face together.

Whatever battles need fighting, I'm at the front ready with my warpaint on.

And whatever beautiful, soft, silent moments we can share, I'm in the circle with my eyes closed and my hands outstretched. I want to receive them all.

CHAPTER 83

The Longest Love Affair

I woke up with a crazy good feeling the other day. It was like when meeting someone new and you wake up, remembering they're in your life. I was skipping around singing, wondering what brought this new joy to my vibe.

It took me most of the day to work out who it was.

You see, my friends, I have been stuck in people-pleasing patterns for a very long time. When I was younger, I had pretty low self-worth and thought I had to give way too much to receive love. Used to give my everything to people who only gave me scraps in return. A childhood of emotional neglect and gaslighting will do that to even the strongest human heart. I used to give and give and give, to my own depletion. Wonder why it never felt like enough.

The people I gave to were often uncomfortable, sometimes took blatant advantage, and for others, it was simply too much, too soon. I loved them like I love puffy, tiny birds—who I delight in—but also the urge to love them till their heads pop off. Yeah, it was a LOT.

Anxious attachment, textbook styles.

All I can say is it has certainly been a journey but I'm at a place where I no longer accept breadcrumbing in my life. No longer accept excuses where there should be apologies. I no longer waste energy trying to work out people's motivations for being dickheads. It's just BYE FELICIA.

Even inconsistency and neglect, which I experienced as 'love' as a child, and kept seeking and hanging onto as an adult, now feels like the warning sign that it is. Now, at the first sign of a major imbalance at the energy and effort between us—I'm out, not deeper in. I'm somewhere else, not hanging on every text, pushing for a different outcome.

For the last few years, I only give my time and energy to people who love and respect me equally and can return a certain level of emotional intelligence and maturity in our relationship. This has meant that some people have not grown with me even if I've known them for 20 years. I'm here to tell you that that is just ok. Not everyone will join you in the places you are going. Not everyone from your past will grow with you.

So, it took most of the day and a few chats with amazing humans to work out that the person that I had met who was giving me that giddy feeling.... WAS ME.

I love myself more now, than trying to get love from anyone else. Liberation is not even the word for it. Reclamation, perhaps? I feel it's time for me to decide who is on my apocalypse list and hold those people close. The ones who only contact me when they want something for themselves are just not in the circle. And it feels bloody incredible. A personal revolution of sorts, and another deepening of this 'work'.

When I learn something, after integrating it, I want to teach everyone else. Everything I have done in my coaching, I have done myself first. I only offer things I can fully stand behind, that I have witnessed, experienced, walked through the fire and healed those scars. Then, I consider myself a new expert in this realm. You cannot preach what you do not do. That's integrity, and it's what's missing from the entire 'coaching' space. Too many snake-oil charlatans preying on other people's sense of 'lack'.

So, I'm thinking of rolling out a new package.

It's something like: 'how to draw healthy boundaries when you come from a people-pleasing and trauma background, and how to deal with the fallout when others refuse to acknowledge those boundaries, instead blaming you and resenting you because you no longer tolerate their shit.'

Any takers? Haha. No, really, this has been an extremely empowering process for me over the last few years.

When your self-worth is rock solid, how others react to you stating your boundaries is way less about you and more about them. It takes emotional maturity to table and then navigate these dynamics, but if not, people can stay locked in a pattern of complacency and enabling each other's shit. 'That's just how I am/they are' etc. Even when it's self-destructive or consistently hurtful to be around.

Your true friends, your true Family—with a capital F—will push you to be better, do better. They will not just allow you the same bullshit and excuses over years. This, I fully believe.

And while it can feel very tricky to state your guidelines for others, people who consistently overstep your boundaries and dysregulate your nervous system, well, after a while it just doesn't feel safe to be around them. Here is a final reminder, you don't get to decide how people treat you… But you can choose whether you will allow that treatment to be ongoing in your life.

I am whole, on my own. There are no buts.

I know what I'm looking for, know how it will feel when I find it, and everything else is just noise.

The longest love affair anyone will ever have, is with ourselves.

FEELING MYSELF AT A FESTIVAL

CHAPTER 84

Fuel for the Fire

LITTLE BO, 1979

I've told you I received a letter from Christie, disowning me, after revealing a couple years before that I was not my father's child. To everyone.

I revisited, processed and unwound a timeline of neglect and emotional abuse, my life peppered with gaslighting and victim blaming. My stories are not for the faint of heart. I share them anyway.

To name it. To unshame it. To transmute it into something beautiful.

I share this journey because we change generational trauma as a community, not as an island.

Now, I choose to surround myself with people who have authentic relationships. Who are emotionally capable of accountability. I am unwilling to entertain anything with a deficit of care and realness. No, thank you.

Since the letter arrived, I have gone no contact.

Tonight, I received an ominous package.

I have already been sent every photo of me from the entire family history, Little Me wiped from the albums and the walls. I still need to go through that box and burn most of them. But I haven't been able to.

So, these can't be photos.

I open it with trepidation.

It is every letter and poem and card I ever gave them. Every Mother's Day card. Every Father's Day card. Every postcard from overseas travels. Every drawing, every story.

Every declaration of love for people who never really loved me. The irony.

As if to say, 'look at all this proof that you once loved us'. I don't read any of it, just let my fingers pass over.

I've been writing since I was able to hold a pen. Found a million ways to say I love you in my lifetime. Little Me tried to say it every which way.. to people who would never hear me.

I now reserve those words for people who deserve it, unequivocally.

Don't feel like calling ten people to process this. I don't need to now.

I will burn all of these in a fire. Will warm my face in the flames. There is no other course of action. Because there is no shortage of words and love and possibility in me. I have shelves full of books of declarations of love on paper and on postcards and on photos and on my phone and on the internet spanning decades. I've done personalised holiday season cards with my animals on the front and me being sexy on the inside for over a decade and sent them to 100 people each year.

Don't need a reminder of how much I have the capability to love. I know.

There are going to be so many words that pour from me every day of my life until I die.

None of them are going in that direction. Not one word.

I have made peace with this, my friends. Have healed from what hurt me so I don't bleed on people who didn't cut me. I don't fall into that pit of despair for longer than a moment anymore.

It's just another chapter in my story.

I get my jacket and my boots on and get ready to crack some kindling.

Pour a glass of wine.

I know who I am and I have pasta to cook, dammit.

I'll celebrate my resilience. Then marshmallows around the fire.

And back to my life being mine cos I made it... and everything/everyone in it is right.

CHAPTER 85

Ten Years Coaching

This year I will have been coaching for 10 years. Reality Check has withstood the test of time, and even though I have still worked in events, in marketing and other places and contracts, I have not had a full-time job working for someone else for a decade. I backed myself hard, and it paid off. It pays off every day when I wake when I want and sit down to build my empire some more.

When I set out to be a 'holistic business coach', I embarked on a journey of levelling-up my knowledge forever—haha. I'm not sure I realised that would be the outcome, that I would commit to learning and betterment of myself, perpetually. I can't make silly excuses when I guide others to face theirs. Can't preach what I don't embody, so I have set goals and reached them for the last decade.

10 YEARS IN BUSINESS, BUY YOURSELF AN OSCAR

I published a deck of cards, self-funded, and then I made them into a free app. These have been my physical offerings to the world. Meanwhile, the clients have kept coming. From institutions, from networks, from conversations in shops and on the street. People have found me, then they talk to others about me, and they want a dose of whatever I'm having, so they book in.

Not only has it been important for me to stay across new business innovations, various industries, grants, funding, tax and investing, but it has also been important for me to learn more about traditional learning, psychology and counselling.

What I find as a coach is that some people come with determination that they want help with their career or business, but we find out quickly there is a relationship that has to move or end first. Sometimes, they have low self-worth or past traumas and, as a result, they stand in the way of their own 'success'. A common story trope I have plenty of lived experience with. Basically, over the years... I now do a lot more than traditional business coaching. Being an intuitive witch with a really, really big heart helps. Even my history, my family trauma, has helped.

You see, trauma makes you hypervigilant, aware of what people say but aren't saying. You learn to read between the lines—both what they say and what's etched in their faces. But harnessed and understood, this fight or flight tendency can be used for good, to be hyper-intuitive, to know exactly what they aren't willing to admit, and gently guide them towards it. I am good at this now.

I have clear and secure boundaries now, am aware of vicarious trauma, am not precious about any advice I give, and fully understand that the client is on a choose-your-own adventure, and I'm merely the guide.

There is only one 'Reality Check' and there is only one me. I don't want to do things like everyone else. Personally, I've had to unpack a lot of trauma in the last few years. Right back to childhood and even before I was born. I often work with 'healers' as their business coach, but I also seek out other professionals to help me regularly on my own personal journey.

I've done everything from intuitive healing from a Maori warrior princess, to reiki, various types of body work, hypnosis, acupuncture, Chinese medicine, years of Western psychology using CBT, and I even tracked down the traditional healer from *Eat, Pray, Love* in Bali, and she gave me 'pretty pills' and put leaves down my underpants. Unsure if it worked... or what worked the most, but here I am.

I'm doing all this so that I am educated. Educated about what things work for me. And educated so that I can help others, from a place of lived experience and embodied knowledge rather than just opinion. I'm hungry for new narratives around trauma-informed work. The old paradigms of 'everything happens for a reason' and 'nobody will love you until you love yourself' have been reassessed as spiritual bypassing and victim-blaming bullshit we don't need where we're going. HUZZAH!

Also, you do not owe your abusers forgiveness. Do you need to see that in caps lock?

YOU DO NOT OWE YOUR ABUSERS FORGIVENESS.

The old adage of 'you forgive them for you, not them' works, but not at the hands of abuse.

You have permission.

I truly believe we are generational cycle breakers. We are unlearning patterns that do not serve us and we are choosing not to pass generational trauma into our kids.

We can heal from the things that hurt us. I feel this is the most important work.

This is what I'm on the planet to do.

Oh, and I'm a killer business and life coach too.

CHAPTER 86

So Many Beautiful Men

It's been 18 months without sex.

There have been dates but with my current, shiny self-worth and elegantly stated boundaries, they have not progressed to the intimacy stage. I know this is actually okay. People tell you to 'just go out and get some', but I know that's not what I'm looking for, and I'm sure that's not what will sustain me. I have seen many cocks and hips and lips, I know what happens next. I could do without any of that and just be in someone's arms watching TV and feel more satisfied. This I know.

There was one who seemed promising, a mechanic who looked at me as if I was a unicorn, and we had two very cute dates to begin with. But then he showed his bi-polar self and freaked out, broke up with me spectacularly, ran away, and sent confusing text messages for a month afterwards. To which I simply declined any further interaction. I know that now, it's just my job to recognise when it's not it. That's my only job until the relationship progresses. Know which ones to fold, and which ones to respond to.

I had a moment last week where I realised just how many beautiful men are around me. I'm at a birthday party for one, then I go to a gig with another, and my phone pings and there's four at once in my inbox, offering up tidbits, asking for my opinion, generally wanting discourse with me, and I see now, that this is where intimacy begins. Not when you take your clothes off. That, my friends, is just sex. That's primal, its chemical, it requires nothing other than pheromones and desire.

Intimacy can be a shared meal, an honest truth, a gentle inquiry. Intimacy is trusting someone to know what's really going on for you, and when I say this, I'm aware that some of the loves I have entertained in the past, were not that. Intimacy is trust. Intimacy is making sure you get home safe, it's recalling what you have happening this week, it's supporting you as you reach your dreams.

And I may not be having sex with any of these men, but we certainly share intimacy.

My friend Brad, who joins me for a plate of $15 dumplings on High Street in Preston, and we come home to watch six episodes of *Alone* in a row, till I'm falling asleep on the couch. He slaps my arse and says, "Time for you to go to bed." Hugs me at the door and leaves.

Or my ex-boyfriend Dan, who has been a friend more than a lover this whole time, who comes over the next evening to show me some travel apps and tell me about his trip overseas, and sends nice messages after about how good it was to see each other.

Or my chosen brother Gerard, my work husband, who calls me most days to rant about work, or politics, or just generally check in. Who I can say anything to—and do—and he will always support me and help me, exactly like a brother would.

Or my other work colleague who became a dear friend. Jason, who came over recently for a spa date with wine and beer and stories, we ate one single magic mushroom together and then potato leek soup later, and he heads off at 8:30pm into the cold autumn night after squeezing me tight at the door.

Or my mate Tom, who for twenty-five years now, has been there for me as a brother when I needed a driveway for my caravan and an open invite to come over anytime.

Or the lovely man up north, who I met at a festival once years ago, and we have stayed in touch on social media, and now we send long, rambly voice messages back and forth to each other updating our lives, supporting each other, even though we have spent a total of 15 hours actually hanging out in person before.

Or the man I affectionately call my 'right wing friend' who I met online four years ago debating politics, and that debate has continued almost daily now for years, because we both approach our views with curiosity, and we have never insulted each other, even when it gets very spicy. One time he said to me, "I would trust you with my house, and my dog", and I felt the same. How many people have you never met that you would trust with your dog?

Recently, I was in his area, a few hours away, and we met for lunch. It felt like we had known each other for years because, well, we have. Just not in person.

Or my 'shady tradie' Ferris, who has been another brother for 15 years, who has quietly followed me into some absolutely crazy adventures and festival work and missions, and always, *always* had my back. Who has never complained at the shit I accidentally put him through, and who was here during lockdown, building a brick wall and a whole garden with me. In the cold. Brick by brick, stone by stone, stealing bluestone bits in buckets from the park with me.

When I think about just how many beautiful men I have to call on, I am grateful.

But also, this is not by accident. They are in my life for me too.

These men are in my life because they choose to be.

Our relationships are not transactional.

They are based on reciprocal effort, on exchange of intel and care and check ins and phone calls and messages. Based on sharing our lives together, over time, and showing up for each other. Even just for dinner or to fix a flat tyre.

My brothers are everywhere, they lift me up, we are real with each other, and their emotions and fears are safe with me. This has way more value than sex.

MITTONS AND ME, RAINBOW MARKET STAGE

CHAPTER 87

My Legacy List

A bucket list is aspirational, which is nice. But also, it's amazing to recognize how far you've already come and what you've already done. Life is precious, and it may end at any moment. So, here I keep a brief record of the things in case it ends tomorrow…

This is my legacy list. I encourage you to make one too.

I started an underground techno club in 1999 where the policy was 'records only' and entry was free.

I danced on a mountain when it was the millennium and hoped for global change.

I protested for things I believe in and locked arms with strangers as riot cops moved in with batons.

I have been Chair of a board, run benefit gigs and volunteered for NGOs to better the world I live in.

I have driven across the Nullarbor (and back) and felt the size and breadth of this land.

I have explored tunnels, drains, and rooftops in secret places.

I have left bondage babies all over the world for others to find.

I booked for two prominent nightclubs in Melbourne, and brought them much success.

I moved across the country for love, and then back when I saw it wasn't right for me. (twice)

I have run my own business helping other people realise their dreams successfully for 10 years.

I trekked the Himalayas at 14 years of age and smoked hash with sadhus.

I have been where the forest meets the sea in FNQ, and believe in it being a type of church.

I have eaten mangoes off my lover in the bath.

I left my family to move to a place that feels like home.

I have ridden horses in the bush and in competition and jumped logs with wild abandon.

I have gotten drunk and hitchhiked home in the cool dawn, singing at the top of my lungs.

I have done graffiti in Hong Kong and got busted tagging a van by cops. They let me go.

I bought kimonos on the street in Tokyo and drank warm sake with my fill of top-class sushi.

I have eaten the best food ever in Taiwan, gotten lost and found again with my internal homing device.

I have walked among the protesting students in Korea and had tiny old men try to pick me up.

I have been the only white person at a temple ceremony in Bali and swam in the spring of eternal life.

I have wandered among the temples at Angkor in Cambodia and felt part of the world's history.

I have shot Glocks in Arizona and ate magic mushrooms in the mountains by the Grand Canyon.

I have been overseas for an internet lover, and cried the whole way home for impossible situations.

I have done nude modelling shoots and been in short films.

I have been a cunt model. Yes, a cunt model. My pussy has been on display in Berlin and Tasmania.

I have dived under the ocean in many places, done freediving and discovered my mermaid self. I had a tail for a while as well.

I have spent many days and nights smiling in Thailand.

I have flown through the forest canopy on ziplines and rappelled down trees over 500 years old.

I have ridden on a motorbike through the mountains of Laos, singing at the top of my lungs in the rain.

I drank Arak with headhunters in Borneo, and went to the only gay club in a Muslim city.

I was born in San Francisco and have left a piece of my heart there eternally.

I jumped out of a plane at 12000 feet, fell to earth at 220kms/hr and loved every minute of it.

I self-published my own magazines (and now a book).

I published a deck of cards to help the world, then made them into a free app for everyone.

I have run my own successful, ethical art gallery for local and underground artists.

I have worked as a teacher, a waitress, stage manager, artist, a production assistant, landscaper, manager, a nightclub promoter, copywriter, curator, an advertising executive, operations manager at festivals, safety officer, a zombie wrangler, a site manager and many other roles.

I have fallen in love and out of love countless times.

I have been a step mother, a friend, a lover, a daughter, a sister, a niece, a confidant, and a loyal supporter of talented people, whether my friends or not.

I have done all of life's missions with honesty and integrity and I choose to speak the truth at all times, even if my voice shakes.

And I'm not done. Yet.

HOLIDAY CARD SHOOT, BY NICOLE CLEARY

CHAPTER 88

You've Got This, Babe

The ultimate glow up isn't physical, it's when you realise every inch of your self-worth, enough so that you waste no time filling your life with love, your spaces with people who give a shit, and give your fucks to problems worth worrying about.

When you have been abused, especially as a child, the things said to you in those formative years leave an imprint. The more you hear that you should 'be quieter' or that you are 'being ridiculous' for expressing feelings or emotions, the more you believe it. The more you mask your behaviour, the more you bury yourself in books where it's 'safe'. Sound familiar to anyone?

The more you doubt your own internal compass, and second guess your instincts too. And the more horrible things people project onto you, and say to you as a child… the more that becomes your internal narrative too, because if the main people who are supposed to love you think that, say that, show you that… well, then it must be true.

When you are small, if you don't have people who love you unconditionally, it can be hard to know what that feels like. It can be hard to know what to think about being loved in general.

I'm here to tell you that love is not shame.

Love is not being put down constantly.

Love isn't feeling less than, or like you have to prove yourself, over and over, to get it.

There was a point in my healing when I noticed my internal dialogue was not my own.

The things told to me as a child—to cover someone else's guilt, to justify other people's actions, lies and behaviour—was actually nothing to do with me. Little Me had taken these things on board as truth, and like a parrot eager to please, repeated them back to myself ad infinitum.

This imprinting is deep. To fully heal, we have to unlearn these 'truths' about us that are not true at all.

For the last ten years, I coach people who sit across from me and offer up their internal narratives. I call it 'can'ts, won'ts and don'ts', when they have every excuse for why they cannot or will not do something or have something which, usually, they really want.

As a practitioner and someone invested in my client's future success, but not emotionally attached to outcomes, this is a very common mental block most humans share, even if what they are blocked about wildly varies.

Over this period, it became obvious to me that my own internal narrative needed shifting. 'There's nobody for me, I don't have a partner because my thighs are big, people only want what they can get from me, people only call me when they need something, I'm not smart, I'm not pretty, I have no value to anyone.'

When you say it all together, it sounds ridiculous, but these are small whispers that circulate.

Then, something happens externally, like a break-up, and your internal voice gets a megaphone, parades around shouting these awful slogans at a deafening roar. Especially when you are already hurting or vulnerable, this is not what you need.

This is not love, and it's certainly not self-love or even being gentle with your dear heart.

Last year, I had a queer punk friend from decades ago visit me from up north. This man has seen me through it all, and I have done the same for him. He's another of those beautiful men in my life, even if we don't see each other much these days.

He remarked that I no longer say self-depreciative things about myself, and with that reflection from an old friend, I realised that it has just been a long process of helping other people to not say negative things about themselves as well. You can't preach 'Reality Check' if you're not checking yourself. Negative self-talk is honestly one of the main things we put in our *own* way. We get stuck in cycles of believing shit things about ourselves that we perpetuate. This is really not useful to either happiness or progressing your life, dreams and goals, and it can be a really tough habit to break.

It takes actual retraining of those neural pathways.

Anyway, last night I caught myself giving a pep talk out loud, in the mirror.

It went something like this:

"You have absolutely fucking got this, babe. You have worked really, really hard for a really long time and you deserve everything that's happening. You don't need to take jobs or clients that don't excite you, you've absolutely done it, girl. And I'm really fucking proud of you."

I understand that I've been doing this for a few years now, but it was the reflection from my friend that made me see that I have reprogrammed this now. I really admire and love myself, and I think I'm a total babe. Am proud of everything I've accomplished, and also, the human I am. I have faced the fear and done it anyway, I have overcome.

When I go to the bathroom, sometimes I catch my reflection in the mirror, and now, always, I say something nice. This is a muscle that you flex, and it gets stronger over time, till it's a habit.

It feels awkward at first, saying, "Hey, gorgeous" to yourself, but now it's second nature.

Sometimes, I do a little dance and say a mantra in a sing-song voice like, "oh yeah, baby, we gonna have a great day and everything is gonna be okay ay ay…" Other times, I literally dance crunk and tell myself I'm fucking amazing.

And why not?

You gotta back yourself first, friends, because if you don't love yourself how in the hell are you going to love somebody else?

(Thanks, Ru Paul, for that slogan that means so so much.)

CHAPTER 89

Goals for Joy

It was after the time I drove back from Far North Queensland after having my heart dashed on the rocks, that I realised the importance of having goals for joy and joy only. Goals that were not for career or financial advancement, for fitness, even travel to faraway places, or to fulfil some idea of who I thought I should become. Just goals for joy. Pure joy. That's what I honed in on.

The first one I ever identified was being a mermaid.

I had already been scuba diving for years, and that was fun, but also, it was a leisure activity. Once you got control of your buoyancy, there wasn't much else to it. I did all the qualifications I could. Deep, Nitrox, Search and Rescue, Wreck diving, right up to Dive Master next. Which is a three-month liveaboard apprenticeship, to become an instructor afterwards and live somewhere tropical, and that wasn't quite it for me.

I decided that freediving was next.

Now, freediving is not a leisure activity by any means, often described as the most dangerous sport in the world. Regular scuba diving is risky under the best of circumstances. In freediving, drowning, blackouts, and severe lung damage make it especially dangerous. Even routine dives can be lethal. Of course, this did not deter me.

I declared this new goal publicly on social media, for accountability and so I didn't chicken out, if I'm honest. Also, to take all my followers on the journey with me of course. To smash those fears, in public, and with it, fulfil a dream for joy which might encourage others to do the same. Everyone loved the 'being a mermaid' goal, it spoke to some whimsical childlike part of all of us. People showed up at my house with concrete mermaid fountains and mermaid jewellery because "you keep inspiring me to reach for dreams". It was something the whole community resonated with.

But it wasn't just about mermaids. It was the reason for it, the hunt for joy. The prioritising of it.

I asked them all directly, "When was the last time you made a goal for joy and joy alone?"

This used to underpin my coaching too. Why spend your entire life working for something that you won't absolutely love doing? Sometimes, asking that question burns new business ventures to dust in an instant.

The mermaid mission was also about striving for the impossible. I went to Amed in north Bali and did my first day of freediving Level 1. It was terrifying, liberating, challenging and exhilarating. I did six dives of around six metres each, and then was overcome by seasickness and a huge wave of emotion like I've hardly ever experienced. I sobbed while bobbing in the ocean with the others supporting me, vulnerability from the depths of my soul poured forth. My snot mixed with my tears and the seawater and I left something of me in the ocean that day.

I swam to shore where I peeled my rashie off and sobbed some more till I was empty. Don't know where it all came from, the urge to do it, the gumption to follow through, the fear I overcame or the well of feeling that poured out of me as a result.

But I didn't give up. I wanted to break my own barriers both physically and mentally.

I took a couple days out of the water, rode the scooter around in the humidity, swam in the pool, ate healthy food and slept early. I went back determined, focused, relaxed, yet surrendered, and I doubled my breath hold from one to two minutes. I made it to a depth of around 11 metres and passed a course only around 50% of students complete. Level 1 freediving qualification achieved.

Everyone cheered for me. She had done it! Look at her go and smash those dreams, even the most dangerous sport in the world, what will she ever do next?

But I didn't want to do more freediving.

That moment in the ocean had rocked me. This sport was no fucking around. I know I love taking risks, but maybe this… <barely audible whispering>… wasn't for me.

The dream went quiet for a few years because deep down, underwater, I felt shame. Shame at not being a 'real' mermaid. At being scared of attempting more freediving qualifications. At saying I was going to do something and feeling like I failed.

Well, fuck shame, I decided! I've had enough of that in my life. And fuck failure while we're at it. Wasn't it Brene Brown who said, "If you're brave enough, you're going to fail."

You gotta reinvent yourself every moment. At the end of lockdown, I decided to do a really non-adult thing, and I bought a mermaid tail. A really fancy one from the Mertailor in California. My first one. Long overdue. It was hot pink and blue and green with extra dorsal fins and matched all my tattoos.

I carried the 20-kilogram technicolour tail across mountains and over rocks. I carted it to clifftops and delighted tourists taking photos of nature. I swam in private pools and took loads of great photos with it, but I didn't swim with it in the ocean once.

It didn't matter. Everyone knew me as a mermaid by now, and so did their kids.

Seven years later, my dream was realised. I was a REAL MERMAID.

Absolute joy.

HAPPIEST MERMAID, KANGAROO ISLAND SA

CHAPTER 10

Earn the Right

After enduring the longest lockdown in the world, there was a lot of reassessment of things.

There were the relationships that fractured due to pressures and division in ethics and ideals. In addition, most of us took career stock, location stock, and wondered if we were really doing everything we could to live our best lives.

For some people, sea change timelines moved forward. Moving back to family-owned lands happened. Friends of mine looked at the dysfunctional rental market and built a tiny house to raise their two small children instead, and drove north to the sunshine so they could take up space.

For me, the message was clear.

Stay right where you are and do exactly what you're doing.

Ten years of coaching and building my businesses with the privilege of stable housing meant I was in a good position, in all the realms. I had five streams of income and a low mortgage after dumping money in it for the lockdown years when there was nowhere to go, nothing to spend on except online shopping, which got tiring pretty quick.

So, what could I do about the gnawing feeling that I was bored and needed a new challenge?

Also, what would I do with all the time not taken up by caring for ageing parents or raising children? I knew I was going to be holding space and giving time and energy to support my community dealing with these things at this stage of life, but what about for me?

What about my quest for limitless joy?

Was I even allowed to have one post-pandemic?

I have never really had 'hobbies' or thought about them in that way. I mean, I guess sticking bondage babies around the world was a 'hobby'. Scuba diving was a hobby, but I lived far from the ocean, didn't really know any divers here in Melbourne and, frankly, was a bit bored of that too after travelling the world to dive destinations alone.

Then I recalled my love of horse riding. Something I had dabbled in as a teenager in the hills when I was allowed to buy a paddock pony for a couple years, and I went to Mylor Pony Club and trained him up to be a Grade 2 Eventer, where we would come last in the dressage and place near the top doing cross country.

Of course, when I was kicked out at 16, the horse dream was over, and my life was very far from any horse action in my twenties when I was immersed in working three hospitality jobs for survival and playing in the still-underground rave scene.

In Guatemala a few years ago, I sought out a riding place, and saddled up for the first time in twenty years on this giant Clydesdale/Criollo who I had to use a ladder to mount. We rode through corn fields that day with volcanoes erupting on the horizon, and I knew I had to do this more.

Post-lockdown, this became very important.

Time in nature, moving the body, and something to do for JOY and joy only.

It was like a siren in my heart, sounding an alarm, I had to do this for my soul.

I found a trainer named Frank who was 35 minutes from my house, and was also trauma-informed with his work with autistic youth. He was the perfect trainer for me, and I started going fortnightly with the goal of showjumping a course again.

I found out that some of my dear friends loved horse riding too, and we got a motley crew together to go trail riding in Upper Plenty at Uncle Nev's, a riding place that was an institution as it's the only place that still lets you go for a big gallop up a hill, risk mitigation be damned.

I proposed a riding holiday in the Snowy Mountains over Easter long weekend, and we trundled off to Mansfield, about two hours out of Melbourne towards the ski fields with our shiny new helmets to saddle up at the base of the mountains in the cold dawn.

On the very first day, my sprightly and giant standardbred horse trotted through thick bush and I smacked my knee hard on a tree, gouging a huge chunk out of it. I cried my eyes out on the mountain, but I saddled up later that afternoon with my knee bandaged and kept going.

For the next four days, we lived *The Man from Snowy River*. Instant coffee on the open fire, and everyone would saddle up on our stocky and tall standardbreds who had their own pecking order, and their own politics happening. These were mountain horses doing their mountain thing, and we were just passengers along for the ride.

We would stop for lunch and hobble to our camp chairs, and it took me a few days to realise the ladies in their fifties and sixties had little bum bags of drugs they were swapping and necking along the trails. Duly noted.

We went up the mountain for two days, and then back down, and there was no way to skip a ride, because what came up, had to come down. I recalled the rhythmic feeling of riding, in silence, for hours at a time. Trail rides regulate your nervous system, it's why Franks' autistic clients kept coming back to the horses. As we rode up and down the tiny trails at a walk, for hours and hours, with incredible mountain views around every corner, it was the first time I had been in the saddle so long since I was fourteen.

I cried quietly, tears mixing with the dust on my face.

I let it come, and go, with every step of my sure-footed horse.

I am good at this now. Up the mountain, down the mountain.

Processing the feelings, letting the trauma move through me, allowing it to pass.

Because I know it does. Trauma is stored in the body, not just your mind and heart.

I thought, and my hips went back and forth with every step, and I got somewhere in all of it.

The tagline for this particular riding place was 'Earn The Right'. After camping in swags for four days with aching bones and a huge gash out of my knee, as well as transmuting more final bits of healing from when I was an innocent teenager, I came back down the mountain having done so.

We earnt the right. And horses were back in my life, in a big way.

AFTER FOUR DAYS RIDING THE SNOWY MOUNTAINS

CHAPTER 91

Safari

Tanzania

It's been a year of planning, saving, and training. I've finally landed in Arusha, Tanzania, East Africa.

After the pandemic, I didn't know where to travel or even why.

It felt like there was nobody to visit, and visiting wonders of the world solo after a couple years alone in the house just wasn't appealing.

Till I discovered the idea of horse-riding travel.

My mermaid dreams had been explored. I'd been diving in Thailand multiple times, to Lombok as well. To the islands of Gili Trawangan and even to the bottom of the Blue Hole in Belize—50 metres down—where only a few Nurse sharks circle and underwater stalactites grow.

But suddenly, on horseback, the world opened up to me again. Even—and especially—some of the places I hadn't been but dreamed of, and some places I probably wouldn't venture on my own with no plan.

In my twenties, a group of friends and I went to Borneo to get our PADI at a water chalet at Singamata in the north Malaysian state of Sabah. We didn't know that one of the world's best dive sites—Sipadan—was there, and instead spent a week on a rickety wooden structure in the ocean learning to scuba dive.

We had gone in a group of five but after diving, we split up. One of my dear girlfriends had more agency than the others and we headed south with no plans and dog-eared Lonely Planets in tow.

We hunted for a real experience, and ended up in Kuching, otherwise known as 'Cat City' in the south-Malaysian state of Sarawak. This was head-hunter land, and we didn't want tourist vibes. We went to the government visitor centre and asked some questions, then somehow the next morning we were loaded up in a minibus full of ambassadors and press on a diplomatic visit to some of the surviving ancestors of head-hunters for the annual Harvest Festival.

We arrived at the longhouse, traditional housing for the indigenous of Sarawak, where 30 families lived under one very long roof. There was a ceremony, which involved the sacrifice of a chicken over a bowl on the threshold, and everyone stepped over to enter. Each door down the length of the longhouse was home to one family group, sometimes 15 people in one room, all ages.

The drink there is Arak, a rice wine distilled in a network of bamboo tubes that is basically rocket fuel. It can be so potent it can kill you, but I only learnt that years later in Bali.

My friend and I got into it, drinking and dancing with the tribe but soon noticed we were almost the only ones drinking. Each family wanted us to try their arak, so to each door we went, with an increasingly raucous, "HEY, HEY, HO!" at each door as another shot went down.

I was sitting with a group of men, getting drunker by the second, when shirts were suddenly coming off and tattoos were being compared, even mine. I grabbed one of the only other Aussies who was on our tour, a photographer, and asked if he would be my surrogate husband for the night.

We were lighting homemade fireworks with the kids in the pig slop under the longhouse, and we ended up wandering around the village at two in the morning. Completely oblivious to the fact that we had caused a diplomatic issue because we were a man and a woman alone together. We went back to our separate accommodation and they unlocked the gates and let us in with a stern talking to.

The next day my hangover was like nothing on Earth. It was over 40°C and I was retching into the cornfields as the second day of cultural activities were rolled out. We were served breakfast of the hard ramen noodles, thick sago ropes, and bone knuckles from some kind of animal. And, of course, we had to eat it with a smile. I pretended like I wasn't holding back more spew.

Anyway, I tell this segway because that was how I used to travel in my 20s, and had a lot of adventures doing it. But now in my 40s, I choose to travel a little differently. When I went to Europe to discover my Italian roots, I had everything pre-booked and it was a totally new experience.

This trip to Africa is no different.

You do not come to Africa as a white woman alone and just wing it. So everything is booked, and tomorrow I head on safari. This is definitely one of the craziest things I've ever done. There feels like a much bigger point than just to see animals from the back of an animal. This mission is part of my healing.

We ride at dawn.

Safari, Day 1

We assemble at the lodge where a gated, stone-paved entrance leads to soft grass and a glistening blue pool. Wide balconies on each side hug a rose-coloured, ranch-style hacienda in South-American style with manicured gardens.

Nine women riders—six from Australia, one from South Africa, an American, and an English woman. Two female guides both living long-term in Tanzania, one Swede named Jo and one born and bred here, Tara. Plus a team of 15 men who are driving ahead to set up camp, cook us three course meals, and care for our horses.

Is this even real?

We set off at 10am from the incredible lodge and I have adrenaline coursing through my body in anticipation. This is no joke. It's experienced riders only, and often not everyone finishes this seven-day camp-out safari in challenging country.

My horse is a 15-hand buckskin Tara bought for $50; he's surefooted, forward, and brave as can be. His name is Gunner. He can turn on a point, has the smoothest canter, and within an hour on his back I trust him fully. He learnt the terrain here as an anti-poaching horse, knows his job as a mountain pony, and does it well. I am laughing with glee as he gallops downhill through lantana, jumping logs with total confidence.

We spend five hours snaking around the bottom of Mt Meru, the smaller of the two mountains in Tanzania, at around 1900 m elevation. It's mountainous rainforest here, layers upon layers of jungle, stranglers enclosing whole trees through the canopy to reach the sky.

We are flying through the narrow trails, ducking branches, weaving through trees, calling out to each other the hazards ahead as our horses smash through the undergrowth with confidence. They are experienced, they know these trails. Luckily, these women are experienced too.

All day, every corner we turn, the landscape changes and unfolds before us. Tracking elephant dung and buffalo footprints, waiting to see some creatures of the forest. We were not disappointed... for a while there's quiet, the rhythmic thud of hooves in soft, fertile soil when you get contemplative, of place and nature and animal and smell and sound... and suddenly something would appear, would call as they noticed us, would shake the trees above us and you would be acutely aware that we are only visiting. Passing through like the tourists we are.

One red Duiker streaking through the bush, colobus monkeys jumping from treetop to treetop with their fluffy white tails, a hippo who was sleeping and begrudgingly woke when our horses trekked past in the sucky mud. Olive baboons grazing in the distance, a waterbuck antelope, a herd of cape African buffalo, a huge string of zebras with their chunky, cute butts.

Moments where I am lost in my own thoughts, of past and future and people. And suddenly, I am hurtling through the forest, every muscle and bone and sinew focused on the horse under me, the branches coming towards me, and the sunlight casting shadows across my face. It was only the moment. Nothing else.

Today was the most technical ride through the most beautiful environment ever in my life (so far). And as I sit here drinking a Kilimanjaro beer around the fire, being waited on by beautiful men, I could die happy tonight.

Safari, Day 2

Everyone sort of slept, and sort of had one ear out for leopards. Apparently, one giant cat passed through camp in the night, but I'll have to take the local guys' word for it.

Dawn wake-up and breakfast, we saddle up and set off across the flatlands below Mt Meru, our trusty ponies navigating the sodden ground with ease. We come across a huge herd of cape African buffalos, maybe 200 or so with calves in tow.

We identify three giant bulls by their fused horns, known as a boss, and the hulk of their bodies.

There's a scuffle, charging, sorting out who's the biggest male in the herd. We stop. We wait. They stare at us. Nobody is giving way. It's the oldest Mexican standoff in the world. Whose herd is bigger, whose herd is more threatening, whose herd will back down first. We watch them. They watch us. They are nonchalant.

After ten minutes or so, our guide Jo approaches slowly, and cracks a giant bull whip above her head. This does the trick. The sound ricochets, emulating a shotgun. She cracks the whip four times while slowly advancing. The bulls turn on their heels and retreat. There's a comment from the posse about Jo's 'giant lady balls' in appreciation. It's not an exaggeration. I know men who won't even ride a horse let alone crack a bullwhip over their head while riding one, and facing off with three bulls and 200 buffalo.

The herd moves aside, and as we follow the edge of the grassland, a few adolescent giraffes appear through the thorny acacias. I am breathless. Seeing them in the wild is not the same as at the zoo. I crane my neck to see more of them; they move quickly despite seeming very non-aerodynamic.

Suddenly, the acacia opens up and there is a journey of 20 giraffes (when they are standing still it's called a 'tower', when they are on the move it's a 'journey') and we dismount to marvel at them loping across the landscape. They are so otherworldly. Long eyelashes and tiny hooves, bobbing through the forest where all the trees are munched to a flat level as high as they can reach.

We snake through the forest, most people getting caught by acacia thorns at some point. My half-chaps and boots are scratched up, thorns embedded in the leather, and I'm grateful for my gear.

After lunch at the most incredible waterfall, unfolding with soft green grass and a small circling creek like a scene out of Jurassic Park, where we stretch and eat and lie in the sun, we pad quietly back down the road through the rainforest to camp. Everyone is silent. It's so peaceful. Just the thud of hooves.

I have nearly cried from overwhelming wonder a few times each day. The world is just so big and also so small, and has so much beauty to uncover. There is no limit to what you can learn and discover if you really want it bad enough.

Safari, Day 3

Today our camp moves, so it's saddle up and ride out by 7am. We leave the verdant rainforest in the lush mountains and head down the paths towards the plains. I'm feeling well rested and ready for it, even if my clothes are quickly running out.

After the rainforest, we head into harsh environment. Even before lunch, we travel about 35 kilometres across the plains through Maasai villages peppered with boma, small areas with nyumba houses within, made with ash and cow dung pressed together, and topped with grass roofs. The Maasai have lived this way for over 400 years.

Chickens and small dogs dot the yards, bougainvillea cascades in hot-pink glory down the sides of porches.

Fields of green beans, of maize, cabbages, tomatoes, red onions; orderly and with channels to direct irrigation through the fields. Everyone comes out to see the muzungu (white people, but actually translates to 'someone who roams around aimlessly') on farasi (horses). We wave and smile, and it's almost like we are a royal procession at one point, all of us doing the half-hand queen wave and calling out "Mambo" (how are you) and "Jambo" (hello). Some of the kids reply in English, "how are you?", "are you okay?" It's a moment of connection for everyone.

Women emerge from huts in their bright orange and red clothes, scores of kids, streaming across the fields with excitement at the horses cantering through. Men with blue cloths wrapped around them, beaded anklets and belts, with small silver discs reflecting the sunlight, stand on one leg with giant, stretched earlobes and call out to us.

The Maasai eat goat milk mixed with cow blood for breakfast—protein rich, and bio available. Jo calls it Maasai champagne. It doesn't sound great to me, but the land is harsh here. Water is precious. Survival is winning. The children run after us through the whole area waving and calling out to us, and one of our group plays a game with them, spinning her big grey mare—Osaka—to chase them. They shriek with a mix of fear and joy then taunt her with the universal: "nah nah", and she does it again. They follow us for a couple kilometres and the game continues. I joke that they will be talking about the "white witch" for days afterwards.

We do long stretches of galloping through flatland dodging the ever present acacia trees, calling out "hole" or "thorns" as a warning to those behind.

There're points where the dust completely obscures vision, I'm galloping flat out in the heat and can barely see the tail of the horse in front of me. There're last minute jumps where Gunner doesn't hesitate for one second, and neither do I. I trust him as I let the reins slip through my hands and he clears each jump with ease; it's hesitating on either of our parts that fucks you up.

Thorns come at you at eye height, and it's fast and furious. It's the longest, hottest, hardest gallop I've done since I was a kid. It's hard work and exhilarating as fuck.

We do long stretches of fast-trot in the dust and I'm exhausted. Heat stroke is near—I know from all the extreme raving at festivals in the Aussie summer. Nausea kicks in. There is no shade, just endless flatlands and dust in the hottest part of the day.

We gallop abreast, the horses kicking up clouds of dust that blow across the plains. The landscape is like the moon… or Mars. It seems endless and relentless, and I've driven across the Nullarbor Plain.

By the time we reach camp at the edge of the treeline across the massive expanse, everyone is filthy and exhausted. The horses are pouring with sweat and dirt, and the minute their saddles are removed, roll in the dust.

We did eight hours in the saddle and covered 65 kilometres. Mt Meru, where we camped last night, appears small in the distance. We are also tough. as. fuck.

Safari, Day 4

We head out and after an hour of walking through tall grasses and dodging acacia thorns, we take off across the plains. We spread into a phalanx and canter together, hooting as the horses stretch and cover ground.

We cross a huge plain, and there are 35 giraffes ahead with babies in tow. We slow, and they watch us approach. There is nothing else to do but take off across the plains, and suddenly we're galloping right behind these incredible creatures, who move swiftly ahead with such elegance. My eyes prick with tears, something so primal about this mission.

We cross the plains and take rest in the shade of some acacias, then walk on foot leading our horses across the cracked marshland—a flood plain that stretches across the horizon. The ground is crunchy with geometric pieces of mud—hardened and brittle—and makes a satisfying sound underfoot. Walking a bit is good for our legs and good for the horses; not so stiff later.

We take them for a drink at the edge of a dam, and Gunner walks right in. I know he's prone to swimming, rolling, so I'm cautious, but when he pulls me in, knee deep in mud over my chaps, I freak out. Feeling so vulnerable; he could just pull me under.

Something happens to me then.

Emotion bubbles up from somewhere deep, and I'm sobbing, pouring with sweat and snot, hyperventilating. Tara takes Gunner from me, and tells me to breathe deeply.

Though that is good advice, I know this isn't a panic attack.

This is what happens when I'm overwhelmed and scared. This is how I've spent a lot of the last eight years since Christie told me who I really am. Since I fully understood that nobody has ever been there to rescue me, to love me no matter what. This is how it feels when I tap into the reality that I didn't have a safe place to rest as a child. I was unwanted, plain and simple. It was always "don't be ridiculous" or "you're fine, stop being dramatic". My emotions were always diminished.

This is what I have to transmute in the process of reparenting myself.

This, my friends, is complex PTSD from family trauma. Even though I now have a label, a diagnosis, coping tools, and know exactly what's happening, I cannot stop it.

Emotion overtakes all rational logic.

It's my own Vietnam flashback, but without the sound of choppers as a trigger. The trigger is often, simply, I'm scared and nobody is coming to save me. That's it. Then guilt hits, and a deep, burning shame because I was taught my emotions aren't real. Which makes it worse. I know this cycle. Know it so well. Even though I am an incredible human who overcomes many things, this is probably something I will deal with for most of my life.

The only thing that stops the sobbing is breathing, weed, or half a Valium, and there ain't no weed here. I breathe, and try not to let my sobbing affect anyone else. Luckily, I have a Valium and I take half, which calms me within 20 minutes.

It has passed. There is no quick fix. No medication to prevent it. You just have to move through it.

It's so uncomfortable for others—PTSD isn't something we feel comfortable talking about, or to give advice. Physical ailments have balms, stretches, medicine, tactics. But this is physical too. It's involuntary. The trauma lives in my body. I think this is why I do the extreme things, to push through. To validate myself. I'm allowed to feel. Even if it's uncomfortable for those around me. I try not to make it so, and withdraw, turn quiet. Go inward and contain my energy.

I don't stay there now.

It's just a place I visit but I don't get to choose when. Learning to validate my own emotions, to regulate them, is my journey. If I have to go across the world to chase giraffes on a galloping horse to do it, well, dammit, I will.

After lunch we set off, and the heat is intense. As we head towards the salt plains, a thick band of cloud crests the mountains from the east heading north. Thunder rumbles. It gets closer. Closer still. Soon, we know it's inevitable.

The rain is coming.

We can smell it. Petrichor.

It hits the salt flat and soaks in. A few drops at first, refreshing after the heat and dust of yesterday. Then suddenly, it pelts down. Sideways. We keep going but it's relentless. It stings as it hits us in the face as we canter across the flat. We pause for a few minutes behind a giant acacia tree, hoping for a bit of respite. All the horses turn their asses towards it. Everyone is saturated through.

We head on, cantering fast across the flat, heads down but having to look where we are headed. It's wild and crazy. Adrenaline to the max. Finally, the rain lessens in intensity and we slow. The wind is freezing and everyone is utterly soaked.

I'm shivering and can't wait to get to camp.

But right as it comes into focus, we are finally rewarded with an elephant spotting. It's a bull with one tusk rolling in the mud. We approach a little closer, and the horses are alert.

It feels like a reward after the rain.

Bring on tomorrow.

Safari, Day 5

I wake after crazy dreams and a very warm night, to pink and purple streaks across the sky. We head out at 8am. Only a half hour from camp, we spot the same big bull we saw the night before, grazing in an acacia grove. We approach silently, at a slow walk.

As we round the corner, he spots us—11 horses with silent riders. We are in a conservation area, right on the border of Kenya. There are no fences here, we are finding these animals in the wild. The big bull spins to face us, and his ears go up and out. Jo and her bay mare, Ella, stand their ground. It's a face off, but it's inquisitive not aggressive.

Yet.

He gestures towards us, a mock charge, and the energy shifts.

Tara says, "with me", and every horse goes back on their haunches to spin 180 degrees to launch away from him. Jo makes a loud, sharp, "Ey" sound, just letting him know we are here and not backing down. He seems satisfied with our retreat, and after a brief ear flap, he turns and goes back to grazing. This happens in slow motion, probably about five minutes that feels like an hour. All of us have adrenaline coursing through our bodies, we can feel the quickened heartbeat of our horses too. I look at one of our group, Emma, and she has tears in her eyes, same as me. It's not fear, it's wonder. We wordlessly clasp hands across our horses' backs. I've never had an experience with wildlife like it.

We come across a string of 60 zebras and 40 giraffes. After they clock us, they begin to move along with us, and it feels like we are part of the pack—100 wild animals and 11 women on horses.

Another magic moment. Something you can't orchestrate. No fences, no idea what we will find and when.

I'm tired deep in my bones today, and after lunch I had the first nap during daylight hours that I've had in 30 years. Riding for so many days in the elements has tapped my mind, body, and soul. Extreme raving doesn't even come close. Going to rest well tonight, this is one of the physically hardest and definitely best things I've ever done.

Safari, Day 6

Today, we headed west over the savannah to visit a Maasai boma, where we were invited by Sekei, one of our night watchmen. This boma is his friends, the chief and his two brothers living together with five wives and about 25 children. The bomas are a mini family village, and this one has been around for thirty years or so.

Maasai are polygamous and measure wealth in numbers of children, cattle, and goats—the entire boma is built around the livestock. In the middle, there is a circular yard where the goats and cattle live, and the outside ring contains the small houses called msonge, where each wife and her children reside. They are made from pressed cow dung and mud walled, straw roofs and very dark inside.

Outside the boundary of the boma, three teenage boys linger, aged about 14-17. They are wearing black and smiling at us, sheepishly. They have just been through initiation, where they are circumcised publicly after a night of dancing and singing and staying awake. The whole boma gathers around to chant and dance as the ritual is performed and they must not show any pain or fear, which is how they prove they are ready to be a man. Then they are cast out of the village for three months with the supervision of an elder, to survive on their own, when they can return to the boma and take a wife.

Women from surrounding bomas have shown up with their wares, with the promise of mzungu visiting. Hand-beaded bracelets and necklaces with dangling chains and small silver discs. They all have stretched earlobes, and wear all the bling at once. It's chaotic and fun selecting jewellery and they put it on me before I can protest. Bling unites me with them, and in twenty minutes I'm jingling and jangling with them all, loving every minute of it. Tara negotiates on behalf of all of us, and I buy about 15 pieces for less than $100 USD. It feels good to buy in this way, there is no middleman, and I'm surrounded by a crush of women all telling Tara whose things are whose as they will split the shillings later.

We canter back across the salt flat and I point Gunner at a dead log to jump, he clears it easily and keeps going, happy to be heading in the direction of camp. I let him gallop into camp, both of us cheeky hotheads who know there are rules but follow them when we feel like it. He's been the perfect horse for me.

The last ride is just plain magic. Nothing special about it, just all of us—11 women cantering across the savannah with our steeds till we get to the bottom of a mountain as the sun sets. We hike up the mountain with a 360 view of the plains, and the champagne pops. We fucking made it. We did it. I've never been prouder of myself, of these women I feel will be friends for life, and of Jo and Tara who led the way and helped make this dream a reality.

My life has changed, I am different. The moon rises and illuminates the landscape and we toast each other's resilience, adventures, and future selves.

We will go back to our lives with something new.

I speak for everyone when I say: we will never forget.

AFTER SEVEN DAYS RIDING SAFARI IN TANZANIA

CHAPTER 92

Coming Home to Yourself

Zanzibar

After the safari, I headed to Zanzibar. My intention was to squeeze a mini tropical holiday out of the 36-hour flight and year of working to get here. It's two degrees in Melbourne right now, and it's been five years on the island colony. That's four straight winters without a break.

In Stone Town, men approach to ask where I'm from. They are tourist touts; it's their job to pick you. Six in a row have said, "Ciao, molto bene, Italiano?" All I can do is say "YES" in response, then, "also Australian" or else they start speaking Italian, and it's too complicated to explain. But I *look* Italian. Finally, I fit into the global fabric of things.

I can't explain how validating this is. My eyes prick with tears at the recognition every time. At the affirmation, the deep knowing, reflected to me on an island off Tanzania in East Africa, of all places. I am Italian. In my heart, in my soul. Though I wish I knew a half-lifetime earlier, I own it now.

Down the east coast in Jambiani, I wander white beaches dotted with coconut palms and the most incredible azure water I've ever seen. Find abandoned palace resorts in decay where I write and photograph. I walk to town and get caught in the rain, hide under an eave with locals and hop a motorbike taxi, my hair streaming in the wind. I spend an hour talking to a young guy with dreadlocks selling shells about magic and manifestation. Listening to the sound of the sea with those shells pressed against our ears, agreeing that magic comes from your heart and your focused intent, no matter your religion.

I used to travel to seek the kind of wild adventures as illustrated in previous chapters of this book but this time, I'm not getting tattooed or dating gangsters or partying with strangers. Though those options have been offered up plenty. Even the cashew seller walking below the stone parapet where I'm sunbaking smiled in a way which let me know he could be mine if I wanted.

But I want more now. More for myself, more from my travel, and way more from my intimate moments.

In addition, I've never had this kind of 'resort' experience, a compound hovering above the masses, totally serene in every way. Loads of shy, lovely staff waiting to serve your any desire. My only company? Three couples lounging in daybeds on the perfectly raked sand with coconut palms rustling in the breeze providing the gentle soundtrack. A safe haven to leave your room unlocked. To decide, swim, snack or cocktail, and nothing else. I gotta say, it's extremely relaxing and I'm so blissed out! Especially with a pina colada or two. Perfection.

Don't worry, I'm still sneaking off in the afternoon to smoke kitu (weed) in the abandoned resort, and playing local hip hop to the chefs loudly in the restaurant, but I have definitely mellowed. And it's good.

Africa as a white woman alone has not been easy. It has been viscerally confronting, tough to both witness and navigate. I've felt raw and vulnerable and tough and bulletproof in different measures at different times. I learnt the phrase, "hapana acha bwana", which means 'leave me alone boy', but only used it once—all the women in earshot cackled. A moment of sisterhood if anything.

It's only me out here—my wits, my wisdom, my intuition. I trust these now. Feel it in my body. A solid NO or YES. I listen to that. It has taken years to tune-in to my internal radio frequency.

Although, it would be nice to share all of it with someone, to not be here alone, I'm content.

I simply no longer feel a desperate longing for a partner. If he arrives, great. If he doesn't, I know what that looks and feels like, and I walk on. I'm not married to potential or possibility now. If he's out there looking for me, he will make himself known.

Note to Australian men: You just walk up and say, "do you have a partner?", wait for the answer, then ask for my number. It happens five, seven, ten times a day here. It's easy.

Regardless, it's crystal clear to me now. I'm not just okay on my own - I'm fucking *fantastic*. And my heart is still wide open.

No matter how challenging, whether it's physical effort like I've never known on safari or the regular harassment of being on my own as a female in the world, the magic is in the overcoming. This applies to every curveball that regular life throws our way.

You gotta risk it to get the biscuit.

You gotta slay the dragon to get the gold.

You don't need to have a DNA-identity revelation to uncover new versions of yourself.

You can do it with a daily, momentary question.

Just ask yourself:

Is this what you really want?

Or is there perhaps, more?

You have permission to seek it.

You're allowed to quest for more, whatever that means.

Society makes you feel as if time is always running out, like other things are more important. As if whatever your heart desired once, it's probably too little or too late.

It's like the adage: when's the best time to plant a tree? The answer: twenty years ago, or today.

There is loads more time to become a myriad more things. For example, I only just discovered 'resort me', who has massages with a view of the sea and wears flowy, dramatic, tropical dresses. I have no idea where she came from but she's kind of fun—I think I'll keep her.

To anyone feeling as if middle age is the end, it isn't. I truly feel as if I'm only just beginning.

Remember all you dreamt you could be in the incredible life you crafted in your mind when you were six, when you were 14, when you're 22, when you're 30, or 45 or 60. Those leylines of desire run deeper than where you were born, where you live now, or who made you.

You can drag your past around like a comfortable but also tattered coat that no longer fits. Or you can decide to be something different. Go for a walk through an African village if you feel like offering up excuses about this. Trust me when I say, if you're reading this book, you probably have way more privilege and agency than many people on this planet.

Despite what cards I've been dealt, I'm acutely aware that my reality is mostly of my own making. I often tell my young clients that life is just a series of choices—one after the other. If you make a wrong one, you can make a different choice next time, but really think about them. Because some can be made only once.

We used to think, "everything happens for a reason" but now we know, this is spiritual bypassing at best and victim blaming at worst.

I prefer the trauma-informed upgrade of "it's not what happens to you, it's what you choose to do with it". The power is ultimately yours. Scary and liberating, right?

I'm personally dedicated to a process of reprogramming, of upgrading my world views and my perception of self, continually. Downloading new software and understanding Matrix style.

I share my life, these stories, as a beacon.

I was terrified of a mediocre life when I was a teenager. If only I knew what was to come.

If you want a life of adventure and honesty and amazing experiences around every corner, you can have it. And you don't need to go to Tanzania or Guatemala or get tattooed all over or dive 50 metres to the bottom of the Blue Hole to find it. (Although maybe I did, to bring this gold back for you.)

Because if I did all this and still made it right here, right now, to tell the story—who knows what else I can do? Who knows what *you* can do!

The happiest ending is one where every day unfolds as a grand exploration. Where you're not bound or constrained by your past. Especially by shame that isn't yours to own, if you don't want it.

Where your heart remains open to love no matter how many times you've been hurt.

Where your worth gets more solid every time you back yourself, and you realise that courage is not the absence of fear but the triumph over it.

Admitting you're not okay is brave as fuck.

Asking for help bravo as fuck.

Expressing your true feelings openly, even when there may be fallout—warrior style.

My vulnerability and open heart, these are my superpowers. I have been rejected for these, even exiled for them, but this is the most precious gem to me.

I've learnt to polish this worth with care so it shines brighter than anything I'd ever dreamed of. It comes from within, not from romantic love or familial validation. From accepting what is, and allowing the becoming of what could be.

We hold the power.

Nobody else does.

The quest for a full life isn't about making stacks of money, nor is it about social status. There are many chapters to your own becoming, it only ends when you take that last breath, and none of us know when that is. So, today is the only day to try! Or if you're exhausted, start tomorrow.

But begin.

This I know.

Every heartbreak and challenge, every moment you've questioned why you're even here is part of your becoming. Every scar has a story, right? They become you, and you can feel it in your bones. Maybe sometimes, as if your heart will physically break from love.

An excavation of self so I may help others do the same, is my life's work.

It might take the form of open-heart surgery via words on social media, or cheerleading you as a coach as you grapple with goals and dreams, or holding space for your broken wings as we heal together into a new form of ourselves.

Or, it might be the feeling of possibility I hope to conjure as you close this book. A moment of magic, of synchronicity from this raw version of my everything, which I offer up to you and the universe.

Thank you for coming on the journey with me.

ONWARDS. ♥

ZANZIBAR 2024

ABOUT THE AUTHOR

Bo Kitty is a take-no-shit business coach, a tattooed, horse-riding freediver and a gonzo anthropologist. An icon in her community, she is known for straight-shooting truth and is not afraid of the dark places we inhabit.

She has danced through the pulsating heart of the rave scene, and her penchant for adventure has led her to travel solo to the farthest corners of the globe, venturing to places that often come with a warning, and returning with tales of extraordinary encounters. A digital pioneer, Bo has been disrupting with her unique blend of wisdom and wit across the internet for nearly three decades, capturing massive audiences with her uncanny ability to tap into the viral zeitgeist. Her writing resonates deeply, often touching on the raw, unfiltered reality of life, love, and the pursuit of authenticity.

Professionally, Miss Kitty has been a marketing guru, an operations manager, a project manager and a Safety Officer with a 30ish year career in the arts and music industries, from nightclubs to festivals and beyond. Currently a formidable business coach at *Reality Check* with clients worldwide, and she also runs a creative agency of B2B solutions—*The Real Army*.

Her life is a testament to living boldly and unapologetically, merging the unconventional with the profound. Bo Kitty is a true force of nature, a modern alchemist whose superpower is turning shit into diamonds. Her work sounds an alarm, calling to those brave enough to walk through the fire to find what lies on the other side.

She lives in Melbourne, Australia, with Bruno the beaglier and Tito Bandito Gatito the rescue cat, and wakes at 6am daily to walk in the bush.

Bo Kitty is available for events, public speaking, workshops and coaching individuals and groups with her brand of effervescent, straight-shooting truth which injects optimism and practical solutions into any environment.

REALITY CHECK—HOLISTIC BUSINESS COACHING FOR REBELS

Bo Kitty is a formidable holistic business and life coach who has worked for over a decade with hundreds of clients worldwide from various walks of life. Along with years of strategic business development and marketing in a range of industries, she is known for honesty, integrity, and cutting through the excuses you tell yourself to reach clarity and understanding. Check out her deck of cards, download her app, read the testimonials, and book a Reality Check session when you are absolutely ready for change.

Reality Check holistic business coaching :
www.checkyoself.com.au

POWER UP CARDS AND APP

The Power Up deck of cards and free mobile app is stacked with next-level business and life advice for entrepreneurs, giving you the ability to stay motivated, set tasks, and think outside the box. You'll receive instantly actionable motivation and game-changing tips straight from the skillset of in-demand business coach and Reality Check founder, Bo Kitty.

Bo Kitty is an entrepreneur with almost 30 years of experience in the creative industries. She believes in empowerment and drawing outside the lines. These cards are her own photos taken from travels around the world, and her best 50 bits of advice for anyone wanting to change their paradigm.

Power Up Cards
https://www.checkyoself.com.au/reality-power-up-deck

Power Up App (search your app store)
https://www.checkyoself.com.au/reality-check-app

THE REAL ARMY — B2B SOLUTIONS BY CREATIVES FOR CREATIVES

Need professional help to drive your project or business forward? At The Real Army, we believe that employing freelancers for their specific skill set is the most effective way to get results and save both time and money. Bo Kitty started this creative agency as a company of one, but now has suppliers across every discipline to drive things forward. From web development to slick graphic design, logos and branding, to set building, event production and experiential requests firmly outside the box, we have you covered.

We can even source a carpet python in 20 minutes from our belly dance community if you need one. Nothing is too weird or too hard because at the Real Army, you get all-killer talent with no-filler bullshit and nobody gets left on the battlefield.

The Real Army
https://therealarmy.com.au

ACKNOWLEDGMENTS

Thanks to:

Sophie, Julie, Clem, Jake : for helping this book live.

Gushi and fam, Ange and Ferris, Bonnita and fam, Stu, Pheelix, Willow, Jake, Mitchio and fam, Ariel and fam, Aubrey and fam, Sammy, Donna, Dan and Sharyn, Timmeh and O, James Bro and Natty, Mel and Steeb, Ocram and Lexis, Cam, Stef and Matt, Kt, Sarah and fam, Karl and fam, Geordie and Grace, Simo and Kelsey, Shar and Josh, Bryan, Kev and Max, Matty and Jarman, Maple and Serena, Mikey Pork and Allan, Nico and Jazzy, PawPaw, Sophia, Alice, Ginny, Nate, Rebecca and fam, Josephine and fam, Peta, Billy, Benji and Fam, Ganga, Savannah, Dyz and fam, Tim and Luna : for the support in all realms at all times, and being my family.

For everyone in my extended Camp Get Fucked family.

For my stellar people and crews over the last 30 years from clubs to festivals to councils.

For the aunties, Deidre and Sue: for choosing me.

For Loretta and family: for accepting me as I am.

And Mother : whose truth set me free and for which I will be forever grateful.

AUTHOR CONTACT PAGE

Email **me@bokitty.com**

Author Website **www.bokitty.com**

Coaching & Training **www.checkyoself.com.au**

B2B Creative Agency **www.therealarmy.com.au**

Facebook **bokitty1**

Linkedin **bokitty**

Instagram **@iambokitty**

www.ingramcontent.com/pod-product-compliance
Lightning Source LLC
Chambersburg PA
CBHW030226100526
44585CB00012BA/258